CONSERVATISM

The Faber Book of
CONSERVATISM

Edited by
KENNETH BAKER

faber and faber
LONDON · BOSTON

First published in 1993
by Faber and Faber Limited
3 Queen Square London WC1N 3AU

Photoset by Parker Typesetting Service, Leicester
Printed in Great Britain by Clays Ltd, St Ives plc

A CIP record for this book is
available from the British Library

ISBN 0-571-14855-7

2 4 6 8 10 9 7 5 3 1

Contents

Preface

I have been putting together the material for a work on Conservatism for a long time. In 1980, I was asked by Heinemann to write a book on 'The Case for Conservatism'. I was working on this when I became a minister in 1981, so I could not continue, and the task was passed on to Chris Patten who brought out a book in time for the 1983 election.

What I have tried to do in this collection is to identify the main principles, ideas and attitudes that make up Conservatism. I have illustrated these with passages from politicians, philosophers, writers and poets. There are eighteen chapters, each dealing with one aspect of Conservatism. The passages in each chapter are in chronological order.

I have selected passages to illustrate the different aspects of Conservatism – such as tradition, the free market, support for the family, patriotism, property, morality, a love of the countryside, less government and a sense of community. Many of these characteristics have been written about by political philosophers over several centuries whose works amount to a huge mass of knowledge and disputation from which to draw. The extracts do not attempt to elaborate on the deep and complex arguments that lie behind these issues but they do attempt to crystallize the essential elements of the Tory tradition.

The great Conservative thinkers and politicians are well represented: Bolingbroke, Burke, Peel, Disraeli, Salisbury, Baldwin, Churchill, Quintin Hogg, Michael Oakeshott and Margaret Thatcher. But there are many less well known who have written or said something which is eloquent or memorable about Conservatism. Not all the authors and poets are Conservative with a large 'C', but the passages I have included from them do express ideas which are conservative with a small 'c'.

It is much easier to compile the collected main texts of socialism, liberalism or communism. These are defined areas of political belief supported by volumes of dogmatic statements, resolutions and declarations amounting to geometrical simplifications of the human condition. It is much more difficult to describe the conservative philosophy, since it is instinctive rather than intellectual; it is subtle rather than simple, and it is close to common sense and the natural feelings of mankind. I have tried to illustrate the various threads that make up the conservative temperament, for people come to be conservative by taking many different paths.

I have not drawn upon the tradition of conservative thought on the Continent or in America, apart from a few passages. The exclusion is quite deliberate: I have sought to trace the origins and development of conservatism in Great Britain and especially in England. The unique nature of Conservatism today in Britain derives from its history, our constitutional arrangements, the Church of England and the social development of the country over the last two hundred years, though its roots go back much earlier.

I would like to thank Mary, my wife, for bearing with me and seeing so much of our time swallowed up in writing another book; Tony Kerpel, who was my Political Adviser at Environment, Education, Central Office and the Home Office, for we have soldiered long together in the good, old cause; and Kathy Hubbard for her patience, and unfailing good humour. I am also grateful to Robert Jackson and David Willetts for reading my manuscript at an advanced stage and making helpful and useful suggestions.

But ultimately the selection is mine, and while I have tried to set out to answer the question, 'What is Conservatism?', I suspect that all I have been able to do is to show why I am a Conservative.

K.B.

Introduction

This book explores why the Conservative Party is the most successful political party which has yet emerged in any democratic country. To acknowledge this success is not to express arrogant defiance, nor boastful complacency, nor triumphalism, it is simply the truth. To be successful, a political party has to be more in office than not; it has to see off its rivals; it has to overcome defeat, and it has to appeal to the young people of each successive generation. All of these things the Conservative Party has done and is continuing to do. It also has to win the battle of ideas. It has to show that it has a more attractive, more coherent, more substantial body of ideas than its rivals. One of the purposes of this anthology is to show how in its long history Conservatism has been explained, defined, discussed and embellished by a glittering collection of political writers and thinkers.

In the nineteenth century the Tories were in power for fifty-seven years, the Whigs for eighteen years, the Liberals for twenty-two years, and various coalitions for three years. In this century, the Conservatives have formed the government for fifty years, the Liberals for ten years, Labour for eighteen years, and coalitions for fourteen years. Since the war, the Conservative ascendancy is even more striking, for up to 1992 the Conservatives have been in office for thirty years and Labour for seventeen years.

The acquisition of office must be the primary test of the effectiveness of any political party but it is, of course, not the final judgement, for that depends upon the use to which that power is put. There is nothing infallible about Tory success; the party was driven out of office or else surrendered power in 1846, 1880, 1906, 1945, 1964 and 1974. But defeat, while dispiriting, did not lead to despair. On each occasion, though with differing time-spans, the party regenerated itself, did not irretrievably fall apart, and managed to fight again for victory.

Survival is nothing new to the Tory Party. It had to see off the Whigs, many of whom actually joined the Tory Party; it had to withstand the Liberal Party with such formidable leaders as Gladstone, Asquith and Lloyd George; it had also to confront socialism and the Labour Party led by Ramsay MacDonald, Attlee and Wilson. During the last two centuries there have been several occasions when the Conservative Party has been written off. After the Reform Bill in 1832, its parliamentary representation fell to just 150 MPs; in 1906 it was overwhelmed by the great Liberal landslide; and in 1966 Harold Wilson was able to boast that the Labour Party had become the natural party of government.

What then explains the staying power of Conservatism? In this book I have tried to identify and illustrate the values, ideas and attitudes that have characterized, and continue to characterize, a Conservative approach to life and to public affairs.

I recognize that it is a good deal easier to spot a Conservative temperament than to define a Conservative philosophy. This does not mean that Conservatives do not have coherent set of beliefs – they do – but their beliefs are more difficult to define than the political ideologies of socialism, liberalism and Marxism with their charters, constitutions and manifestos. That set of beliefs and attitudes has been transformed by each succeeding generation into policies and proposals to deal with the particular problems of that generation, and the agent for this over the last 160 years has been the Conservative Party. There is, however, a continuity derived from tradition. The characteristics that distinguish a Conservative have a durability; they are recognizably the same over the centuries, although the events against which they are measured, tested and pitted have been so very different.

I could not resist reminding those who read this book that Conservatives like to enjoy life. Bagehot went as far to say that 'the essence of Toryism is enjoyment'. You will not find hairshirts on general issue at Central Office. The true Tory knows that politics is simply not the be-all and end-all. There are many other aspects of life that are more important. He knows that 'there is good news yet to hear and fine things to be seen/Before we go to Paradise by way of Kensal Green'.

I hope that the readers of this book will take away with them a greater understanding of what makes a Conservative. They will soon realize that I have not tried to chart the history of the Conservative Party nor to set out the practical details of policies which are included in our party's manifestos. You will not find the soul of the Conservative Party in a manifesto. Manifestos merely say what has to be done in the immediate future so as to maintain and support a Conservative society. It is the realization that that society is worth sustaining and must be saved which leads people to commit themselves to the Conservative cause.

I say Conservative rather than Tory for the simple reason that the former word is now more widely used. It was first coined in the 1830s and became so quickly established that in 1832 an arch-opponent, Daniel O'Connell, said that the word Conservative was 'the fashionable term, the new-fangled phrase now used in polite society to designate the Tory ascendency'. The word Tory is still used, usually with an accompanying sneer by a political opponent. But it is also used by some as a badge of pride and independence, and as an assertion of the older, more traditional verities. Randolph Churchill robustly defended it saying, ' "Tory" has always possessed an essentially popular flavour ... it denotes great historical struggles.'

There are differences implicit in the two words. For example, Peel was much happier describing himself as a Conservative – that is, more of a reforming spirit – and Wellington as a Tory – that is, showing a greater reluctance to change. Indeed, throughout the history of the party there has been an internal tug-of-war between the more active and the more cautious; between intervention in the market and allowing the free play of market forces; between those who accept change and those who want to die in the last ditch; between the withdrawers from the Empire and the holders-on; between the European enthusiasts and the European sceptics. It has been the good fortune, some would say the genius, of Conservatism that it has been able, often with considerable strain and with spells in opposition, to survive these internal disputes and find a way of living and pulling together.

I have selected passages from politicians, thinkers and authors (some of whom were not themselves Conservative) to answer the question, 'What is Conservatism?' This anthology, however, no less than any other, is above all a personal selection – essentially it reflects my own approach to Conservatism and explains why I'm a Conservative and have spent much of my life promoting the Conservative cause.

Let me start by saying what Conservatism is not. First, it is not the blind and insensitive defence simply of what exists. If the Conservative Party only existed to defend the *status quo* it would, like a sand-castle, have been washed away by the irresistible tides of progress. Secondly, it is not the protection of unbridled vested interests. If this had been its purpose, it would have suffered the fate of the many parties of the right in Europe which became repositories of the minority pleadings of the privileged and closeted. Thirdly, it is not the bastion against all change. If this had been its inspiration then it would have become a museum for the moribund.

Conservatism cannot – like so many of the rationalist codes of political theory – be learnt from a series of textbooks. Michael Oakeshott, the most perceptive of Conservative thinkers this century, has drawn the distinction between the technical knowledge that so many of the '-isms' of political science sell to the public and the practical knowledge that is instinctive rather than intellectual. In 1948 he wrote: 'Reputable political behaviour is not dependent upon sound philosophy ... In general, constitutional tradition is a good substitute for philosophy.' Socialism, communism, and liberalism all purport to have a set answer to the many problems of our society, each of which is derived from what is claimed to be a rational analysis. All too often human nature is left out. The Conservative approach is not as intellectual; but it is a good deal more intelligent.

The young Disraeli, writing in defence of the English constitution in 1835, said that:

The formation of a free government on an extensive scale is not to be found ensconced behind a revolutionary barricade or floating in the bloody gutters of an incendiary metropolis. It cannot be scribbled down – this great invention – in a morning on the envelope of a letter by some charter-concocting monarch, or sketched with ludicrous facility in the conceited commonplace book of an Utilitarian sage. With us it has been the growth of ages, and brooding centuries have watched over and tended its perilous birth and feeble infancy.

The question is often asked – it was posed in Disraeli's novel *Coningsby* – 'What will you conserve?' This is an entirely fair question which demands an answer. Mine is this. We should conserve those institutions in our society which contribute towards harmony and stability; we should encourage those instincts which lead towards responsibility and a generosity of spirit; we should protect individual freedom and open the doors of opportunity to all; and we should cherish that love of community which in transcending mere selfishness makes us proud to belong to our society. These are my criteria for conservation. In practice, it means strong and continuing support for the family as the basic unit in our society of interlocking communities. It means a defence of the main pillars of our constitution – parliamentary government, the rule of law and the independence of the judiciary. It means policies to promote private enterprise and to reward personal initiative. It means the encouragement of self-reliance, but also a ready acceptance of the obligation to help the needy. It means increasing the opportunities for every individual to thrive and prosper by exercising his or her talents. It means creating a wider choice for everyone to live their own lives in their own homes and to spend their savings as they wish. It means limiting the role of government and allowing the spontaneity of individuals as full a range as possible.

At the heart of Conservatism is a deep respect for the individual. Many would claim that this derives from the fact that man is made in the image of God, and each individual soul is special and important. The various dogmas of the right and left have never respected the separate sanctity of each individual. In his book *Mortal Danger* Alexander Solzhenitsyn said that the aim of 'Communist authorities is to force the people to serve them unfailingly as a work-force, or if need be as a fighting force'. This concept of people as so many pawns, capable of manipulation, is totally alien to our way of life. A totalitarian state organizes society to make people do what it wants them to do. A democracy is engaged in the much more difficult task of sustaining a society in peace and harmony by allowing people to do what they themselves want to do.

The simplistic approach is to say that Conservatives believe in authority and protecting the established order including property rights; the Liberals believe in freedom; and the Socialists believe in interventionist policies designed to promote social justice. These are wide and misleading summaries of the much more complicated and diverse concepts which lie behind the three parties. Macaulay tried to identify the difference between Conservatism and Whiggery when he wrote:

If, rejecting all that is merely accidental, we look at the essential characteristics of the Whig and the Tory, we may consider each of them as the representatives of the great principle, essential to the welfare of nations. One is, in an especial manner, the guardian of liberty, and the other of order. One is the moving power, and the other the steadying power of the State. One is the sail, without which society would make no progress; the other the ballast, without which there would be no safety in a tempest.

It suited Macaulay, from his Whig standpoint, to make such a clear distinction, but a moment's reflection shows that what he says is simply not true. One of the great strands of Conservatism has been its support for individual liberty. Pitt and Lord Liverpool followed policies of economic liberalism. Peel made the great conversion to free trade in 1846 and Rab Butler reduced income tax after 1951 to encourage enterprise by rewarding individuals. Margaret Thatcher, inspired by Enoch Powell and Keith Joseph, put individual consumers making their own decisions in the market place at the centre of her economic policy.

All of these policies were centred on increasing individual choice, freedom and liberty. They were nearly all opposed by the Liberals or earlier by the Whigs. The classic liberalism of J. S. Mill allowed each individual as much freedom as possible. But liberalism had social aims which could only be met by restricting the freedom of the individual and increasing the role of government. The present-day Liberal Party advocates the State's intervention in a whole manner of ways that makes it virtually indistinguishable from the Labour Party.

A Conservative will seek a more open and competitive society where choice and opportunity are given free play. But he also recognizes that in certain areas the State has a duty to intervene and exercise its authority. This is seen most clearly in his strong support for law and order and his giving high priority to the defence of the country. The market too needs effective rules to ensure fair play and the elimination of restrictive practices whether they are operated by monopolies or trade unions. He is also aware that the moral authority of society is under constant challenge and needs his support. It is never easy to get the balance right between freedom and authority, but I believe that Conservatives have been rather better at striking a balance than other parties. They know instinctively that the power of government should be limited, and therefore seek ways of restraining its expenditure. They are mindful of Dr Johnson's thunderous growl, 'A Tory does not want to give more real power to Government.' I have tried to show the complicated skein of interrelated ideas that make up the Conservative approach and how the tensions are resolved and reconciled.

To find a balance can involve a paradox, as I discovered in my own political career when confronted by the need for reform in education. On the one hand, the National Curriculum was prescriptive – it laid down what children should be taught at schools, the levels of attainment which they should reach and how they were to be tested at various ages. Setting national standards necessarily involves a good degree of centralization, and this departure from past practice was justified only because of the poor and uneven standards provided in many schools. On the other hand, by introducing delegated budgets, by increasing the role of governing bodies, by enhancing parental choice and by introducing grant-maintained schools, my reforms dispersed power away from the Department and the local education authorities. I spoke frequently of the need to pass power away from the hub of the wheel to the rim.

Conservatives have always been suspicious of the power exercised at the centre and conscious of the corrupting influence of office as well. In the eighteenth century, more often out of office than in, they gladly adopted the name of the Country Party, which summed up their suspicious hostility to the Court and the interfering power of London. Edmund Burke talked of the 'little platoons' as being the essential elements in society – close, familiar, local, with which people could identify. And in the twentieth century, Oakeshott had no doubt that the liberties which we enjoy are due to the 'absence from our society of overwhelming concentrations of power'.

Individual liberty and freedom are therefore enhanced by this spread of power, but they are buttressed by the ownership of property. The possession of private property goes much deeper than a selfish desire to acquire – it reflects a deep instinct in human nature that has to do with privacy, independence and the family. It also conveys certain political strengths. A society where personal ownership is widely spread will be more stable and more able to resist, in the words of Evelyn Waugh, 'the majority, the public man, the State, the spirit of the age – the many-headed, many-named monster'.

The spread of home ownership has become a central aim of Conservative policy. Anthony Eden coined the phrase (it's the only one he's remembered for) 'a nation-wide property-owning democracy'. In the 1970s and 1980s this aim was largely fulfilled. Home ownership, personal savings, share ownership and private pensions all expanded. In 1991 John Major spoke of the importance of inheritance: 'I want to see wealth cascading down the generations'.

But the ownership of property carries with it obligations. Boling-broke was one of the first English Conservative thinkers to inveigh against the situation where 'public want and private wealth abound'. Dr Johnson, writing some fifty years later, stated bluntly that 'a decent provision for the poor' was 'the true test of civilisation'. So in this book, I deal with the responsibilities and duties of individuals which Conservatives recognize must accompany the enjoyment of wealth, position and property.

Conservatives are proud of the many measures enacted by Conservative governments in the nineteenth and twentieth centuries to improve the social condition of the country. Disraeli as usual put the point pungently and simply: 'Power only has one duty – to secure the social welfare of the people.' That tradition runs through Baldwin, Neville Chamberlain, Leo Amery, Keith Joseph and Ted Heath. When John Major spoke of his ideal of 'a country at ease with itself', he was speaking of a Toryism that strikes a chord with all generations. It is rooted in decency, it opens opportunity, it encourages ownership, and although it is essentially based on the liberal free market, it is also sensitive to individual needs.

Some of those needs can be met by the welfare state. But the Conservative also believes that the individual and the family must be the main providers of their own welfare. Many need help either from the State or from other individuals, but the first and hopefully the most abiding source of support will be the family. Chris Patten saw that stronger support for the family was the linchpin of any policy for encouraging community care. Margaret Thatcher, often wrongly accused of being uncaring, set out, in her speech to the General Assembly of the Church of Scotland, her support for the family not as a vehicle of civic virtue but as the very foundation on which a government built its policies for welfare, education and social responsibility.

Such sentiments can be dismissed as quintessentially middle class and, as Chesterton pointed out, it is always easy to sneer at the middle classes. But Conservatives have unashamedly supported the middle classes throughout the centuries. Quintin Hogg robustly declared, 'I am a defender of the middle classes.' Keith Joseph, with somewhat less enthusiasm, said that a bourgeois society is, on the whole, 'the least bad yet invented'. Certainly many of the values which were previously middle class have now spread far beyond the middle classes, and therein lies one of the reasons for the success of Conservatism.

Orwell put his finger on it in 1941. He saw that the middle classes and the working classes were drawing together through the development of the consumer society and the opportunities opened up by the radio, the motor car and *Picture Post*. He said that the germ of the future of England would be found in towns like Slough, Dagenham, Barnet, Letchworth and Hayes. How right he was. But it wasn't the Labour Party that benefited. In the 1992 election, four of those five towns returned a Conservative Member of Parliament.

The Labour Party had not shaken off its identification with the old working classes. It was the old working classes incorporated into a new, and more classless society, which had shaken off their identification with Labour. Socialism is less the villain that it was, not because it has modified its beliefs but because it has so manifestly failed and been rejected by the millions of people who have suffered at its hands. The socialist planned economy died in Russia and Eastern Europe. But the hope lingers on that socialism, somehow transformed as it crosses the Channel, will bring a better life. Liberalism is an altogether more sinuous collection of uncertainties. To those Conservatives who are tempted to dabble with liberalism, I would recommend reading Malcolm Muggeridge's withering scorn on the 'great liberal death wish'.

This book also examines how Conservatives have handled – not always easily – the push of freedom and the pull of authority in the area of economic policy. The balance between the individual and the State has not been one of perfect equilibrium! In the 1930s the long slump led Harold MacMillan to advocate in his book, *The Middle Way*, a strong interventionist role for the Government by creating a planned economy. During the Second World War, in order to marshal all the forces of the nation against Hitler and fascism, the power of the State was greatly increased. The greatest powers of intervention that we had ever experienced in our history were largely retained and used by Attlee's government from 1945. Conservative thinking up until 1950 largely accepted that *status quo* and modified it only marginally.

The assumption was that the clock could not be turned back, and that the ratchet of socialism could not be reversed. Little was done to reduce the state sector which Attlee had substantially extended through his huge nationalization programmes. The One Nation group of MPs, in two pamphlets published in 1950 and 1954, sought to redress the balance. They advocated more private enterprise, more competition and the unleashing of market forces. Denationalization was advocated, though little was done. A few brave measures were undertaken, like Ted Heath's ending of resale price maintenance in 1963. But on the whole there was not a great departure from the post-war consensus.

During the 1960s it was clear that the corporatist State was not working, and the Conservatives won the 1970 election on a very liberal market-orientated policy drawn up at a hotel in Croydon, Selsdon Park, which added a new phrase to the political vocabulary – 'Selsdon Man'. This was really a return to the much earlier ideas of Conservatism – less State intervention, less State spending, less State control, getting the State off the backs of industry, denationalization, reducing the public sector and the size of the bureaucracy. All these policies were followed by Ted Heath's government of 1970–72, but economic problems caused by the second miners' strike in 1972 led his government to engage in a highly interventionist policy of wage, price, rent and dividend control which came to grief some eighteen months later.

I was a junior minister at that time, trying to implement a prices and incomes policy and learning the hard way that such a policy goes against the grain of human nature. What it came down to was that a group of ministers met on a Friday afternoon in the Cabinet Office to determine the pay of plumbers, new tariffs for taxi drivers, and the price of petrol. This process was accompanied by tripartite meetings between the unions, the CBI and the government. Anybody who was engaged in this experiment learnt that, however desperate an economic situation may be, there could be no solution down that route.

The Tory defeat in February 1974 showed that action was needed to deal with the power of the trade unions. They had emasculated Harold Wilson, forced Ted Heath to hold an election which he lost, and were to drive Jim Callaghan out of office during the 'winter of discontent'.

The Conservatives learned their lessons. By 1979 Mrs Thatcher had fashioned a different way of running the economy which was much more in accord with traditional Conservative policies. It was based upon attacking inflation and returning to sound money through a strict monetary policy. Direct taxes were reduced to stimulate individual enterprise; the proportion of GDP taken by public expenditure fell; major public utilities were privatized; the consumer was listened to more than the producer; trade union reform reduced the power of the union bosses.

But it is one of the paradoxes of the 1980s that action was taken in certain areas where the market would have responded only sluggishly.

Powerful new bodies with wide-ranging powers were set up to regenerate the inner cities. The mixture certainly worked, since more wealth was created than ever before – and was spread more widely. Four election victories in a row have shown the popularity of Conservatism in the 1980s. Already that decade is acquiring the glow of a golden age.

Margaret Thatcher responded to the problems of the day in much the same way as Robert Peel had done in 1846. He then rejected the traditional protectionist attitude of the Tory Party because it was not working and was proving to be against the national interest. He recognized the benefits that would flow from free trade and less State intervention.

'Thatcherism' has sometimes been called 'the new Conservatism'. Whenever I hear that phrase I reach for my tin hat, since I know that I will soon be showered with rhetorical shrapnel. The word 'new' is used to favour the one part of Conservatism that the author likes; and it could just as well be appropriate to use the word 'old'. 'New' was used to describe the paternalistic and interventionist policies of immediate post-war Conservatism. But there was nothing particularly new about them: Neville Chamberlain had built up his domestic reputation in following just such policies before the war, and they can be traced back to Joseph Chamberlain and to the traditional paternalism of the old squirearchy. Thatcherism, with its advocacy of individual choice and private enterprise, and its attacks upon socialist collectivism, was not breaking new ground but returning to one of the most important elements in Conservatism since Burke. As Iain McLeod said to the Party Conference in 1962, 'There is no new Conservatism, only a restatement of old beliefs in modern terms.' Indeed it would be surprising if 'newness' appealed to Conservatives. The essence of Conservatism is its respect for the continuity of thought and attitude. Tradition is the shadow behind us and also a lodestar for the future. We should therefore beware of heeding the appeal to 'newness' – for this is the cry of the tinker as he displays his wares on his tray. Chesterton put it well: 'We grow conservative as we grow old, it is true. But we do not grow conservative because we find so many new things spurious. We grow conservative because we find so many old things genuine.'

The Conservatives' respect for tradition and sense of history are not quaint antiquarianism but a recognition that the problems of today are not unique and that something is to be learnt from knowing how other people in earlier ages had dealt with similar ones. Also, we should shun the answer that begins with pulling down everything and starting with a completely clean slate. Clarendon warned against that in 1647: 'Take heed of removing landmarks and destroying foundations.'

I remember Edward Boyle telling the story at the Oxford Union of a Frenchman and an Englishman sitting together, when the news was brought to them that at last it had been definitely proved that God did not exist. The Frenchman threw up his hands in delight and exclaimed, 'At last Voltaire has been justified.' The Englishman stared moodily ahead and sighed, 'Ah well, another old landmark gone.' Many Conservatives have a landmark mentality, and that is something recognized by Orwell in the extract I have included from *Coming Up For Air*. They also have a respect for custom and habit, which are deeply rooted in human nature. It is no accident that we like ceremonies and ceremonial occasions – they are collective celebrations of the continuity of traditional behaviour, whether they be christenings, weddings, coronations or funerals. They serve to remind us of the shared feelings and interests of mankind. These are not snobbish gatherings for the middle class. Shared and passionately held loyalties are felt as much by pigeon fanciers as by polo players, no less in working-class men's clubs than in the Long Room at Lords.

A belief in the importance of tradition creates a certain humility. Conservatives are deeply suspicious of any grandiose designs to improve the lot of man – as Norman St John Stevas remarked, 'Utopias are not for us.' Socialists believe that utopias can be made to exist – they use the rhetoric of 'the new Jerusalem' – and that some superior power or intellect can divine the goals and devise the way that mankind can be directed to achieving them. This utopian approach to politics usually leads to a sad curtailing of the freedom of the pilgrims as they are made to tread the path to the promised land. At its noblest the talk is of 'the general good', and at its most mundane it comes down to 'the gentlemen in Whitehall knowing best'. The Conservative is a good deal more humble. He may, like Quintin Hogg, be deeply conscious of man's original sin; like Burke he may warn against 'the caprices of weak and giddy men'; like Halifax he may recall that 'our pride makes us over-value our stock of thought, so as to trade much beyond what it is able to make good'. He will be suspicious of abstractions, preferring the solid though more modest ground of what can be done simply and precisely for particular people in a particular situation. In *Jerusalem*, William Blake (not usually quoted in the Conservative cause) describes the earthy common sense of the typical Conservative approach:

He who would do good to another man must do it in Minute Particulars: General Good is the plea of the scoundrel, hypocrite and flatterer,
For Art and Science cannot exist but in minutely organised particulars,
And not in generalising Demonstrations of the Rational power.

This respect for the past makes it easier for Conservatives to respond to the need for change. As Burke said, 'A State without the means of some change is without the means of its conservation.' Some Tories have spent much of their lives looking for a last ditch in which to die. Others, having a keener sense of survival and a more practical bent, realize that some change is inevitable, and if Conservatism can influence the outcome of change then it is likely to be more bearable, more successful and more palatable. It is a cautious and measured approach drawn from experience which George Bernard Shaw summarized in the words that he put into the mouth of King Magnus in *The Apple Cart* – 'I stand for the evolutionary appetite against the day's gluttony.'

One area where this has been the guiding spirit of the Conservatives is in the defence of the constitution and its 'glorious institutions', as Disraeli described them. Conservatives have always been aware that there is no greater 'fiend than anarchy' and that the barbarian is always at the gate. One of the principal tasks of Conservatism is the preservation of those institutions, practices, procedures and ceremonies that together buttress the stability of the nation. Bolingbroke, Peel, Disraeli, Salisbury and Baldwin all defended the essential elements of the constitution of their day. The task is just as relevant today, when the Liberals and some socialists want to abandon our electoral system, which does produce stable governments, in favour of one which has reduced most governments in Europe to confusion or chaos. It also finds a contemporary expression in John Major's robust defence of the unity of the United Kingdom.

Deep in Conservatism lies a love of country, manifested in a respect bordering upon reverence for the existing traditions, the familiar customs and the age-old institutions of Great Britain. At the heart is the monarchy, the enduring symbol of national unity. The singing of the national anthem at the Conservative Party Conference is no mere formality. And there is an attachment to the land itself, our national heritage of a beautiful, green countryside, historic buildings, busy cities and quiet suburbs.

There is a pride, too, in being British, which transcends class, colour or creed. People do want to belong to and be identified with a wider community, and the widest is the nation itself. A patriotic spirit enriches a strong sense of allegiance and unity and it holds our country together. It is one of the reasons why we have not torn ourselves apart in a civil war for over 300 years.

We are proud that our small island has given to the world parliamentary government, the independence of the law and the integrity of public administration. In seeing these civilizing influences spread across the world, Conservatives have not suffered from the qualms and handwringing of socialists or liberals. Nor has our country been solely preoccupied, even in the nineteenth century, with the Empire or the Commonwealth. Our proximity to Europe has meant that we have been and will be inextricably linked with the political and economic developments on the continent of Europe. The great debate in the Conservative Party in the 1990s is what sort of Europe does Britain want to see. The answer is certainly not a centralized and federal Europe – the vitality of Europe springs from the separate nation states. Their collective strength derives from the single common market, which is a great force for cohesion. The prevailing view of Conservatives is to see not a United States of Europe but a united Europe of states. But even so, we should not be so preoccupied with the inland waterways of Europe that we forget that there are broad seas, wide oceans, and countries outside Europe where British interests and British diplomacy still have a role to play.

Pride and confidence derive from a love of one's land, a love that has united and bound people together to secure great results in peace and in war. Ford Maddox Ford expressed the strength of this ennobling spirit in a poem he wrote during the First World War:

> What is love of one's land?
> Ah, we know very well,
> It is something that sleeps for a year, a day,
> For a month, something that keeps
> Very hidden and quiet and still,
> And then takes,
> The quiet heart like a wave,

The quiet brain like a spell,
The quiet will
Like a tornado, and that shakes
The whole being and soul . . .
Aye the whole of the soul.

1

'People will not Look Forward to Posterity, who never Look Backwards to their Ancestors'

History is important to Conservatives and there is no better study for a politician than the history of his own country. The past has shaped but not predetermined our present-day society. Traditions also shape the future. As Burke wrote, 'people will not look forward to posterity, who never look backwards to their ancestors'.

Much can be learned from the past, not least a sense of humility. The pressing problems of today which seem about to overwhelm us, are seen from a historical perspective to be not so special, not so novel and not so unique. Historical perspective also leads us to the realization that our liberties, laws, institutions, and customs of political behaviour have not sprung up in the twentieth century; rather they derive from the traditions and practices of the past, and draw their strength from that endurance. The veneration that Conservatives have for the past is a very practical thing. Our legal and constitutional arrangements have stood the test of time and survived through the challenges and dangers in successive generations. So custom and tradition are good guides, and respect for the dead creates a constraint.

History should not simply be a romantic, Madame Tussaud tableau, providing an escape from the pressing problems of today. Nostalgia cannot be the spine of a manifesto. Roger Scruton reminds us that 'there is no sound politics of antiquarianism'. To preserve anything requires a positive act, a commitment, and a conviction that what has been passed down to us is worthy of being passed on to others. What has served us well should not be lightly discarded or destroyed, whether it be old buildings, ancient woodlands, traditional ceremonies or the very unity of the United Kingdom. If any changes need to be made, then the spirit of innovation should be imbued by the traditions of the past.

'Take heed of removing landmarks'

Take heed of removing landmarks and destroying foundations, whilst you insist upon these you have a place to fix your feet upon ... Abandon your principles and there is no judge of reason left but plurality of votes and strength of hands.

EDWARD HYDE, EARL OF CLARENDON
Letter to Sir John Berkeley in his negotiations with the Army, 1647

'Those that went before'

The wise minister sees, and is concerned to see, further, because government has a further concern; he sees the objects that are distant as well as those that are near, and all their remote relations, and even their indirect tendencies ... He considers his administration as a single day in the great year of government; but as a day that is affected by those that went before, and that must affect those that follow.

HENRY ST JOHN, VISCOUNT BOLINGBROKE
Letter to Sir William Windham, 1717

'People will not look forward to posterity, who never look backward to their ancestors'

You will observe, that from Magna Charta to the Declaration of Right, it has been the uniform policy of our constitution to claim and assert our liberties, as an *entailed inheritance* derived to us from our fore-fathers, and to be transmitted to our posterity; as an estate specially belonging to the people of this kingdom without any reference what-ever to any other more general or prior right. By this means our constitution preserves an unity in so great a diversity of its parts. We have an inheritable crown; an inheritable peerage; and an house of commons and a people inheriting privileges, franchises, and liberties, from a long line of ancestors.

This policy appears to me to be the result of profound reflection; or rather the happy effect of following nature, which is wisdom without reflection, and above it. A spirit of innovation is generally the result of a selfish temper and confined views. People will not look forward to posterity, who never look backward to their ancestors. Besides, the people of England well know, that the idea of inheritance furnishes a sure principle of conservation, and a sure principle of transmission; without at all excluding a principle of improvement. It leaves acquisition free; but it secures what it acquires. Whatever advantages are obtained by a state proceeding on these maxims, are locked fast as in a sort of family settlement; grasped as in a kind of mortmain for ever. By a constitutional policy, working after the pattern of nature, we receive, we hold, we transmit our government and our privileges, in the same manner in which we enjoy and transmit our property and our lives. The institutions of policy, the goods of fortune, the gifts of Providence, are handed down, to us and from us, in the same course and order. Our political system is placed in a just correspondence and symmetry with the order of the world, and with the mode of existence decreed to a permanent body composed of transitory parts; wherein, by the disposition of a stupendous wisdom, moulding together the great mysterious incorporation of the human race, the whole, at one time, is never old, or middle-aged, or young, but in a condition of unchangeable constancy, moves on through the varied tenour of perpetual decay, fall, renovation, and progression. Thus, by preserving the method of nature in the conduct of the state, in what we improve, we are never wholly new; in what we retain we are never wholly obsolete.

EDMUND BURKE

Reflections on the Revolution in France, 1790
This is one of the great texts of Conservatism.

'With us it has been the growth of ages'

The formation of a free government on an extensive scale, while it is assuredly one of the most interesting problems of humanity, is certainly the greatest achievement of human wit. Perhaps I should rather term it a super-human achievement; for it requires such refined prudence, such comprehensive knowledge, and such perspicacious sagacity, united with such almost illimitable powers of combination, that it is nearly in vain to hope for qualities so rare to be congregated in a solitary mind. Assuredly this *summum bonum* is not to be found ensconced behind a revolutionary barricade, or floating in the bloody gutters of an incendiary metropolis. It cannot be scribbled down – this great invention – in a morning on the envelope of a letter by some charter-concocting monarch, or sketched with ludicrous facility in the conceited commonplace book of an Utilitarian sage. With us it has been the growth of ages, and brooding centuries have watched over and tended its peril-ous birth and feeble infancy. The noble offspring of liberty and law now flourishes in the full and lusty vigour of its proud and perfect manhood. Long may it flourish! Long be its life, venerable its age, and distant its beatified euthanasia! I offer this prayer for the sake of human nature, as much as for my country; not more for Britain, than for the world, of which it is the ornament and honour.

BENJAMIN DISRAELI

A Vindication of the English Constitution, 1835

This romantic effusion by the young Disraeli owes a lot to Burke and it is not surprising to find that late in his life he adopted a title which was associated with Burke. This passage is a passionate defence of tradition and of historical continuity which contrasts with the practical and down-to-earth approach of Peel.

'Customs and manners of a sensitive and highly-trained race'

The customs and manners of a sensitive and highly-trained race are always Vital: that is to say, they are orderly manifestations of intense life (like the habitual action of the fingers of a musician). The customs and manners of a vile and rude race, on the contrary, are conditions of decay: they are not, properly speaking, habits, but incrustations; not restraints, or forms, of life; but gangrenes; – noisome, and the beginnings of death.

And generally so far as custom attaches itself to indolence instead of action, and to prejudice instead of perception, it takes this deadly character, so that thus

Custom hangs upon us with a weight
Heavy as frost, and deep almost as life.

This power and depth are, however, just what give value to custom, when it works with life, instead of against it.

JOHN RUSKIN

Essays on Political Economy, 1867

'Things as they are'

I believe in my father, and his father, and his father's father, the makers and keepers of my estate; and I believe in myself and my son and my son's son. And I believe that we have made the country, and shall keep the country what it is. And I believe in the Public Schools, and especially the Public School that I was at. And I believe in my social equals and the country house, and in things as they are, for ever and ever.

JOHN GALSWORTHY
The Country House, 1907

'An organized body of thought'

Although they believe, I daresay quite honestly, that they will defeat the Labour party by making a Coalition, not founded on principle, against the Labour party, I think the government will find in the end that there is only one way of defeating revolutionary tactics and that is by presenting an organized body of thought which is non-revolutionary. That body of thought I call Conservatism. If the government will be loyal to Conservatism, loyal indeed to any one policy of coherent thought, they will succeed.

LORD HUGH CECIL
An attack on the Liberal-Conservative coalition after the First World War.

'We grow conservative'

We grow conservative as we grow old it is true. But we do not grow conservative because we find so many new things spurious. We grow conservative because we find so many old things genuine.

G. K. CHESTERTON

'A definite creed and a cast-iron code of morals'

Nobody has any business to use the word 'progress' unless he has a definite creed and a cast-iron code of morals. Nobody can be progressive without being doctrinal; I might almost say that nobody can be progressive without being infallible – at any rate, without believing in some infallibility. For progress by its very name indicates a direction; and the moment we are in the least doubtful about the direction, we became in the same degree doubtful about the progress ... But it is precisely about the direction that we disagree. Whether the future excellence lies in more law or less law, in more liberty or less liberty;

whether property will be finally concentrated or finally cut up; whether sexual passion will reach its sanest in an almost virgin intellectualism or in a full animal freedom; whether we should love everybody with Tolstoy, or spare nobody with Nietzsche; – these are the things about which we are actually fighting most. It is not merely true that the age which has settled least what is progress is this 'progressive' age. It is, moreover, true that the people who have settled least what is progress are the most 'progressive' people in it. The ordinary mass, the men who have never troubled about progress, might be trusted perhaps to progress. The particular individuals who talk about progress would certainly fly to the four winds of heaven when the pistol-shot started the race. I do not, therefore, say that the word 'progress' is unmeaning; I say it is unmeaning without the previous definition of a moral doctrine, and that it can only be applied to groups of persons who hold that doctrine in common.

G. K. CHESTERTON

ANCESTRAL HOUSES

Surely among a rich man's flowering lawns,
Amid the rustle of his planted hills,
Life overflows without ambitious pains;
And rains down life until the basin spills,
And mounts more dizzy high the more it rains
As though to choose whatever shape it wills
And never stoop to a mechanical
Or servile shape, at others' beck and call.

Mere dreams, mere dreams! Yet Homer had not sung
Had he not found it certain beyond dreams
That out of life's own self-delight had sprung
The abounding glittering jet; though now it seems
As if some marvellous empty sea-shell flung
Out of the obscure dark of the rich streams.
And not a fountain, were the symbol which
Shadows the inherited glory of the rich.

Some violent bitter man, some powerful man
Called architect and artist in, that they,

Bitter and violent men, might rear in stone
The sweetness that all longed for night and day,
The gentleness none there had ever known
But when the master's buried mice can play.
And maybe the great-grandson of that house,
For all its bronze and marble, 's but a mouse.

O what if gardens where the peacock strays
With delicate feet upon old terraces,
Or else all Juno from an urn displays
Before the indifferent garden deities;
O what if levelled lawns and gravelled ways
Where slippered Contemplation finds his ease
And Childhood a delight for every sense,
But take our greatness with our violence?

What if the glory of escutcheoned doors,
And buildings that a haughtier age designed,
The pacing to and fro on polished floors
Amid great chambers and long galleries, lined
With famous portraits of our ancestors;
What if those things the greatest of mankind
Consider most to magnify, or to bless,
But take our greatness with our bitterness?

W. B. YEATS
Meditations in Time of Civil War, 1928

In including this beautiful poem I am not attempting to recruit Yeats as an English Conservative, but he does have deep conservative instincts. It was written at a time when the very basis of society was being threatened and weakened by civil war: 'Things fall apart; the centre cannot hold; Mere anarchy is loosed upon the world.' War is a great destroyer of the established order. For a conservative the centre has to hold. Otherwise the calm gentleness and culture of the past, represented in this poem by the great ancestral homes and the people who live in them, are lost for ever.

'A feeling of continuity'

Christ! What's the use of saying that one oughtn't to be sentimental about 'before the war'? I *am* sentimental about it. So are you if you remember it. It's quite true that if you look back on any special period of time you tend to remember the pleasant bits. That's true even of the war. But it's also true that people then had something that we haven't got now.

What? It was simply that they didn't think of the future as something to be terrified of. It isn't that life was softer then than now. Actually it was harsher. People on the whole worked harder, lived less comfortably, and died more painfully. The farm hands worked frightful hours for fourteen shillings a week and ended up as worn-out cripples with a five-shilling old-age pension and an occasional half-crown from the parish. And what was called 'respectable' poverty was even worse. When little Watson, a small draper at the other end of the High Street, 'failed' after years of struggling, his personal assets were £2 9s. 6d., and he died almost immediately of what was called 'gastric trouble', but the doctor let it out that it was starvation. Yet he'd clung to his frock coat to the last. Old Crimp, the watchmaker's assistant, a skilled workman who'd been at the job, man and boy, for fifty years, got cataract and had to go into the workhouse. His grandchildren were howling in the street when they took him away. His wife went out charing, and by desperate efforts managed to send him a shilling a week for pocket-money. You saw ghastly things happening sometimes. Small businesses sliding down the hill, solid tradesmen turning gradually into broken-down bankrupts, people dying by inches of cancer and liver disease, drunken husbands signing the pledge every Monday and breaking it every Saturday, girls ruined for life by an illegitimate baby. The houses had no bathrooms, you broke the ice in your basin on winter mornings, the back streets stank like the devil in hot weather, and the churchyard was bang in the middle of the town, so that you never went a day without remembering how you'd got to end. And yet what was it that people had in those days? A feeling of security, even when they weren't secure. More exactly, it was a feeling of continuity. All of them knew they'd got to die, and I suppose a few of them knew they were going to go bankrupt, but what they didn't know was that the order of things could change. Whatever might happen to themselves, things would go on as they'd known them.

GEORGE ORWELL
Coming up for Air, 1939

'In my beginning is my end'

In my beginning is my end. In succession
Houses rise and fall, crumble, are extended,

Are removed, destroyed, restored, or in their place
Is an open field, or a factory, or a by-pass.
Old stone to new building, old timber to new fires,
Old fires to ashes, and ashes to the earth
Which is already flesh, fur and faeces,
Bone of man and beast, cornstalk and leaf.
Houses live and die: there is a time for building
And a time for living and for generation
And a time for the wind to break the loosened pane
And to shake the wainscot where the field-mouse trots
And to shake the tattered arras woven with a silent motto.

    T. S. ELIOT
    'East Coker', *The Four Quartets*, 1942

THE DEBTOR

I am debtor to all, to all am I bounden,
Fellowman and beast, season and solstice, darkness and light,
And life and death. On the backs of the dead,
See, I am borne, on lost errands led,
By spent harvests nourished. Forgotten prayers
To gods forgotten bring blessings upon me.
Rusted arrow and broken bow, look, they preserve me
Here in this place. The never-won stronghold
That sank in the ground as the years into time,
Slowly with all its men steadfast and watching,
Keeps me safe now. The ancient waters
Cleanse me, revive me. Victor and vanquished
Give me their passion, their peace and the field.
The meadows of Lethe shed twilight around me.
The dead in their silences keep me in memory,
Have me in hold. To all I am bounden.

    EDWIN MUIR, 1949

'A political party may find that it has had a history'

A political party may find that it has had a history, before it is fully
aware of or agreed upon its own permanent tenets; it may have arrived
at its actual formation through a succession of metamorphoses and

adaptations, during which some issues have been superannuated and new issues have arisen. What its fundamental tenets are, will probably be found only by careful examination of its behaviour throughout its history and by examination of what its more thoughtful and philosophic minds have said on its behalf; and only accurate historical knowledge and judicious analysis will be able to discriminate between the permanent and the transitory; between those doctrines and principles which it must ever, and in all circumstances, maintain, or manifest itself a fraud, and those called forth by special circumstances, which are only intelligible and justifiable in the light of those circumstances.

T. S. ELIOT
The Literature of Politics, 1955

'Neither fixed nor finished'

My own attitude to politics, as I have made clear in writing of Cambridge days, had been strongly influenced by my uncle Geoffrey Butler's essays on *The Tory Tradition*. In his preface to these, written in 1914, he had declared, 'Resistance to predatory attacks upon property, and the like, will always form important items in the Tory programme. But Tory doctrine loses all that is ennobling in its appeal, if it confines itself to these; if it fails, that is, to get down to the principles which lie beneath all such resistance. The great Tory leaders of the past challenge us to something more, and by their challenge show us the secret of their own irresistible example. The captains of Toryism in the past can be made the instructors of Toryism in the present: and the Tory tradition is the Tory hope.' Many years later I wrote my own preface to a revised edition of the book in which I sought to identify the legacy of these captains of Toryism. What they had left us, I insisted, was not a collection of causes for which we were obliged to die in the last ditch, nor a set of premises by whose consistent application we might infallibly regulate our conduct, but a mature tradition of political thought and behaviour which is neither fixed nor finished. This tradition at its best is responsive to the demands of each new age, empirical as to method, resourceful in expressing itself in popular idiom, though deeply conscious that the 'councils to which Time is not called, Time will not ratify'.

R. A. BUTLER
The Art of the Possible, 1971

But not everything in the past is glorious . . .

People who are always praising the past
And especially the times of faith as best
Ought to go and live in the Middle Ages
And be burnt at the stake as witches and sages.

    STEVIE SMITH
    'The Past'

'There is no sound politics of antiquarianism'

It is perhaps not a happy description of this task as a search for 'roots', for although that word captures the ideas of tradition and allegiance which the conservative requires, it also suggests a kind of nostalgia which he cannot afford. Naturally, nostalgia for the past is more reasonable than nostalgia for the future; nevertheless it is, like every form of sentimentality, a way of 'standing back', a refusal to engage in the practice of rational life. It consigns its subject to inaction, and its condition is that of Dante's Limbo: without hope, living in desire. While the love of country and tradition is to some extent confirmed in the nostalgia with which the Englishman views his eccentricities, his countryside, his architecture, and the ghostly presences of England, this nostalgia depends upon the possibility of something more concrete – of a deliberate activity of citizenship of which it provides only a sepia-toned reflection. Here we see the distinction between true conservatism and mere 'conservation'. There is no sound politics of antiquarianism. It does not matter whether the 'antique drum' sounds from the pastures of rural England, or from the warm backyards of the slums. You can follow it, but you cannot lead it.

    Our search, then, is for the immediate forms of social participation, those forms which intelligibly present to the citizen the fact of his public life, and so generate his values.

    ROGER SCRUTON
    The Meaning of Conservatism, 1980

THE COMMONPLACE

A commonplace is good for nothing now
Yet that is how the world goes, all the same:

Nothing is what you had when you set out,
And nothing you will have when you go home.
C. H. SISSON, 1980

'Preserving "old England" is not some quirky passion'

The monarchy, of course, is one institution which pretty well everybody thinks worth preserving. It is worth preserving, above all, because
it symbolises the continuity of our national life – in a word, the past.
How does one quantify the value of the past? One can't, any more than
one can quantify the value of a poem. Nor can one quantify the value
of Westminster Abbey or of the Royal Parks. All one knows is that a
country which has preserved its past as well as Britain has done is far
better off than one that has not. Most people love the familiar and it is
no accident that when the soldiers in the First World War put their
thoughts to paper before going over the top, more often than not they
were thinking of some familiar domestic English landscape which for
them represented what they were fighting and dying for. Preserving
'old England' is not some quirky passion felt only by genealogists or
nostalgic romantics. It is something vitally important, above all to
ordinary people for whom belonging to an ancient nation is their only
privilege. Too few Thatcherite lieutenants understand this. They have
even suggested, for example, that the Royal Parks should be privatised,
so as to be run more efficiently and to bring in more revenue. In the old
Tory Party, controlled by inheritors of wealth in whom the habits of
custodianship come as second nature, such a lack of understanding
about the value of continuity would have been inconceivable.

PEREGRINE WORSTHORNE
The Politics of Manners, 1988

2

'The Cause of our Glorious Institutions'

One of the principal tasks of Conservatism is the preservation of those institutions, practices, procedures and ceremonies that together buttress the stability of the nation. For those forces which challenge custom, which deride tradition and convention, which undermine legitimate authority and aim at destabilization, are always at the gate.

Shakespeare warned that once degree, priority, place, office and custom were rejected then the stability of the State was threatened: 'Untune that string and see what discord follows'. Burke saw the preservation of the Constitution as a solemn trust which each generation had to bear; its vision for the future strengthened by the wisdom that it drew from the past.

The Constitution to be defended has itself changed over the years. In the seventeenth century, it was the struggle between the executive, the King, and the legislature, Parliament. I have included a passage from Clarendon's great history of the Civil War which describes Falkland's conversion from the parliamentary to the King's cause. It is one of the earliest examples of someone following their conscience in the defence of the Constitution.

In the first session of the Long Parliament, November 1640 to July 1641, Falkland, together with Pym and Hampden, led the attack upon the court, Laud and Stafford condemning the whole period of the 1630s as a 'malevolent conspiracy'. However he soon became suspicious of the parliamentarians' true motives. Both he and Clarendon decided to join the King in order to defend the Constitution from being undermined by the parliamentary demands of Pym. They saw the King as being the sovereign of the whole Constitution, not absolute but pervasive. The constitutionality of Parliament's decisions was guaranteed by the royal assent and the very existence of the royal power ensured that by working in unison the moral ends of society were met. Both Falkland and Clarendon had seen Pym manipulate the London mob to cow the members sitting at Westminster and they foresaw that this would develop into the absolute power of a vindictive parliamentary majority. They both feared the development of a democratic tyranny and the ensuing political terror which would take away the liberty and life of people. To avoid this the King's authority had to be defended at all cost, but that authority had to be exercised in a moderate way.

For Clarendon the basis of a political settlement was its morality. To him good order was essential rather than order itself. Hobbes on the other hand believed that peaceful despotism was a quite satisfactory goal since it stopped the drift into chaos. For Clarendon and Falkland power had to be derived from morality; that was the only justification for it and a guarantee of peace, harmony and wisdom.

Falkland and Clarendon wanted to fashion a constitutional monarchy. The pitiful tragedy of their cause was that the King was simply not up to it. They knew full well that the personal sacrifice they made in attaching themselves to Charles could well lead to disaster because of his fallibility. Falkland soon realized the hopelessness of the task and in one of the early battles of the Civil War at Newbury he rode into the enemy committing a very brave act akin to suicide.

Later in the seventeenth century James II was overthrown when he attempted to return the country to Roman Catholicism through the use of non-parliamentary powers and armed force. The decisive factor in the Glorious Revolution of 1688 was the defection of certain key Tories. The constitutional settlement of that year rested upon the balance of power between the House of Commons, the House of Lords, and the Crown. The Tories, however, did not benefit. Bolingbroke's contribution to Toryism was to resist the Whig supremacy of these earlier Hanoverian years. He saw that this balance of power was being destroyed by Walpole through patronage and placemen and through his extensive personal corruption, which led to him amassing a huge fortune. He promoted the interests of his own family to such an extent that his government was called the 'Robinocracy'. Together with the Crown, Walpole undermined the independence of the Commons through the manipulation of MPs. Free and regular elections were placed in jeopardy. But Bolingbroke, by defending the constitutional settlement of 1688, gave spirit, heart and intellectual distinction to the Tories.

In the eighteenth and early nineteenth centuries, the Constitution was monarchical, aristocratic and Protestant. The Tories resisted the 1832 Reform Act which extended the suffrage, but they quickly came to accept its consequences. The search throughout was for a system that produced stability and gave authority to the Government. Following the Reform Act the number of Conservative MPs was reduced to 150. Peel set about picking up the party, insisting that the cries of the ultras be rejected and that the party must reconcile itself to the reality of reform. At the election in 1841 the Tories won 367 seats. One of the steps along the road to success had been the publication in 1834 of the Tamworth Manifesto, which was the first statement of a party's policies issued by an incumbent Prime Minister and approved by his Cabinet. Peel realized that the purpose of the Conservative Party was to defend the existing Constitution; the Crown, the aristocracy, the Commons, and the Church of England. Some change was necessary but not too much. It is the earliest expression of liberal conservatism, and was condemned by Disraeli as an attempt to construct a party without principle which would lead to political infidelity.

The Tories promoted and enhanced the extension of the suffrage in the nineteenth century. A minority government, led by Derby in the Lords and Disraeli in the Commons, put on to the statute book the second great Reform Act of the nineteenth century which extended the franchise to all householders. Disraeli's motives, as usual, were complex. He wanted to outwit Gladstone whose Reform Bill of 1866 had failed and he wanted to assert his claim to be the next leader of the Conservative Party; to do this he became the spokesman in the Cabinet for the backbenchers who wanted a more radical change. Above all he always cherished a romantic view that the Conservative Party alone could unite the aristocracy and the working class against commercial and industrial interests.

The 1867 bill, as a result of amendments in the House of Commons, went much further than anyone had foreseen. Derby called it 'a leap in the dark'. It is, however, a good example of the Conservative Party being in charge of reform. It wasn't just a surrender to the radicals for some significant safeguards were built in, especially the retention of the difference between county and borough status which helped the Tories to win seats. Disraeli also ensured that the ensuing boundary changes placed the suburbs firmly back within the cities, thereby preserving the exclusive character of the county electorate.

In the following election the Liberals won a decisive victory, doing rather better than forecast in the counties, but Disraeli drew some consolation from the fact that the Tories won a lot of support in the cities; that was the bedrock upon which he was to build.

Today, more than a century later, the Conservative Party defends the existing electoral arrangement of 'first past the post' since it produces a greater stability than other electoral systems which may seem at first sight to be fairer. So historically, the main tenet of Conservatism has not simply been a defence of the status quo or of the established order. As Sir Walter Scott pointed out, these inherited institutions have to demonstrate their effectiveness. But once that is proved, they have to be defended, upheld and, if necessary, fought for. Evelyn Waugh warned that Conservatives always had to be active in the defence of civilization, for 'we are all potential recruits for anarchy. Unremitting effort is needed to keep men living together in peace'.

Institutions wear out and circumstances change. A good example of this is our criminal justice system. In the late 1980s it became clear that parts of it were not functioning well. The clear evidence of this was the spate of cases involving miscarriages of justice. It is very important to maintain public confidence in the criminal justice system for otherwise public order is at risk. That is why, after the Court of Appeal had decided to set aside the verdicts in the case of the Birmingham Six, I set up a Royal Commission in 1991 under Lord Runciman to examine the whole criminal justice system and to recommend changes in it.

Roger Scruton reminds us that 'the Constitution and the institutions which sustain it will always lie at the heart of conservative thinking'. In the 1992 election the constitutional question of devolution became an important issue, indeed north of the border it was the central issue. But the creation of a Scottish Assembly with executive authority and tax-raising powers raised fundamental questions which were just as important to Londoners as to Glaswegians. In a speech to a large rally in Wembley at the end of the general election campaign, John Major urged Britain to 'wake up' to the fact that the very unity of the United Kingdom was at risk.

'No greater fiend'

There lives no greater fiend than Anarchy.
She ruins states, turns houses out of doors,
Breaks up in rout the embattled soldiery.
SOPHOCLES
Antigone, c. 495–406 BC

The Divine Order

The heavens themselves, the planets, and this centre
Observe degree, priority and place,
Insisture, course, proportion, season, form,
Office and custom, all in line of order;
And therefore is the glorious planet Sol
In noble eminence enthron'd and spher'd
Amidst the other, whose med'cinable eye
Corrects the ill aspects of planets evil,
And posts like the commandment of a king,
Sans check, to good and bad. But when the planets
In evil mixture to disorder wander;
What plagues and what portents, what mutiny,
What raging of the sea, shaking of earth,
Commotion in the winds! Frights, changes, horrors,
Divert and crack, rend and deracinate,
The unity and married calm of states
Quite from their fixture! O, when degree is shak'd,
Which is the ladder of all high designs,
The enterprise is sick! How could communities,
Degrees in schools, and brotherhoods in cities,
Peaceful commerce from dividable shores,
The primogeniture and due of birth,
Prerogative of age, crowns, sceptres, laurels,
But by degree, stand in authentic place?
Take but degree away, untune that string,
And hark, what discord follows! Each thing meets
In mere oppugnancy: the bounded waters
Should lift their bosoms higher than the shores,
And make a sop of all this solid globe;

Strength should be lord of imbecility,
And the rude son should strike his father dead;
Force should be right; or rather, right and wrong –
Between whose endless jar justice resides –
Should lose their names, and so should justice too.

WILLIAM SHAKESPEARE

Troilus and Cressida, 1609

In the famous speech which he gives to the character of Ulysses, Shakespeare emphasizes to his Jacobean audience the importance of an authority which is divinely ordained and which is maintained by the hierarchical nature of society. It is not quite a text for the Divine Right of Kings, but it does offer a clear warning of what would happen should the state of things be undermined.

'The Character of Falkland'

But I must here take leave a little longer to discontinue this narration: and if the celebrating the memory of eminent and extraordinary persons, and transmitting their great virtues, for the imitation of posterity, be one of the principal ends and duties of history, it will not be thought impertinent, in this place, to remember a loss which no time will suffer to be forgotten, and no success or good fortune could repair. In this unhappy battle was slain the lord viscount Falkland; a person of such prodigious parts of learning and knowledge, of that inimitable sweetness and delight in conversation, of so flowing and obliging a humanity and goodness to mankind, and of that primitive simplicity and integrity of life, that if there were no other brand upon this odious and accursed civil war, than that single loss, it must be most infamous, and execrable to all posterity . . .

For this reason, when he heard it first whispered, 'that the king had a purpose to make him a privy counsellor,' for which there was, in the beginning, no other ground, but because he was known sufficient, (*haud semper errat fama, aliquando et eligit,*) he resolved to decline it; and at last suffered himself only to be overruled, by the advice and persuasions of his friends, to submit to it. Afterwards, when he found that the king intended to make him secretary of state, he was positive to refuse it.

Two reasons prevailed with him to receive the seals, and but for those he had resolutely avoided them. The first, the consideration that his refusal might bring some blemish upon the king's affairs, and that

men would have believed, that he had refused so great an honour and
trust, because he must have been with it obliged to do somewhat else
not justifiable. And this he made matter of conscience, since he knew
the king made choice of him, before other men, especially because he
thought him more honest than other men. The other was, lest he might
be thought to avoid it out of fear to do an ungracious thing to the
house of commons . . .

For these reasons, he submitted to the king's command, and became
his secretary, with as humble and devoted an acknowledgment of the
greatness of the obligation, as could be expressed, and as true a sense of
it in his heart.

EDWARD HYDE, EARL OF CLARENDON
History of the Rebellion in England, 1704
This passage refers to events in 1643.

'Rebels, who base aims pursue'

Who ne'er consented to our father's fall?
Then kings are slaves to those whom they command
And tenants to their people's pleasure stand.
Add, that the power for property allow'd
Is mischievously seated in the crowd:
For who can be secure of private right,
If sovereign sway may be dissolv'd by might?
Nor is the people's judgment always true:
The most may err as grossly as the few?
And faultless kings run down by common cry,
For vice, oppression, and for tyranny.
What standard is there in a fickle rout,
Which, flowing to the mark, runs faster out?
Nor only crowds but Sanhedrims may be
Infected with this public lunacy,
And share the madness of rebellious times,
To murder monarchs for imagin'd crimes.
If they may give and take whene'er they please,
Not kings alone (the Godhead's images,)
But government itself at length must fall
To nature's state, where all have right to all.
Yet grant our lords the people kings can make,

What prudent men a settled throne would shake?
For whatsoe'er their sufferings were before,
That change they covet makes them suffer more.
All other errors but disturb a state;
But innovation is the blow of fate.
If ancient fabrics nod, and threat to fall,
To patch their flaws, and buttress up the wall,
Thus far 'tis duty; but here fix the mark:
For all beyond it is to touch our ark.
To change foundations, cast the frame anew,
Is work for rebels, who base ends pursue;
At once divine and human laws control,
And mend the parts by ruin of the whole.
The tampering world is subject to this curse,
To physic their disease into a worse.

    JOHN DRYDEN
    Absalom and Achitophel, 1681

This is the greatest political poem in the English language. Dryden defended
Charles II and the right of his unpopular brother to succeed him. Here he warns of
the anarchy that would flow from any usurpation of the throne. James did succeed
but threw away the crown by changing too much.

'The world's great harmony'

'Twas then the studious head or generous mind,
Follower of God or friend of humankind,
Poet or patriot, rose but to restore
The faith and moral nature gave before;
Re-lumed her ancient light, not kindled new;
If not God's image, yet his shadow drew;
Taught pow'r's due use to people and to kings;
Taught not to slack nor strain its tender strings,
The less, or greater, set so justly true
That touching one must strike the other too;
Till jarring interests of themselves create
Th' according music of a well-mixed state.
Such is the world's great harmony, that springs
From order, union, full consent of things:
Where small and great, where weak and mighty made

To serve, not suffer, strengthen, not invade;
More pow'rful each as needful to the rest
And, in proportion as it blesses, bless'd;
Draw to one point, and to one centre bring
Beast, man, or angel, servant, lord or king.

ALEXANDER POPE

An Essay on Man, 1733

'The genius of our nation'

If liberty be that delicious and wholsome fruit, on which the British
nation hath fed for so many ages, and to which we owe our riches, our
strength, and all the advantages we boast of; the British constitution is
the tree that bears this fruit, and will continue to bear it, as long as we are
careful to fence it in, and trench it round, against the beasts of the field,
and the insects of the earth. To speak without a figure, our constitution is
a system of government suited to the genius of our nation, and even to
our situation. The experience of many hundred years hath shewn, that
by preserving this constitution inviolate, or by drawing it back to the
principles on which it was originally founded, whenever it shall be made
to swerve from them, we may secure to ourselves, and to our latest
posterity, the possession of that liberty which we have long enjoyed.

But happily this kind of progression from a free to a slavish constitution of government, was stopped at the revolution, and the notions
themselves are so exploded in the course of six and forty years, that they
are entertained at this hour by no set of men, whose numbers or
importance give them any pretence to be reckoned among our national
parties. It is as true, that there are now men who pursue the very same
design by different methods. The former attacked, these undermine our
liberty. The former were the beasts of the field hinted at above; these are
the insects of the earth; and like other insects, tho sprung from dirt, and
the vilest of the animal kind, they can nibble, and gnaw, and poison;
and, if they are suffered to multiply and work on, they can lay the most
fruitful country waste. Corruption and dependency are their favourite
topics.

LORD BOLINGBROKE

A Dissertation upon Parties, 1735

James II's attempt to subvert the Constitution by increasing the power of the
Crown led to the revolution of 1688. Bolingbroke was one of the most gifted and

eloquent politicians of his time. By the age of thirty-six, he had been Secretary of War in the Whig government during Marlborough's great victories and had then become a leading Tory minister who personally negotiated the Treaty of Utrecht which ended the war with Louis XIV. He was a close, personal friend of Pope and Swift, who thought he was 'the greatest young man I ever knew'. He fell from power on Queen Anne's death; fled to exile in France and schemed with the son of James II in the Jacobite rebellion of 1715. He was only allowed to return to England in 1723, when, from outside Parliament, he led the Tory attack upon the Whig government of Robert Walpole. He returned disappointed to France in 1735, realizing there was no prospect of office, and he spent the rest of his life writing his works of political philosophy and history.

'The highest degree of opulence'

Little else is requisite to carry a state to the highest degree of opulence from the lowest barbarism but peace, easy taxes, and a tolerable administration of justice: all the rest being brought about by the natural course of things.

ADAM SMITH, 1755

'Manners are of more importance than laws'

Manners are of more importance than laws. Upon them, in a great measure, the laws depend. The law touches us but here and there, and now and then. Manners are what vex or soothe, corrupt or purify, exalt or debase, barbarise or refine us, by a constant, steady, uniform, insensible operation, like that of the air we breathe in. They give their whole form and colour to our lives. According to their quality, they aid morals, they supply them, or they totally destroy them.

EDMUND BURKE

'This union of liberty with the law'

We have enjoyed ... the benefit of those original principles of our constitution ... It is this union of liberty with law, which, by raising a barrier equally firm against the encroachments of power, and the violence of popular commotion, affords to property its just security, produces the exertion of genius and labour, the extent and solidity of credit, the circulation and increase of capital; which forms and upholds the national character, and sets in motion all the springs

which actuate the great mass of the community through all its various
disciplines.

WILLIAM PITT, 1792

'The proper season for granting requests'

J[effrey] also says [in the *Edinburgh Review*, January 1818] that there
ought to be a reform in Parliament, because the people wish for it. If
the two propositions contained in this sentence form part of the Whig
creed, all I can say is that I am a Tory ... I am by no means persuaded
that the people's wishing for reform is a reason for *immediately* granting it to them. A *long continued* and *strongly expressed* wish of the
people of every country ought, no doubt, to be gratified; but it is the
part of a wise and strong Government to resist popular clamour, to
choose the proper season for granting requests, and to wait till it has
had time to distinguish between the real permanent will of the country
and a mere transitory cry.

J. R. WARD, later Lord Dudley, 1818

'The only unerring test'

An established system is not to be tried by those tests which may with
perfect correctness be applied to a new theory. A civilized nation, long
in possession of a code of law, under which, with all its inconveniences,
they have found means to flourish, is not to be regarded as an infant
colony, on which experiments in legislation may, without much danger
of presumption, be hazarded. A philosopher is not entitled to inves-
tigate such a system by those ideas which he has fixed in his own mind
as the standard of possible excellence. The only unerring test of every
old establishment is the *effect* it has actually produced; for that must be
held to be good, from whence good is derived. The people have, by
degrees, moulded their habits to the law they are compelled to obey;
for some of its imperfections, remedies have been found, to others they
have reconciled themselves; till, at last, they have, from various causes,
attained the object which the most sanguine visionary could promise to
himself from his own perfect *unembodied* system.

SIR WALTER SCOTT
Essay on Judicial Reform

'The foundation of a great party'

My object for some years past, that which I have most earnestly laboured to accomplish, has been to lay the foundation of a great party, which, existing in the House of Commons, and deriving its strength from the popular will, should diminish the risk and deaden the shock of a collision between the two deliberative branches of the legislature – which should enable us to check the too importunate eagerness of well-intending men, for hasty and precipitate changes in the constitution and laws of the country, and by which we should be enabled to say, with a voice of authority, to the restless spirit of revolutionary change, 'Here are thy bounds, and here shall thy vibrations cease.' Gentlemen, I was deeply impressed with a conviction of the necessity of forming such a party from the period when a great change was made in the representative system of the country . . .

If you ask me what I mean by conservative principles – as we have heard something like a vague and unsatisfactory description of them – I will, in conclusion, briefly state what I mean by conservative principles. By conservative principles I mean, and I believe you mean, the maintenance of the Peerage and the Monarchy – the continuance of the just powers and attributes of King, Lords, and Commons, in this country . . .

By conservative principles I mean, a determination to meet every threatened danger to the protestant establishment – nay, I mean more, I mean that we are determined upon the infliction – if we can inflict it – of 'a heavy blow and a great discouragement' to those principles which are antagonist to the establishment of the protestant faith. By conservative principles I mean, a maintenance of the settled institutions of church and state, and I mean also the maintenance, defence, and continuation of those laws, those institutions, that society, and those habits and manners which have contributed to mould and form the character of Englishmen, and enabled this country, in her contests and the fearful rivalry of war, to extort the admiration of the world, and in the useful emulation of peaceful industry, commercial enterprize, and social improvement, have endeared the name of England and Englishmen in every country in the world to those who seek the establishment of liberty without oppression.

ROBERT PEEL
Speech at Merchant Taylor's Hall, 1838

'The cause of our glorious institutions'

'If any fellow were to ask me what the Conservative Cause is, I am sure I should not know what to say,' said Buckhurst.

'Why, it is the cause of our glorious institutions,' said Coningsby. 'A Crown robbed of its prerogatives; a Church controlled by a commission; and an Aristocracy that does not lead.'

'Under whose genial influence the order of the Peasantry, "a country's pride," has vanished from the face of the land,' said Henry Sydney, 'and is succeeded by a race of serfs, who are called labourers, and who burn ricks.'

'Under which,' continued Coningsby, 'the Crown has become a cipher; the Church a sect; the Nobility drones; and the People drudges.'

'It is the great constitutional cause,' said Lord Vere, 'that refuses everything to opposition; yields everything to agitation; conservative in Parliament, destructive out of doors; that has no objection to any change provided only it be effected by unauthorised means.'

'The first public association of men,' said Coningsby, 'who have worked for an avowed end without enunciating a single principle.'

'And who have established political infidelity throughout the land,' said Lord Henry.

BENJAMIN DISRAELI
Coningsby, 1844

The Reform Act of 1867

Household suffrage will produce a state of things in many boroughs the results of which I defy any one to predict. In Leeds for example the present number of electors are about 8,500. With household suffrage they will become about 35,000. Is there any one who dares to say what will be the character & tendency of that constituency. It may be good or bad; but it is a revolution.

LORD CAERNARFON, 1867

We have inaugurated a new era in English politics this session, and depend upon it, the new fashion will henceforth be the rule and not the exception. This session we have not had what we before possessed – a party of attack and a party of resistance. We have instead two parties of competition who, like Cleon and the Sausage-seller of Aristophanes, are both bidding for the support of Demos.

ROBERT LOWE

Final debate on the Reform Bill, 1867

'The end of our poor Old England'

Inexpressibly delirious seems to me, at present in my solitude, the puddle of Parliament and Public upon what it calls the 'Reform Measure'; that is to say, The calling in of new supplies of block-headism, gullibility, bribeability, amenability to beer and balderdash, by way of amending the woes we have had from our previous supplies of that bad article. The intellect of a man who believes in the possibility of 'improvement' by such a method is to me a finished-off and shut-up intellect, with which I would not argue: mere waste of wind between us to exchange words on that class of topics. It is not Thought, this which my reforming brother utters to me with such emphasis and eloquence; it is mere 'reflex and reverberation,' repetition of what he has always heard others imagining to think, and repeating as orthodox, indisput-able, and the gospel of our salvation in this world. Does not all Nature groan everywhere, and lie in bondage, till you give it a Parliament? Is one a man at all unless one have a suffrage to Parliament? . . .

A superlative Hebrew Conjuror, spell-binding all the great Lords, great Parties, great Interests of England, to his hand in this manner, and leading them by the nose, like helpless mesmerised somnambulant cattle, to such issue, did the world ever see a *flebile ludibrium* of such magnitude before? Lath-sword and Scissors of Destiny; Pickleherring and the Three *Parcæ* alike busy in it. This too, I suppose, we had deserved. The end of our poor Old England (such an England as we had at last made of it) to be not a tearful Tragedy, but an ignominious Farce as well!

THOMAS CARLYLE

'Shooting Niagara: and After', *Macmillan's Magazine*, 1867

Carlyle was not the natural spokesman of the Conservative Party but he expressed the view that the extension of the suffrage was not a universal panacea and that Disraeli, the villain of the piece, betrayed the basic interests of the country. This is the voice of true reaction and I have included it because it was not heeded by the Conservative Party.

'Confidence'

If I were asked to define conservative policy, I should say that it was the upholding of confidence.

ROBERT CECIL, MARQUESS OF SALISBURY

'Chaos, Cosmos! Cosmos, Chaos!'

Chaos, Cosmos! Cosmos, Chaos! once again the sickening game;
Freedom, free to slay herself, and dying while they shout her name.

Step by step we gain'd a freedom known to Europe, known to all;
Step by step we rose to greatness, thro' the tonguesters we may fall.

You that woo the Voices – tell them 'old experience is a fool,'
Teach your flatter'd kings that only those who cannot read can rule.

Pluck the mighty from their seat, but set no meek ones in their place;
Pillory Wisdom in your markets, pelt your offal at her face.

Tumble Nature heel o'er head, and, yelling with the yelling street,
Set the feet above the brain and swear the brain is in the feet.

Bring the old dark ages back without the faith, without the hope,
Break the State, the Church, the Throne, and roll their ruins down the slope.

Authors – atheist, essayist, novelist, realist, rhymester, play your part,
Paint the mortal shame of nature with the living hues of Art.

Rip your brothers' vices open, strip your own foul passions bare;
Down with Reticence, down with Reverence – forward naked – let them stare.

Feed the budding rose of boyhood with the drainage of your sewer;
Send the drain into the fountain, lest the stream should issue pure.

Set the maiden fancies wallowing in the troughs of Zolaism,
Forward, forward, ay and backward, downward too into the abysm.

Do your best to charm the worst, to lower the rising race of men;
Have we risen from out the beast, then back into the beast again?

Only 'dust to dust' for me that sicken at your lawless din,
Dust in wholesome old-world dust before the newer world begin.

ALFRED LORD TENNYSON
'Locksley Hall Sixty Years After', 1886

This was written towards the end of Tennyson's life and is in stark contrast to the optimism of 'Locksley Hall', which was written forty years earlier. Here Tennyson warns of the dangers of a too liberal society, of a press that is too intrusive and of democracy destroyed by a lawless din.

THE SECOND COMING

Turning and turning in the widening gyre
The falcon cannot hear the falconer;
Things fall apart; the centre cannot hold;
Mere anarchy is loosed upon the world,
The blood-dimmed tide is loosed, and everywhere
The ceremony of innocence is drowned;
The best lack all conviction, while the worst
Are full of passionate intensity.

Surely some revelation is at hand;
Surely the Second Coming is at hand.
The Second Coming! Hardly are those words out
When a vast image out of *Spiritus Mundi*
Troubles my sight: somewhere in sands of the desert
A shape with lion body and the head of a man,
A gaze blank and pitiless as the sun,
Is moving its slow thighs, while all about it
Reel shadows of the indignant desert birds.
The darkness drops again; but now I know
That twenty centuries of stony sleep
Were vexed to nightmare by a rocking cradle,
And what rough beast, its hour come round at last,
Slouches towards Bethlehem to be born?

W. B. YEATS
The Cat and the Moon and Certain Poems, 1924

'A conservative has positive work to do'

A conservative is not merely an obstructionist who wishes to resist the introduction of novelties; nor is he, as was assumed by most nineteenth-century parliamentarians, a brake to frivolous experiment. He has positive work to do, whose value is particularly emphasized by the plight of Mexico. Civilization has no force of its own beyond what is given it from within. It is under constant assault and it takes most of the energies of civilized man to keep going at all. There are criminal ideas and a criminal class in every nation and the first action of every revolution, figuratively and literally, is to open the prisons. Barbarism is never finally defeated; given propitious circumstances, men and women who seem quite orderly will commit every conceivable atrocity. The danger does not come merely from habitual hooligans; we are all potential recruits for anarchy. Unremitting effort is needed to keep men living together at peace; there is only a margin of energy left over for experiment however beneficent. Once the prisons of the mind have been opened, the orgy is on. There is no more agreeable position than that of dissident from a stable society. Theirs are all the solid advantages of other people's creation and preservation, and all the fun of detecting hypocrisies and inconsistencies. There are times when dissidents are not only enviable but valuable. The work of preserving society is sometimes onerous, sometimes almost effortless. The more elaborate the society, the more vulnerable it is to attack, and the more complete its collapse in case of defeat. At a time like the present it is notably precarious. If it falls we shall see not merely the dissolution of a few joint-stock corporations, but of the spiritual and material achievements of our history.

EVELYN WAUGH
Robbery under Law, 1934

'A continuous parley'

From William's day onwards the key to our constitutional evolution is to be found in the interaction between the Crown, i.e. the central governing, directing, and initiating element in the national life, and the nation in its various 'estates', i.e. classes and communities, as the guardian of its written and unwritten laws and customs. The ambitions or needs of the Crown continually demanded changes in the law which the nation was only prepared to accept after discussion or parley with its representatives and on terms. Out of that parley, progressively more continuous and more intimate as needs increased, and out of those terms, grew our system, as we know it, of Government in and with Parliament, subject to the ever increasing influence of public opinion and to periodic review by the nation as a whole . . .

All the same, throughout the evolution of that system the two main elements of our political life have remained distinct, though progressively harmonized and integrated. Our Constitution is still, at bottom, based on a continuous parley or conference in Parliament between the Crown, i.e. the Government as the directing and energizing element, and the representatives of the Nation whose assent and acquiescence are essential and are only to be secured by full discussion. The whole life of British politics, to quote Bagehot, 'is the action and reaction between the Ministry and the Parliament'.

LEO AMERY
Thoughts on the Constitution, 1947

'The first duty'

The first duty of government is to uphold the law, and if it tries to bob, weave and duck round that duty when it is inconvenient the governed will do exactly the same thing, and then nothing will be safe, not home, not liberty, not life itself.

MARGARET THATCHER, 1975

'Liberty under law'

I must, of course, now unmask the philosophy underlying the gist of these remarks. I believe that there is a golden thread which alone gives meaning to the political history of the West, from Marathon to Alamein, from Solon to Winston Churchill and after. This I choose to call the doctrine of liberty under law. It is not a static doctrine claiming to be true for all time, like the gospel according to Hegel or Marx, or for that matter like the original language of the Nicene and Athanasian creeds. It offers no utopias and attempts to define no ideal state of society. It is rather an evolving and living tradition to which there is no exact orthodoxy or precise formula. Moreover, the body of doctrine and tradition is not, and never will be, complete. At different times and at different places it has been interpreted differently ...

In addition, there are direct and earlier sources of the living tradition quite outside the Christian and Jewish tradition. Some lie in Athens where the idea of freedom first found articulate expression and exercised her liberating force. Some lie in Rome with her tradition of definite legal principles and impartial judicial administration following in the wake of military conquest. It is strange, is it not, that three cities, none of which, at their zenith, can have numbered as many inhabitants as modern Birmingham, should have had an influence so disproportionately great? But in this pantheon of moral origins shall we not add that of the inhabitants of the little island moored off the coast of Europe which, inspired by the other three, first pioneered representative government, first insisted upon an independent judiciary irremovable at the caprice of a sovereign, first placed judgements of fact in the hands of a modern jury, first erected compromise and moderation into a principle and, besides all else, sought to interpret positive law in the light of the application of accepted moral principles?

QUINTIN HOGG, VISCOUNT HAILSHAM
The Door wherein I Went, 1975

'The heart of conservative thinking'

Authority, in the sense that we have considered, is an enormous artefact. By which I mean, not that authority is intentionally constructed, but rather that it exists only in so far as men exercise, understand and submit to it. The condition of society presupposes this general connivance, and a conservative will seek to uphold all those practices and institutions – among which, of course, the family is pre-eminent – through which the habits of allegiance are acquired ... The conservative believes in the power of state as necessary to the state's authority, and will seek to establish and enforce that power in the face of every influence that opposes it. However, his desire is to see power standing not naked in the forum of politics, but clothed in constitution, operating always through an adequate system of law, so that its movement seems never barbarous or oppressive, but always controlled and inevitable, an expression of the civilized vitality through which allegiance is inspired. The constitution, therefore, and the institutions which sustain it, will always lie at the heart of conservative thinking. The conservative places his faith in arrangements that are known and tried, and wishes to imbue them with all the authority necessary to constitute an accepted and objective public realm. It is from this that his respect for tradition and custom arises, and not from any end – such as freedom – towards which these practices are seen as a means.

ROGER SCRUTON
The Meaning of Conservatism, 1980

'The threat of a new barbarism'

A generation could quickly grow up ignorant and uncertain of our ethical and cultural heritage. This I characterize as the threat of a new barbarism. Today's barbarian is not outside the city walls but within them. He wears no bearskin and carries no club and may be armed with nothing more lethal than a ball-point pen. The nearest he may get to the primeval forest is the quadrangle of an Oxford (or a Cambridge) college but he is a barbarian none the less if he undermines the religious and moral values on which our traditions of civility are based.

This undermining may be done in a number of different ways. Moral and spiritual issues may be judged and resolved solely by their practical results, or they may be reduced to the status of linguistic problems and disposed of by an analysis of language, or they may be treated as being matters of wholly subjective feeling. All these approaches reject implicitly or explicitly what for centuries has been the foundation of western society – the belief in an order of values both objective and universal, the following of which constitutes the good life and its rejection the bad. The rejection of reason as a sure guide in human affairs destroys not only liberty but equality and fraternity. There can be no liberty without self-restraint, no equality without recognition of others as being endowed with reason and rights like ourselves, no fraternity without a sense of shared values. Without brotherhood society is reduced to a conglomeration of warring atoms in which conflicts are decided by force not law. Warfare such as this destroys in the end the very idea of community – that form of society in which what is shared is more important than what divides and in which men remain locked in argument but not in battle or fratricidal strife.

Society's concern with moral values springs then not only from their intrinsic worth but from the perceptions of the connection between the moral and social orders. One rests upon the other. The state borrows from above and below itself: it looks upwards to religion and morality as well as downwards to history and sociology. An earlier age produced the aphorism 'No Bishop No King'. Our own would do well to ponder on another, 'No morality: no law'. To deny or to lose sight of the ethical nature of political freedom is folly but it is a folly characteristic of our time.

NORMAN ST JOHN STEVAS
'The Moral Basis of Conservatism', 1980

'A pact with the devil'

As Home Secretary, responsible for keeping the good race relations we enjoy in Britain, I am determined that what we have seen in Germany and France will not happen here. But that depends upon having tough immigration and asylum laws which control the numbers coming into Britain. Such laws will only come from the Conservatives. Asylum control is an issue in this country, and in this election, just as much as in Germany. Mr Hattersley does not dare to speak about it. Mr Ashdown does not care to speak about it. But we do. It is our duty as Conservatives to speak about it.

The fascists in Baden Wurtemburg received 11 per cent of the vote. In Britain, that would not give them power. But in Germany, which has proportional representation, that 11 per cent will catapult the fascists into a powerful role in the State Parliament. I have warned many times that proportional representation makes it easier for extremist minorities to gain power. That has now happened in Germany, as it has happened with the fascist National Front in France.

Proportional representation has helped the fascists to march again in Europe. It is a terrible warning to us about what could happen if we threw away our system of first-past-the-post elections. That is what Mr Ashdown wants to do. It is what Mr Kinnock is prepared to do as the price for power. If proportional representation turned out to have the same results in Britain, it would be a pact with the devil.

Mr Kinnock and Mr Ashdown are preparing for Britain a deadly political cocktail. The ingredients are Labour and Liberal Democrat unconcern about increasing levels of economic migrants and asylum seekers entering Britain, coupled with the introduction of a political system which would unleash extremists who fed upon public concern about this issue. The Conservative Party will fight with all its strength against such a prospect. We are proud of the tolerance and stability of our ancient democracy which has allowed us as a nation to absorb over time people from different countries and cultures. We respect the character of the British people which has allowed this to happen. But no party can ignore the fact that this tolerance is based on a firm and fair control of numbers entering Britain.

The upheavals in eastern Europe and elsewhere in the world must not be allowed to trigger that scale of migration to Britain which has aroused the public anxieties we are now seeing in France, Germany and Austria. The wheelings and dealings of the Labour and Liberal Democrat parties, squabbling over power they have not yet won at the ballot box, must not be allowed to destroy our particular system of parliamentary democracy. For it is this system which has kept us in Britain free from the poisonous politics we are now seeing elsewhere in Europe.

KENNETH BAKER

Stroud election speech, 1992

In the general election in 1992, proportional representation became a most important issue because for most of the campaign it was thought that the result would be a hung parliament. The Liberal Democrat Party like the old Alliance strongly advocated it and insisted as a condition of the probable coalition that PR be introduced for Westminster in time for the next election. Neil Kinnock, the leader of the Labour Party, announced PR for the Scottish and Welsh Assemblies and the European Parliament as well as a full inquiry for parliamentary elections. John Major and other senior ministers pointed out the dangers of PR: the disproportionate power it gives to minorities, the instability from shifting coalitions, and the entrance it provides for extremist parties. I made this speech on the last Monday of the campaign in Stroud, referring to the successes of the extreme right candidates in the German regional elections the previous day. The Conservative Party continues to fulfil its historic role of defending the Constitution by resisting PR.

'Wake up, my fellow countrymen'

I want to turn first to a key issue at the very heart of this Election. It is the sleeping issue – but it matters more than anything. It hasn't been much talked about, but it's always been there. It is something that grips our very being as the British people. I speak of the unity of the United Kingdom – the rock of our constitution. We take it for granted – but at this Election it is at risk. Let me therefore speak to you simply, directly and, through you, to every part of the country. As your Prime Minister, yes, but as a Briton, too. Let me speak in plain, unvarnished terms.

The first issue arises in Scotland. At this Election, there is a nationalist party which proposes to tear Scotland away from our union. It is a negative case, a socialist case, a separatist case. It is the fast route to divorce between two great nations. The exchange of Great Britain for a little Scotland and a lesser union. Our admirers and our rivals across the world would think we were mad. The Labour and Liberal parties see short-term advantage in seeking to appease, not to wrestle with, this demon. They propose a new tax-raising parliament in Scotland. Such a plan would shake the balance of our constitution. Set us on the road to bitterness, conflict and separation.

There will be no further debate, no referendum. Just a headlong plunge into something of disastrous consequences to Britain. Scarcely a soul in England or Wales is aware of it. But, in the consequences of these changes, our whole nation would be caught. We could be no longer a United, but, a Disunited Kingdom – an outcome which would diminish us all. To imperil the tried and successful Union of our four nations for party benefit, as our opponents do, is unforgivable. To toss aside the Union through which, over three hundred years, this country has moulded the history of the world. That is unbelievable.

Can you, dare you, conceive of it? Consider the outcome. The walls of this island fortress that appear so strong, undermined from within, the United Kingdom untied, the bonds that generations of our enemies have fought and failed to break, loosened by us ourselves. But that is what is at risk on 9th April. Labour and Liberal policy could break up Britain.

This party, and this party alone, will defend our union. I ask you – go out and tell the people of the danger we face. If I could summon up all the authority of this office I would put it into this single warning – the United Kingdom is in danger. Wake up, my fellow countrymen. Wake up *now*, before it is too late.

JOHN MAJOR
Wembley party rally, 5 April 1992

3

'Change is our Ally'

At the heart of Conservatism are the opposing instincts of a reluctance to accept change and a recognition that change is inevitable, even necessary. To resist necessary change is as futile as resisting the force of gravity. One can try, but the apple will always fall to the ground, never soar upwards. The question for the Conservative, therefore, is how change should be handled, assimilated, influenced or controlled. A person or an institution with a strong sense of identity, and with the self-confidence which flows from that, can grapple all the more effectively with change than one which is only a weathercock turning indifferently to accommodate each and any wind which blows.

In the 1950s, the One Nation Group of Tory MPs produced a pamphlet with the title 'Change is our Ally'. They drew upon Burke's realization that 'A State without the means of some change is without the means of its conservation'. Disraeli said much the same in 1867, and Cardinal Newman drew comfort from his observation that 'Here below to live, is to change often.' Roger Scruton in 1980 advocated change, though Evelyn Waugh regretted that the Conservative Party had never turned the clock back.

For Sir Keith Joseph, who so influenced Margaret Thatcher's thinking, change was not to be pursued in the direction in which 1970s corporatism and socialism had led Britain. He spoke of 'the ratchet effect' of socialism, that the Conservatives were failing because they were accommodating the changes brought about by socialism, not reversing them. As a result, the Conservative governments led by Margaret Thatcher were marked by their radicalism, especially in the dismantling of State-owned monopoly services. It is ironic that political figures popularly regarded as being on the right of the political *spectrum demonstrated more real radicalism than was evinced by the figures of the Left when they were in power.*

One of the reasons that the Conservative Party has survived during periods of massive political and economic change, indeed survived much better than many centre-right parties on the Continent, is its reasonable, pragmatic and sensible approach to change. For the Conservative, change should be rooted in popular response, and derive from a deep respect for tradition, custom and the practices of the past.

To Conserve and Improve

A disposition to preserve and an ability to improve taken together,
would be my standard of a statesman.
    EDMUND BURKE
    Reflections on the Revolution in France, 1790

A state without the means of some change is without the means of its
conservation. Without such means it might even risk the loss of that
part of the constitution which it wished the most religiously to
preserve.
    EDMUND BURKE
    An Appeal from the New to the Old Whigs, 1791

'Can't you let it alone?'
    WILLIAM LAMB MELBOURNE, 2ND VISCOUNT
    This was Melbourne's habitual question.

Those who resist indiscriminately all improvements as innovations
may find themselves compelled to submit to innovations although
they are not improvements.
    GEORGE CANNING

'Nothing so dangerous as innovation'

'That is the beauty of it,' said Seithenyn. 'Some parts of it are rotten
and some parts of it are sound.'
    'It is well,' said Elphin, 'that some parts are sound: it were better
that all were so.'
    'So I have heard some people say before,' said Seithenyn, 'perverse
people, blind to venerable antiquity; that very unamiable sort of
people who are in the habit of indulging their reason. But I say that
the parts that are rotten give elasticity to those that are sound: they
give them elasticity, elasticity, elasticity. If it were all sound it would
break by its own obstinate stiffness ... There is nothing so dangerous
as innovation ... This immortal work has stood for centuries and will
stand for centuries more if we let it alone. It is well: it works well: let
well alone. Cupbearer fill. It was half rotten when I was born, and

that is a conclusive reason why it should be three parts rotten when I die.'

THOMAS LOVE PEACOCK

The Misfortunes of Elphin, 1829

Peacock satirizes the attitude of the Wellington Tories to the Reform Bill. In this extract the attention of the Welsh Prince Seithenyn is drawn by Elphin to the condition of an embankment on his property, which was supposed to keep out the sea. 'Elasticity' was considered to be the prime virtue of the old Constitution.

'All that I hope for'

All that I hope for is, that the change in the position of the country may be gradual, that it may be effected without civil war, and may occasion as little sudden destruction of individual interests and property as possible. We may all by degrees take our respective stations in the new order of things, and go on until further changes take place *ad infinitum.*

ARTHUR WELLESLEY, DUKE OF WELLINGTON, 1836

The best measures to avert a great calamity'

Now, all of you admit that the real question at issue is the improvement of the social and moral condition of the masses of the population. We wish to elevate, in the gradation of society, that great class which gains its support by manual labour. That is agreed on all hands. The mere interest of the landlords, the mere interest of the occupying tenants, important as they are, are subordinate to the great question – what is calculated to increase the comforts, to improve the condition, and elevate the social character of the millions who subsist by manual labour, whether they are engaged in manufactures or in agriculture . . . I will not hesitate to say my firm belief is, that it is most consistent with prudence and good policy, most consistent with the real interests of the landed proprietors themselves, most consistent with the maintenance of a territorial aristocracy, seeing by how precarious a tenure, namely, the vicissitude of the seasons, you hold your present protective system; I say that it is my firm belief that it is for the advantage of all classes, in these times of comparative comfort and comparative calm, to anticipate the angry discussions which might arise, by proposing at once a final settlement of the question . . .

I always will assert the right to give that advice which I

conscientiously believe to be conducive to the general well-being. I was
not considering ... what was the best bargain to make for a party. I
was considering first what were the best measures to avert a great
calamity and, as a secondary consideration, to relieve that interest,
which I was bound to protect, from the odium of refusing to acquiesce
in measures which I thought to be necessary for the purpose of averting
that calamity. Sir, I cannot charge myself or my colleagues with having
been unfaithful to the trust committed to us.

ROBERT PEEL

House of Commons, 15 May 1846

This is Sir Robert Peel's famous defence of his change of heart when he abandoned
the Tories' long commitment to protective duties on the import of corn. In 1846 he
repealed the Corn Laws in the belief that free trade would bring greater wealth to
the country and its people. It did. It also brought defeat to the Tories, who
remained out of power for most of the following twenty years. But Peel was
reverting to the traditional standpoint of the Tories that there should not be any
artificial barriers to trade.

'An unflinching conservative'

In politics, Mr Thorne was an unflinching conservative ... When that
terrible crisis of free trade had arrived, when the repeal of the corn laws
was carried by those very men whom Mr Thorne had hitherto regarded
as the only possible saviours of his country, he was for a time paralysed
... now all trust of human faith must for ever be at an end. Not only
must ruin come, but it must come through the apostasy of those who
had been regarded as the truest of true believers. Politics in England, as
a pursuit for gentlemen, must be at an end.

ANTHONY TROLLOPE

Barchester Towers, 1846

'The homage due'

I will not withold the homage due to the progress of reason and to
truth by denying that my opinions on the subject of protection have
undergone a change.

ROBERT PEEL

Debate on the Address, 1846

'What is conservatism?'

But you say you are conservative – eminently conservative – while we are revolutionary, destructive, or something of the sort. What is conservatism? Is it not adherence to the old and tried, against a new and untried? We stick to, contend for, the identical old policy on the point in controversy which was adopted by 'our fathers who framed the Government under which we live'; while you with one accord reject, and scout, and spit upon that old policy and insist upon substituting something new. True, you disagree among yourselves as to what that substitute shall be. You are divided on new propositions and plans, but you are unanimous in rejecting and denouncing the old policy of the fathers. Some of you are for reviving the foreign slave trade; some for a Congressional slave code for the Territories; some for Congress forbidding the Territories to prohibit slavery within their limits; some for maintaining slavery in the Territories through the judiciary; some for the 'gur-reat pur-rinciple' that 'if one man would enslave another, no third man should object,' fantastically called 'popular sovereignty'; but never a man among you in favor of Federal prohibition of slavery in Federal Territories, according to the practice of 'our fathers who framed the Government under which we live.' Not one of all your various plans can show a precedent or an advocate in the century within which our Government originated. Consider, then, whether your claim of conservatism for yourselves, and your charge of destructiveness against us, are based on the most clear and stable foundations.

ABRAHAM LINCOLN

'Change is constant'

In a progressive country change is constant; and the question is not whether you should resist change which is inevitable, but whether that change should be carried out in deference to the manners, the customs, the laws, and the traditions of a people, or whether it should be carried out in deference to abstract principles and arbitrary and general doctrines.

BENJAMIN DISRAELI, Edinburgh, 1867

'To reconcile change with that respect for tradition'

Throughout my public life I have aimed at two chief results. Not insensible to the principle of progress, I have endeavoured to reconcile change with that respect for tradition, which is one of the main elements of our social strength; and in external affairs I have endeavoured to develop and strengthen our Empire believing that the combination of achievement and responsibility elevates the character and condition of a people.

    BENJAMIN DISRAELI
    'Letter to the Electors of Buckinghamshire', 1876

'To live is to change'

The development then of an idea is not like an investigation worked out on paper, in which each successive advance is a pure evolution from a foregoing, but it is carried on through and by means of communities of men and their leaders and guides; and it employs their minds as its instruments, and depends upon them while it uses them. And so, as regards existing opinions, principles, measures, and institutions of the community which it has invaded; it develops by establishing relations between itself and them; it employs itself, in giving them a new meaning and direction, in creating what may be called a jurisdiction over them, in throwing off whatever in them it cannot assimilate. It grows when it incorporates, and its identity is found not in isolation, but in continuity and sovereignty ... It changes with them in order to remain the same. In a higher world it is otherwise, but here below to live is to change, and to be perfect is to have changed often.

    CARDINAL J. H. NEWMAN

To Newman change was a great continuing process whereby the old was transformed by the new through a natural assimilation. A good justification for a man who started as a priest in the Church of England and ended as a prelate in the Church of Rome.

'We change our blood or we perish'

The danger would be in not letting it be progressive, and there's a little danger too at times in our slowness. We change our blood or we perish.
GEORGE MEREDITH
Beauchamp's Career, 1876

'We must work at less speed'

The Tory party is composed of very varying elements; and there is much trouble and vexation of spirit in trying to make them work together. I think the 'classes and dependents of class' are the strongest ingredients in our composition: but we have so to conduct our legislation that we shall give some satisfaction to both classes and masses. This is specially difficult with the classes – because all legislation is rather unwelcome to them, as tending to disturb a state of things with which they are satisfied. It is evident, therefore, that we must work at less speed and at a lower temperature, than our opponents. Our Bills must be tentative and cautious; not sweeping and dramatic.
ROBERT CECIL, MARQUESS OF SALISBURY, November 1886
Salisbury and his Chancellor of the Exchequer were temperamentally unsuited. Churchill was hyperactive and conceited in the belief that he was the darling of the masses. In this letter Salisbury issued a stinging rebuke, and rather cynically stated the reason why Tories should be slower. He, however, acted very quickly in accepting immediately Churchill's resignation, thereby denying him any opportunity of withdrawing it. It is also one of the paradoxes of Conservatism that Salisbury did put on to the Statute Book several major measures of social reform, such as the creation of the county councils, free elementary education and the Workman's Compensation Act.

'Rooted in original realities'

We therefore come back to the primary truth, that what is right with the world has nothing to do with future changes, but is rooted in original realities. If groups or peoples show an unexpected independence or creative power; if they do things no one had dreamed of their doing; if they prove more ferocious or more self-sacrificing than the wisdom of the world had ever given them credit for, then such inexplicable outbursts can always be referred back to some elementary and absolute doctrine about the nature of men. No traditions in this world are so ancient as the traditions that lead to modern upheaval and innovation. Nothing nowadays is so conservative as a revolution. The men who call themselves Republicans are men walking the streets of deserted and tiny city-states, and digging up the great bones of pagans. And when we ask on what republicanism really rests, we come back to that great undemonstrable dogma of the native dignity of man. And when we come back to the lord of creation, we come back of necessity to creation; and we ask ourselves that ultimate question which St Thomas Aquinas (an extreme optimist) answered in the affirmative: Are these things ultimately of value at all?

    G. K. CHESTERTON, 1910

'I was a Tory'

I was a Tory in the sense that I disliked change unless the need for it was amply proved, and that I desired to preserve continuity with the past and keep whatever of the old foundations were sound.

    JOHN BUCHAN

'The evolutionary appetite'

KING MAGNUS: I stand for the future and the past, for the posterity that has no vote and the tradition that never had any. I stand for the great abstractions: for conscience and virtue; for the eternal against the expedient; for the evolutionary appetite against the day's gluttony; for intellectual integrity, for humanity, for the rescue of industry from commercialism and of science from professionalism, for everything that you desire as sincerely as I, but which in you is held in leash by the Press, which can organize against you the ignorance and superstition, the timidity and credulity, the gullibility and prudery, the hating and hunting instinct of the voting mob, and cast you down from power if you utter a word to alarm or displease the adventurers who have the Press in their pockets.

    G B SHAW
    The Apple Cart, 1930

G. B. Shaw despised Conservatism, all that it stood for and all that it had done. In the Fabian Society, he helped to fashion an intellectual force which he hoped would sweep it away. He was a formidable opponent but in this passage as a playwright he was able to empathize with the Tory approach to life.

'History is not the study of origins'

If we see in each generation the conflict of the future against the past, the fight of what might be called progressive versus reactionary, we shall find ourselves organizing the historical story upon what is really an unfolding principle of progress, and our eyes will be fixed upon certain people who appear as the special agencies of that progress. We shall be tempted to ask the fatal question, To whom do we owe our religious liberty? But if we see in each generation a clash of wills out of which there emerges something that probably no man ever willed, our minds become concentrated upon the process that produced such an unpredictable issue, and we are more open for an intensive study of the motions and interactions that underlie historical change. In these circumstances the question will be stated in its proper form: How did religious liberty arise? The process of the historical transition will then be recognized to be unlike what the whig historian seems to assume – much less like the procedure of a logical argument and perhaps much more like the method by which a man can be imagined to work his way out of a 'complex'. It is a process which moves by mediations and those mediations may be provided by anything in the world – by men's sins or misapprehensions or by what we can only call fortunate conjunctures. Very strange bridges are used to make the passage from one state of things to another; we may lose sight of them in our surveys of general history, but their discovery is the glory of historical research. History is not the study of origins; rather it is the analysis of all the mediations by which the past was turned into our present.

HERBERT BUTTERFIELD
The Whig Interpretation of History, 1931

A Critic Speaks ...

The trouble with the Conservative Party is that it has never turned the clock back a single second.

EVELYN WAUGH

'But for reactionaries'

If you wanted to be in the advance guard of political thinking in the 1830s you had to believe that if only the state ceased altogether to control man's economic activities, perfect harmony and perfect justice would result. Equally, if you wanted to be in the front rank of progress in the 1890s, or if you wanted to have any sort of reputation for intelligence and virtue in the period between the two last great wars, you had to believe that nothing was necessary to the realisation of the Kingdom of Heaven except that the state should forthwith control all man's economic activities.

One of the great merits of the Conservative Party, which is normally accounted to it as a vice, is that it never accepted either of these sweeping opinions. In the days when free enterprise was the intellectual fashion, it concentrated on pointing out the limitations of this philosophy, and today, when state control is the fashion, it concentrates on pointing out the limitations of *this* idea. This is what is meant by being a reactionary, that is to say a man with a capacity and a tendency to react against the particular ideas which happen to be in vogue at the moment. But for reactionaries, there would be no kind of continuity in British politics. Quite apart from this, there is probably something to be said for the view that the exact amount of freedom which men ought to have differs substantially at different times and in different places, and that there is no abstract principle which in itself affords a mathematically certain way of determining the degree of personal liberty which can safely be tolerated in, say, a prison colony and a republic of Quakers. This distrust of abstract principles as infallible guides on the subject of personal liberty is another Conservative characteristic known philosophically as empiricism and polemically as 'opportunism'. It is another thing to which Britain owes much, including the existence and steady evolution of the British Commonwealth, and of course it is another thing which the Left classifies as Tory stupidity.

T. E. UTLEY, 1953

4

'The World Seems Ever More Free-Market'

Modern democratic politics is about economics. The word was not used much by the Tories in the eighteenth and nineteenth centuries, they preferred 'trade', 'industry' and 'commerce'. In the twentieth century it is all very different, economic management covers not only those three things but also the level of government spending, monetary policy, interest rates, exchange rates and demand management.

In this chapter, I give prominence to those elements in Conservative thinking which have been constant over the years. But there has been at different times varying emphasis between interventionist policies and the free market. Conservatives have consistently supported policies that are based on sound money, private enterprise, lower taxes and less State involvement. As early as 1735, Bolingbroke castigated the high tax policies of Walpole; Adam Smith warned of the danger of excessive government expenditure, and Lecky, at the end of the nineteenth century warned that high taxes led to intrusive bureaucracy and less personal freedom. In the 1950s, Rab Butler reduced taxes to breathe new life into the economy and each of the Chancellors of the Exchequer under Margaret Thatcher abolished taxes and reduced income tax significantly. She made it an object of policy to reduce government spending as a percentage of the country's wealth and for three years running the Government was able to reduce taxes, repay debt and increase social spending.

So, there is a distinct thread running through Conservative economic thinking over the centuries. More government expenditure means less choice for the individual. Socialism, on the other hand, looks upon high government spending, with its consequent high tax levels, as a virtue and as a means of changing society. Adam Smith and Edmund

Burke, two of the founding fathers of Conservative thought, argued that commerce flourished, industry prospered and wealth multiplied if the State did as little as possible. It had, of course, to raise revenue for the defence of the realm, the maintenance of justice, and to help the needy, but that done, Adam Smith was certain that a country's interests were best served by a 'hidden hand', the decisions of countless people in the market place.

This policy prevailed in the nineteenth century though the State did introduce laws to regulate and control business activity. The central policy of socialism as it developed in the late nineteenth century was the use of State power to intervene in the markets, to plan, and to control. The Conservatives, on the other hand, aimed to strike a balance between the untrammelled laissez-faire roundly condemned by Carlyle and the controlled, planned economy. But the slump of the 1930s led Conservatives like Harold Macmillan to advocate greater intervention. The re-shaping of Conservative policy immediately after the war, in such documents as the Industrial Charter, was in much the same vein. Rab Butler, the author of the charter, was none the less at pains to point out in his memoirs that when he became Chancellor of the Exchequer he did introduce measures to stimulate business and create an enterprise culture.

One issue that split the Tories in the nineteenth century was free trade. In 1846 Peel and free trade won. In 1906 Joseph Chamberlain and protection won but at the price of dividing the party so sharply that it lost the election. This is no longer a matter of contention. Free trade has won and the party is united in wanting to see tariff barriers, artificial restraints of trade and all manner of restrictive practices disappear. Churchill, T. E. Utley and Michael Oakeshott all warned against monopolies and trade unions distorting the market in favour of privileged interests. That too, has been a strong Conservative theme.

In the introduction I wrote about Ted Heath's ill-fated experiment in intervention. Nigel Lawson's Mais lecture in 1984 summarized the policies followed by the Thatcher Government after 1979. They were certainly more market orientated: in particular, the State's respon-sibilities for the great public utilities were transferred to the market and to the regulator. State assets were sold to the public for billions of pounds. But, as Keith Joseph said, 'Monetarism was not enough', and the Conservatives have showed once again their ability to reconcile two strands that seemed to pull in different directions. What has emerged from the Thatcher years is not a completely free-for-all market, rather the market sustains a system which recognizes the social obligations for those who are less able, or less lucky.

'The increase and continuance of taxes'

The increase and continuance of taxes acquire to the crown, by multiplying officers of the revenue, and by arming them with formidable powers against the rest of their fellow-subjects, a degree of power, the weight of which the inferior ranks of our people have long felt, and they most, who are most useful to the commonwealth, and which even the superior ranks may feel one time or other; for I presume it would not be difficult to shew how a full exercise of the powers that are in being, with, or even without some little additions to them, for the improvement of the revenue, that stale pretence for oppression, might oblige the greatest lord in the land to bow as low to a commissioner of the customs, or excise, or to some subaltern harpy, as any nobleman or gentleman in France can be obliged to bow to the intendant of his province. But the establishment of public funds, on the credit of these taxes, hath been productive of more and greater mischiefs than the taxes themselves, not only by increasing the means of corruption, and the power of the crown, but by the effect it hath had on the spirit of the nation, on our manners, and our morals.

HENRY ST JOHN, VISCOUNT BOLINGBROKE, 1735

A desire to reduce taxes has a long and honourable pedigree. Bolingbroke opposed taxation since it gave the government too much power, and the tax collectors bore down too heavily on the taxpayers.

'Prodigality and misconduct'

Great nations are never impoverished by private, though they sometimes are by public, prodigality and misconduct. The whole, or almost the whole public revenue, is in most countries employed in maintaining unproductive hands.

ADAM SMITH

Inquiry into the Nature and Causes of the Wealth of Nations, 1776

'Led by an invisible hand'

Every individual ... generally, indeed, neither intends to promote the public interest, nor knows how much he is promoting it. By preferring the support of domestic to that of foreign industry he intends only his own security; and by directing that industry in such a manner as its produce may be of the greatest value, he intends only his own gain, and he is in this, as in many other cases, led by an invisible hand to promote an end which was no part of his intention.

ADAM SMITH
Inquiry into the Nature and Causes of the Wealth of Nations, 1776

'Uniform, constant and uninterrupted effort'

A desire which, though generally calm and dispassionate, comes with us from the womb and never leaves us until we go into the grave. In the whole interval which separates those two moments, there is scarce perhaps a single instant in which any man is so perfectly and completely satisfied with his situation as to be without any wish of alteration or improvement of any kind. An augmentation of fortune is the means by which the greater past of men propose and wish to better their condition . . . The uniform, constant, and uninterrupted effort of every man to better his condition, the principle from which public and national, as well as private opulence is originally derived, is frequently powerful enough to maintain the natural progress of things towards improvement, in spite both of the extravagance of government and of the greatest errors of administration.

ADAM SMITH
Inquiry into the Nature and Causes of the Wealth of Nations, 1776

'One of the shabbiest Gospels ever preached'

In brief, all this Mammon-Gospel of Supply and Demand, Competition, Laissez-faire and Devil take the hindmost, begins to be one of the shabbiest Gospels over preached, or altogether the shabbiest . . . Farthing cheaper per yard! No great Nation can stand at the apex of such a pyramid. Screwing itself higher and higher; balancing itself on its great toe! . . . The inventive genius of England is not a Beaver's or a Skunk's or a Spider's genius; it is a Man's genius, I hope with a god over him.

THOMAS CARLYLE
Past and Present, 1843

'More massive and more colossal productive forces'

The bourgeoisie, during its rule of scarce one hundred years, has created more massive and more colossal productive forces than have all preceding generations together. Subjection of Nature's forces to man, machinery, application of chemistry to industry and agriculture, steam-navigation, railways, electric telegraphs, clearing of whole continents for cultivation, canalization of rivers, whole populations conjured out of the ground – what earlier century had even a presentiment that such productive forces slumbered in the lap of social labour?

KARL MARX AND FRIEDRICH ENGELS
The Communist Manifesto, 1848

'How the gluttony of business is punished'

The law of wise life is, that the maker of the money should also be the spender of it, and spend it, approximately, all before he dies; so that his true ambition as an economist should be, to die, not as rich, but as poor, as possible, calculating the ebb tide of possession in true and calm proportion to the ebb tide of life. Which law, checking the wing of accumulative desire in the mid-volley, and leading to peace of possession and fulness of fruition in old age, is also wholesome, in that by the freedom of gift, together with present help and counsel, it at once endears and dignifies age in the sight of youth, which then no longer strips the bodies of the dead, but receives the grace of the living. Its chief use would (or will be, for men are indeed capable of attaining to this much use of their reason), that some temperance and measure will be put to the acquisitiveness of commerce. For as things stand, a man holds it his duty to be temperate in his food, and of his body, but for no duty to be temperate in his riches, and of his mind. He sees that he ought not to waste his youth and his flesh for luxury; but he will waste his age, and his soul, for money, and think it no wrong, nor *delirium tremens* of the intellect any evil. But the law of life is, that a man should fix the sum he desires to make annually, as the food he desires to eat daily; and stay when he has reached the limit, refusing increase of business, and leaving it to others, so obtaining due freedom of time for better thoughts. How the gluttony of business is punished, a bill of health for the principals of the richest city houses, issued annually, would show in a sufficiently impressive manner.

JOHN RUSKIN

Essays on Political Economy, 1867

Ruskin is not usually cited in aid of Conservatism, but, his contempt for the aggressive acquisition of wealth finds a sympathetic welcome with many traditional Tories.

'Stop competition, and you stop the struggle of individualism'

All life is a struggle. Amongst workmen, competition is a struggle to advance towards high wages. Amongst masters, to make the highest profits . . . Stop competition, and you stop the struggle of individualism . . . Under competition, the lazy man is put under the necessity of exerting himself; and if he will not exert himself, he must fall behind. If he do not work, neither shall he eat . . . There is enough for all, but do your own share of work you must.

SAMUEL SMILES

'A question of liberty'

The expansion of the authority and the multiplication of the functions of the State in other fields, and especially in the field of social regulation, is an equally apparent accompaniment of modern democracy. This increase of State power means a multiplication of restrictions imposed upon the various forms of human action. It means an increase of bureaucracy, or, in other words, of the number and power of State officials. It means also a constant increase of taxation, which is in reality a constant restriction of liberty. One of the first forms of liberty is the right of every man to dispose of his own property and earnings, and every tax is a portion of this money taken from him by the force and authority of the law. Many of these taxes are, no doubt, for purposes in which he has the highest interest. They give him the necessary security of life, property, and industry, and they add in countless ways to his enjoyment. But if taxes are multiplied for carrying out a crowd of objects in which he has no interest, and with many of which he has no sympathy, his liberty is proportionately restricted. His money is more and more taken from him by force for purposes of which he does not approve. The question of taxation is in the highest degree a question of liberty, and taxation under a democracy is likely to take forms that are peculiarly hostile to liberty. I have already pointed out how the old fundamental principle of English freedom, that no one should be taxed except by his consent, is being gradually discarded; and how we are steadily advancing to a state in which one class will impose the taxes, while another class will be mainly compelled to pay them. It is obvious that taxation is more and more employed for objects that are not common interests of the whole community, and that there is a growing tendency to look upon it as a possible means of confiscation; to make use of it to break down the power, influence, and wealth of particular classes; to form a new social type; to obtain the means of class bribery.

W. H. LECKY
Democracy and Liberty, 1898
The Victorian historian Lecky questioned whether true freedom was really compatible with parliamentary government. Here he echoes Mill's concern that minority interests would be submerged and penalized by an executive purporting to act in the interests of the majority.

'This peaceful evolution'

But I do not propose to employ this defence of private enterprise in the fields for which it is best suited in order to condone or excuse the poverty and insecurity in the basic necessities of life, which we have today as a legacy of unrestrained competition and uneconomic waste and redundancy. I shall advocate all the more passionately on grounds of morality, of social responsibility, as well as of economic wisdom, a wide extension of social enterprise and control in the sphere of minimum human needs. The satisfaction of those needs is a duty which society owes to its citizens. In carrying out that responsibility it should adopt the most economical methods of large-scale co-operative enterprise. The volume of the supply of these necessities, the prices at which they are sold, and the power of the consumer to buy them should not be left to the determination of the push and pull of competitive effort. We have to evolve a new system by which the supply of those articles which we have classified as being of common need and more or less standardised in character, would be absorbed into an amplified conception of the social services . . .

Britain has been moving along the road towards economic planning for many years now in accordance with the traditional English principles of compromise and adjustment. Unless we can continue this peaceful evolution from a free capitalism to planned capitalism, or, it may be, a new synthesis of Capitalist and Socialist theory, there will be little hope of preserving the civil, democratic, and cultural freedom which, limited as it may be at the moment by economic inefficiency, is a valuable heritage. It is only by the adoption of this middle course that we can avoid resorting to measures of political discipline and dictatorship.

HAROLD MACMILLAN
The Middle Way, 1938

'Dangerously close to totalitarianism'

If the state does not interfere, then other semi-political organisations such as monopolies, trusts, unions, etc., may interfere, reducing the freedom of the market to a fiction. On the other hand, it is most important to realise that without a carefully protected market, the whole economic system must cease to serve its only rational purpose, to satisfy the demands of the consumer ... Economic 'planning' that does not plan for economic freedom in this sense will lead danger-ously close to totalitarianism.

KARL POPPER, 1945

'Defend the general public against abuses of monopolies'

It is an essential principle of Conservative, Unionist and Tory policy to defend the general public against abuses of monopolies and against restraints on trade and enterprise, whether these evils come from private corporations, from the mischievous plans of doctrinaire governments, or from the incompetence and arbitrariness of depart-ments of State.

WINSTON CHURCHILL, 1946

'Strong central guidance over the operation of the economy'

Our first purpose was to counter the charge and the fear that we were the party of industrial go-as-you-please and devil-take-the-hindmost, that full employment and the Welfare State were not safe in our hands. We therefore took our cue less from our historic philosophy, though that would indeed have been relevant, than from the existing complexity of modern industry and Britain's position as a debtor country which made reversion to *laissez-faire* impossible. 'In economic matters the government has very important functions', we insisted in the accents of Keynesianism . . . The Charter was, therefore, first and foremost an assurance that in the interests of efficiency, full employment and social security, modern Conservatism would maintain strong central guidance over the operation of the economy.

Our second purpose was to present a recognizable alternative to the reigning orthodoxies of Socialism – not to put the clock back, but to reclaim a prominent role for individual initiative and private enterprise in the mixed and managed economy . . . what stands out very plainly is the extent to which we foresaw and foreshadowed the characteristically Conservative measures of the post-1951 period, with many of which I was myself to be associated as Chancellor – the improvement of incentives through reduced taxation, the encouragement of a high level of personal savings, the steady and orderly reduction of physical controls, the overhauling of the top-heavy administrative machine and the shrinking of the Civil Service, the reopening of commodity markets, the sharpening of competition by bringing what we called 'the floodlight of publicity' to bear upon restrictive practices, and the empirical approach to denationalization. All these are to be found in the Charter; and if they were not the ingredients which gave it its most distinctive flavour, this was because an assertion of freedom may be taken for granted in the Conservative faith, whereas our imperative need was to establish what was then very far from being taken for granted: the Conservative intention to reconcile individual effort with a proper measure of central planning and direction and no less important to 'point to a way of life designed to free private endeavour from the taint of selfishness or self-interest'.

R. A. BUTLER

The Art of the Possible, 1971

After its substantial and unexpected defeat in 1945 Rab and a group of talented young men in the research department – Maudling, Macleod, Powell and Angus Maude – decided that it was essential for the party to distance itself from its traditional free-market, open-competition and non-interfering approach. This policy was most eloquently expressed in the Industrial Charter in 1947. The Tories had to accept the post-war settlement and this paid off for within six years they were in power. Rab took credit in his memoirs for the liberalizing measures he introduced as Chancellor after 1951, but it fell to Margaret Thatcher's

governments to dismantle the architecture of the planned and State-owned
economy which Attlee had established.

'All monopolies are prejudicial to freedom'

Collectivism is indifferent to all elements of our freedom and the enemy
of some. But the real antithesis of a free manner of living, as we know
it, is syndicalism. Indeed, syndicalism is not only destructive of freedom; it is destructive, also, of any kind of orderly existence. It rejects
both the concentration of overwhelming power in the government (by
means of which a collectivist society is always being rescued from the
chaos it encourages), and it rejects the wide dispersion of power which
is the basis of freedom. Syndicalism is a contrivance by means of which
society is disposed for a perpetual civil war in which the parties are the
organized self-interest of functional minorities and a weak central
government, and for which the community as a whole pays the bill in
monopoly prices and disorder. The great concentrations of power in a
syndicalist society are the sellers of labour organized in functional
monopoly associations. All monopolies are prejudicial to freedom, but
there is good reason for supposing that labour monopolies are more
dangerous than any others, and that a society in the grip of such
monopolies would enjoy less freedom than any other sort of society. In
the first place, labour monopolies have shown themselves more capable
than enterprise monopolies of attaining really great power, economic,
political and even military. Their appetite for power is insatiable and,
producing nothing, they encounter none of the productional dis-
economies of undue size. Once grown large, they are exceedingly
difficult to dissipate and impossible to control. Appearing to spring
from the lawful exercise of the right of voluntary association (though
as monopolistic associations they are really a denial of that right), they
win legal immunities and they enjoy popular support however scandal-
ous their activity. Enterprise monopolies, on the other hand (not less to
be deplored by the libertarian), are less dangerous because they are less
powerful. They are precariously held together, they are unpopular and
they are highly sensitive to legal control. Taken separately, there is no
question which of the two kinds of monopoly is the more subversive of
freedom. But in addition to its greater power, the labour monopoly is
dangerous because it demands enterprise monopoly as its complement.
There is a disastrous identity of interest between the two kinds of

monopoly; each tends to foster and to strengthen the other, fighting together to maximize joint extractions from the public while also fighting each other over the division of the spoils. Indeed, the conflict of capital and labour (the struggle over the division of earnings) is merely a sham fight (often costing the public more than the participants), concealing the substantial conflict between the producer (enterprise and labour, both organized monopolistically) and the consumer.

MICHAEL OAKESHOTT, 1949

'The normal environment in which nations live'

To a Tory the nation is not primarily an economic entity. It may place political and social ends above purely economic ones, and for their sake may justifiably on occasions seek to prevent change or divert it. Yet economic change is the normal environment in which nations live, and successful adjustment to it is a condition of their well-being. In six years of war and six of Socialism this important truth was dangerously obscured and overlaid. We doubt if it yet claims sufficient attention.

'A Tory Approach to Social Problems', One Nation Pamphlet, 1950

'The pendulum must swing back'

Political thought and practice during the last 40 years have swung away from laissez-faire toward the opposite extreme of centralised planning and control ... In the second half of the twentieth century the creation of new wealth has become our most urgent need. If this is to be achieved we believe that the pendulum must swing back to a more competitive system ... This means a reversal of the trend of the pre-war era. In the 1920s and '30s, rationalisation, whether under public or private control, was the order of the day. Employers and owners of capital saw in it an insurance against sudden and complete defeat; employees thought that it offered some guarantee against the worst forms of unemployment. The whole emphasis was on the defence of the status quo ... Since the war the economic setting has become utterly different ... The emphasis has thus shifted from stability to change.

'Change is our Ally', One Nation Pamphlet, 1954

'The best judges'

The first of these themes is that efficient co-ordination depends not on centralised planning but on the exercise of consumer choice based on economic costs competitively determined.

It has been fashionable for many years to respond to talk about the virtues of competition with dark warnings of anarchy and waste, and to emphasise the need for co-ordination in economic effort. This attitude has, we have seen, been by no means confined to Socialists, and it has left us with many harmful anachronisms in our economy. We do not believe that any group of men can be wise enough, or can command sufficient executive resources, to direct the whole economy or a very large sector of it. This is so whether the planners belong to a government department, a nationalised board, or some private trade association.

These views can, or course, be misrepresented as an attack on all forms of planning. They are nothing of the kind. The planning and co-ordination which are essential in modern industry are a part of the apparatus of management. They are, however, not the creative forces of industry. Every industry has its customers, and it is they who must be presumed to be the best judges of what they want. They are the most effective co-ordinating force, provided they can choose between different goods and services offered at true economic cost.

This argument for co-ordination by competition is not an argument for a pure *laissez-faire* economy. While it is normally harmful from an economic point of view to distort the natural interaction of the forces of supply and demand, it may well be beneficial to control the speed of this reaction by raising or lowering the economic temperature. This may be needed to mitigate the effects of economic change for social purposes; but it may also be needed in order to protect the country's economy against world conditions in general and the actions of other individual countries in particular.

'Change is our Ally', *One Nation Pamphlet*, 1954
This CPC pamphlet was edited by Angus Maude and Enoch Powell.

'Money is a passport for free men'

This is why I do not share the prevailing belief in the validity of what is called socialism. That the State should act as umpire and, when necessary, temper excessive wealth by remedial taxation, that one man should not be fantastically rich and another helplessly poor, I can believe. But to widen the exercise of free choice is one thing; to by-pass it altogether and substitute for it authoritarian dictation is to reverse the entire course of our history and open the flood-gates of tyranny. Money is a passport for free men; compulsory purchase and the whole modern mechanism of statutory confiscation the dungeon key of the servile state. The use of the first produces a community of men capable of realising that others have rights and viewpoints which must be respected. The other breeds men, like the totalitarian dictators, who are incapable of any bargain except one in which they obtain everything they want. It is this that Lord Acton had in mind when he wrote that all power tends to corrupt, but that absolute power corrupts absolutely.

The truth is that without the instrument of money-choice a free society cannot operate or a free man subsist. Money is the means with which, at the expense of conceding to some other a like freedom of choice, we purchase our own. Money gives us the liberty to satisfy our needs and wishes in our own way: to help others, to do what we regard as just or our duty, to do good, or to do evil. It is the only social alternative to a state either of anarchy or despotism, to a world in which the strong exert their will by violence or one in which Government ordains what everyone must do, suffer or enjoy. There is no other mechanism save money by which the individual can enjoy freedom of choice in a law-abiding and peaceful society.

ARTHUR BRYANT, 1966
in *The Lion and the Unicorn*, 1970

'The presence of self-interest, the fear of failure and the hope of success'

Now, I yield to no one in my admiration for businessmen and industrialists. I recognise that, as a mere politician, I am not worthy to unloose the latchet of the businessman's shoe – when he is about his business. We who believe in private enterprise, and the competitive capitalist society, believe that the businessman and the industrialist when they are at their job, even if they are not always right, are right more often than anyone else would be – far more often.

The mistake arises when we take two or more businessmen or industralists, put them together on a committee, set them to manage or advise on other people's businesses or industries, and then expect that they will be twice as good at it collectively as each of them is separately at this own job. The expectation is vain. At the very moment when we took them, so to speak, from the plough or the forge, at the very moment when we cut the umbiblical cord of self-interest which attached them to the nourishing forces of profit and competition, they became different beings. They became, in short, committee men like other committee men, or administrators like other administrators, or even politicians like other politicians – but at all events no longer businessmen or industrialists. They apply themselves to the matter in hand with a zealous concern for the public weal, 'laying aside', as our House of Commons prayer has it, 'all private interests, prejudices and partial affections'. But there precisely is the rub. It is the presence of self-interest, the fear of failure and the hope of success, which endows the businessman and the industrialist, acting and reacting with others similarly situated, with his significance to the community, with the probability that upon the whole his business judgments will be overwhelmingly superior to those arrived at by other means.

ENOCH POWELL
Freedom and Reality, 1969

'A social evil'

Inflation is no mere monetary inconvenience. It is a social evil, an injustice between man and man and a moral evil, a dishonesty between government and people, between class and class ... The highest national interest, overtopping all others in the economic sphere, is honest money – money that holds its value. Growth, full employment, expanding public services – all these are worth nothing unless that first and great condition is fulfilled.

ENOCH POWELL, 1973

The Unacceptable Face of Capitalism

MR GRIMOND: When the Prime Minister talks to the CBI, will he ask it to condemn unequivocally the sort of goings on that we have all read about at Lonrho which are fatal to any counter-inflation policy? Will he also point out to the CBI that greed does not now seem to be a monopoly of the trade unions?

THE PRIME MINISTER [Edward Heath]: It would not be necessary for me to ask the CBI to make a statement of that kind, and as a responsible body it should be prepared to make its own statement. I hope that the right hon. Member for Orkney and Shetland (Mr Grimond) will not exaggerate to the extent of saying that an incident of this kind is fatal to the counter-inflation policy. It is the unpleasant and unacceptable face of capitalism, but one should not suggest that the whole of British industry consists of practices of this kind.

House of Commons, 15 May 1973

The international trading and mining company Lonrho had been accused of offering bribes to secure contracts. Duncan Sandys, a former Cabinet minister and a consultant to the company, felt compelled to resign, and paid his £130,000 compensation into a tax-free account in the Cayman Islands. This was not illegal, but such ingenious loopholes were embarrassing to the Government, which was pursuing a statutory incomes policy. The Prime Minister, Ted Heath, distanced himself from his old friend, and his celebrated phrase has since been applied to any aspect of capitalism which the user wants to condemn. The phrase was actually coined by Heath's political adviser, Douglas Hurd.

'Monetarism is not enough'

Monetarism is not enough. This is not intended as a counsel of despair, but a warning note. Government's intention to contract the money supply is welcome and potentially beneficial to all. But it is not enough unless there is also the essential reduction of the state sector and the essential encouragement of enterprise. We are over-governed, over-spent, over-taxed, over-borrowed and over-manned. If we shirk the cure, the after-effect of continued over-taxation will be worse than any thing we have endured hitherto. Our ability to distinguish between economic reality and economic make-believe will decline further. We shall experience accelerated worsening of job prospects, the growing flight of those with professional skills, talent and ability to other countries, and an increase in the shabbiness and squalor of everyday lives.

That is why, by itself, the strict and unflinching control of money supply though essential is not enough. We must also have substantial cuts in tax and public spending and bold incentives and encouragements to the wealth creators, without whose renewed efforts we shall all grow poorer.

KEITH JOSEPH

Stockton Lecture, 1976

'Make tax collecting a declining industry'

Our aim is to make tax collecting a declining industry. There are more civil servants in the Inland Revenue than there are sailors in the British Navy. If governments do not cut what *they* spend, we have to cut what *we* spend. There is one hand-out that the people really want today. That is the government's hand out of their pocket.

MARGARET THATCHER
Conservative Party Conference, 1977

'Jobs will multiply'

Every human being is a consumer: most are also producers, of services as well as goods – or potential or former producers. The consumers vary in number, tastes and effective demand. There are more consumers than producers. As the capacity to produce increases, so does the scope for consumption. Since God sends with every pair of hands a mouth and a whole range of actual and potential appetites, including voluntary leisure, the population as consumers will keep occupied the population as producers provided, of course, that the financial system is so managed as to allow this to happen.

The reverse is *not* true; producers will not satisfy consumers by producing the same pattern of goods and services. Consumers change their demands because of changing income, fashion, awareness, taste, invention, innovation, advertising and cannot be prevented from changing except by the coercion practised in socialist societies.

The trading sector of our economy has a double function. It has to trade effectively enough at home and abroad to buy the raw materials, as well as the goods and services that we need and want from abroad.

But it is also the profit-making part of the trading sector which provides the source of most of the taxes for government services. So jobs in the government sector, as well as jobs in the private, depend on the profitability and competitiveness of private enterprise. Overload the private sector by placing a top-heavy government sector on its back and the long-term job prospects in both will dwindle. We shall not have better hospital services, for instance, if we ignore this relationship.

Conversely, the more profitably competitive the trading sector, the more jobs it will provide in a growing number of firms – and the more government sector jobs we can afford.

The danger lies in treating either sector as if its function was to employ rather than to satisfy customers at home and abroad. Paradoxically, insofar as we focus on people as workers, rather than as consumers we shall destroy jobs because consumers here and abroad will buy from more competitive sources overseas. If we focus on consumers – both at home and abroad – then jobs will multiply.

KEITH JOSEPH

'Conditions of full employment', Speech to Bow Group, 1978

'The cloth-capped colonels of the TUC'

Inside Britain there is a parallel threat from the Marxist collectivist totalitarians too.

Small in number, those anti-democratic forces have gained great power through the trades union movement.

Just to state that fact is to be accused of 'union-bashing' – often by people who know it to be true. Such people are to be found in the Conservative, Liberal and Labour Parties.

Their politics may be different but such people share the morality of Laval and Pétain ... they are willing not only to tolerate evil, but to excuse it ... and to profit by so doing.

The trades unions, like the press, the BBC, the CBI or the Army, are neither good nor bad in themselves.

They must be judged by their actions.

What would we say if the red-capped colonels of the Army used their military power for political ends? What if they insisted on conscription as part of their price for allowing a government to stay in office?

Would it be 'Army-bashing' to criticise that?

Yet today the cloth-capped colonels of the TUC use their industrial power for political ends. They insist on the conscription of the closed shop as part of their price for allowing a government to stay in office.

Is it 'union-bashing' to criticise that?

NORMAN TEBBIT, September 1978

Norman Tebbit relished his reputation as a union-basher. One of the reasons for his hostility to the abuse of union power was that his wife Margaret was once denied admission to an NHS hospital by NUPE action and he had to send her to a private hospital which he could ill afford. Similar incidents were to occur frequently during the winter of discontent and led to the Thatcher Government trimming back the power of the trade-union bosses and removing the protection of union funds from actions for damages caused by union action. In this speech

Tebbit entered the dispute between the hawkish Keith Joseph and the dovish Jim
Prior. He wanted to avoid a bitter quarrel and said these healing words at the
conference later that year: 'I'm a hawk but not kamikaze. – And Jim's a dove – but
he's not chicken.'

'To protect people against exploitation'

Conservatives have always sought to protect people against exploit-
ation by powerful individuals or combinations. The fundamental rights
of freedom of contract and freedom of association have therefore been
circumscribed. Social reform of the nineteenth century included the
establishment of trade unions and the prohibition of unacceptable
working conditions, and legislation of the twentieth century has provided remedies against the excesses of union power. Conservatives also
recognise that capitalism contains the seeds of its own destruction, to
the extent that unregulated enterprise may lead to injustice and even
oppression. Hence their support for legislation to control monopolies,
restrictive trade practices and other forms of anti-competitive
behaviour.

T. E. UTLEY
Capitalism, the Moral Case, 1980

'No prouder word in our history than "freeholder"'

Wherever we can we shall extend the opportunity for personal ownership and the self-respect that goes with it. Three hundred and seventy
thousand families have now bought their own homes from councils,
new towns and housing associations. That is the result of this Government's housing policy carried through in the teeth of opposition from
the Labour Party. We have fought them all the way and we won. Half a
million more people will now live and grow up as freeholders with a
real stake in the country and with something to pass on to their
children. There is no prouder word in our history than 'freeholder'.

This is the largest transfer of assets from the State to the family in
British history and it was done by a Conservative Government. And
this really will be an irreversible shift of power to the people.

MARGARET THATCHER, 1982

'The climate is changing'

It is the conquest of inflation, and not the pursuit of growth and employment, which is or should be the objective of macroeconomic policy. And it is the creation of conditions conducive to growth and employment, and not suppression of price rises, which is or should be the objective of microeconomic policy . . .

In the field of microeconomic policy, too, what we are seeking to do is to change a psychology, to change a business culture. The abolition of pay controls, price controls, dividend controls, foreign exchange controls, bank lending controls, hire purchase controls, industrial building controls – all these have been beneficial in themselves, but will bring even greater benefit to the nation as part of the process of rediscovering the enterprise culture.

A process that will be carried further by progressive reductions in the burden of taxation – provided we maintain, as we must, the downward trend of public expenditure as a proportion of GDP. And one that will be further promoted by the onward march of privatization and the breaking up of monopolies and restrictive practices – not least in the City of London.

In this context, moreover, the labour market is clearly of vital importance; and the labour legislation already enacted, and that currently before Parliament, present a long overdue start in a key area of the national economy. On almost all of these fronts we are opposed, inevitably, by vested interests of one kind or another. On almost all of them it will take time for the changes to have their full effect. But the climate *is* changing: of that there can be no doubt.

NIGEL LAWSON
'The British Experiment', Fifth Mais Lecture, 1984

'Liberalizing Conservative policies'

The 1987 general election was the crucial step from a period when the reversal of the Conservative revolution always seemed possible, to one where it is almost inconceivable. It was a watershed between a party crusade for a property-owning democracy and the establishment of a new national common ground of politics. The foundations for national recovery have been firmly laid. The results are coming through. And there is no political, moral or intellectual challenge in sight to the liberalising Conservative policies which have released the spirit and the talent of our nation.

SIR GEOFFREY HOWE, 1987

'The world seems ever more free-market'

Reading ingenious theories showing why capitalism cannot survive, one is left wondering why the world seems ever more free-market. The theories of the pessimists who feared the decay of capitalism are out of touch with reality. Capitalism is a more powerful, political and economic movement now than at any other time this century. The advanced Western world remains resolutely committed to Smith's 'system of natural liberty'. The old Eastern bloc and the impoverished third world have not only abandoned Lenin and Che Guevara, but also Dubček and Tito. Adam Smith, Friedrich Hayek, Margaret Thatcher convey the spirit of the age.

Conservative capitalism must have more effective mechanisms to protect itself against the erosion of its moral capital than the pessimists allow for. Our review of postwar conservatism suggested what some of these mechanisms might be. Free-market economies generate growth and prosperity which are nowadays so important in sustaining any democratic polity. Detailed government intervention in the economy fails to deliver the economic growth which modern electorates expect. More fundamentally, it sets us in direct competition with each other for government favours and subsidies. A government which steers clear of heavy-handed intervention eases the pressures of overload and ungovernability which we saw in Britain in the 1970s. And even if we are all tempted to indulge our appetites and to borrow rather than to save (as happened in Britain in the late 1980s) we are soon brought to face the unpalatable reality – that you cannot carry on borrowing to live beyond your means for ever. Painful lessons in prudent borrowing and lending are re-learned.

If one turns to normal people's everyday experience, those fears about the destructive forces unloosed by free markets seem absurd and hysterical. The British suburb is not a place of rootless, miserable apathy. People admittedly, do pursue their material aspirations – to own their house, to pay off the mortgage, to be able to afford a good holiday – but these are not immoral or shameful. And at the same time the latest sociological researchers confirm what one may anyway have suspected: that suburbs comprise rich networks of voluntary association, from Rotary Club to British Legion, from the rota for driving the children to school to the firm's social club. Even that urge to home ownership, satisfied more successfully in the 1980s than in any other decade, has given people new and stronger ties to their neighbourhood. Ownership and belonging go together. Our civic culture is under greatest strain not in the suburbs but in the inner cities from where so many businesses have fled. It is the absence of a modern capitalist economy which brings the real problems, not its success.

So conservatives can happily value both the historic traditions of this country and the values of freedom and the free market. There is no need to become bogged down in arguments about which of these ideas should take precedence – because we have the good fortune to live in a society which has a long historical tradition of freedom and individualism.

DAVID WILLETTS
Modern Conservatism, 1992

'The era of corporatism has long passed'

NEDO's potential value is high, as the one forum where ministers regularly meet senior representatives of industry, the unions and the City.

MICHAEL HESELTINE
Where There's a Will, 1987

The National Economic Development Council and the National Economic Development Office were established in 1962. In the 1960s and 1970s, they provided a helpful forum in which the overall economy and the performance of individual sectors could be discussed and debated. Much useful work was done then, and successive Governments in that period valued the role that NEDC played.

But the era of corporatism has long passed. In the last decade, Governments, not just in Britain but across the world, have pursued more market-oriented policies, the promotion, and the smooth functioning of market mechanisms. There have been radical changes to the structure of business and industry. The number of small firms and of the self-employed has grown rapidly. Large parts of the former public sector have been privatised, and international markets are increasingly integrated.

The British work force have become more skilled and more specialised, with more flexible working practices and more varied career patterns. Trade union membership has declined, and in the private sector, decentralised wage bargaining has become the norm rather than the exception.

Against that background, it is clear that the NEDC no long reflects the needs and realities of the British economy in the 1990s. Since its inception, the council has been dominated by producer interests, but its membership and structure cannot hope to represent fully the interests and views of the whole range of industry or of the work force. And paradoxically, the continued existence of the NEDC in those changed circumstances may actually have inhibited, rather than encouraged, the development of direct contact on specific issues between the Government and trade unions and other employee associations. Accordingly, and after careful consideration, the government have decided that the National Economic Development Council should now be abolished.

NORMAN LAMONT

House of Commons, 16 June 1992

Selwyn Lloyd set up NEDO in 1961 as a forum where both sides of industry could meet the government. It was meant to be a new way of doing things but all it did was to spawn sector working groups which had no effect on our industrial efficiency or our industrial relations. It was only a talking shop; Nigel Lawson cut back its work and Norman Lamont cut it out altogether.

5

'A Nation-wide Property-Owning Democracy'

Conservatives believe that ownership of property is one of the cornerstones of a free and contented nation. The desire to own the roof over one's own head, and to be able to pass that on to one's own children, is rooted in human nature. This applies to the mighty and to the humble, to the celebrated and the unknown. Shakespeare, after his success in London and the court, wanted only to return to his home town and own a house there. Throughout our history the individual has not only asserted his right to liberty and freedom but has also acquired, as the most practical manifestation of that liberty, property which he can call his own.

The personal ownership of property is a tangible stake in society to be defended against political threat and personal intruders. It is a social anchor which helps form resistance to radical change. It is the independence of the owner as against the tenant's dependence. It encourages self-reliance and confers responsibility. In all these respects, the ownership of property is a manifestation of attitudes which Conservatives are keenest to promote.

Much of our law protects property, and the privacy and independence which derive from it. We have not had for over 500 years a peasant class; there was the sturdily independent yeoman farmer. Then the Industrial Revolution created in our towns and cities huge developments where manual workers and the lower middle classes could afford only to pay rent. But as soon as they acquired the means, they too set about owning their own homes. Dickens reflected this desire in the attitude of the lawyer's clerk, Wemmick, in Great Expectations.

It has been the particular success of the Conservative Party in this century to allow many millions of ordinary people to become home *owners. Since 1946, when Anthony Eden spoke of 'a nation-wide property-owning democracy', home ownership has spread to 70 per cent of the population. Under Margaret Thatcher's government, council tenants were given the right to purchase their own homes and 1,500,000 families did so.*

The Thatcher Government also ensured that property ownership meant share ownership as well as bricks and mortar. The great privatizations of the 1980s – Cable & Wireless, Rolls Royce, British Airways, British Steel, British Telecommunications, gas, water and electricity – saw an expansion from 3 million shareholders in 1979 to 11 million in 1992. More people than ever before now had a direct stake in the nation's economic welfare. As Adam Smith had forecast 200 years earlier, 'Sale of crown lands would bring untold benefit.'

'A moderate but adequate amount of property'

For this reason it is a happy state of affairs when those who take part in the life of the state have a moderate but adequate amount of property; for where one set of people possesses a great deal and the other nothing, the result is either extreme democracy or unmixed oligarchy or a tyranny due to the excesses of the other two. Tyranny often emerges from an over-enthusiastic democracy or from an oligarchy, but much more rarely from middle-class constitutions or from those very near to them.

ARISTOTLE
Politics, Book IV, *c.* 335 BC

'The Condition of Humane Life'

God gave the World to Men in Common; but since he gave it them for their benefit, and the greatest Conveniencies of Life they were capable to draw from it, it cannot be supposed he meant it should always remain common and uncultivated. He gave it to the use of the Industrious and Rational, (and *Labour* was to be *his Title* to it;) not to the Fancy or Convetousness of the Quarrelsom and Contentious ... The Law Man was under, was rather for *appropriating*. God Commanded, and his Wants forced him to *labour*. That was his *Property* which could not be taken from him where-ever he had fixed it. And hence subduing or cultivating the Earth, and having Dominion, we see are joyned together. The one gave Title to the other. So that God, by commanding to subdue, gave Authority so far to *appropriate*. And the Condition of Humane Life, which requires Labour and Materials to work on, necessarily introduces *private Possessions*.

The measure of Property, Nature has well set, by the Extent of Mens *Labour, and the Conveniency of Life:* No Mans Labour could subdue, or appropriate all: nor could his Enjoyment consume more than a small part; so that it was impossible for any Man, this way, to intrench upon the right of another, or acquire, to himself, a Property, to the Prejudice of his Neighbour, who would still have room, for as good, and as large a Possession (after the other had taken out his) as before it was appropriated. This *measure* did confine every Man's *Possession*, to a very moderate Proportion, and such as he might appropriate to himself, without Injury to any Body in the first Ages of the World.

JOHN LOCKE
The Second Treatise of Government, 1690

'The best judges'

The possessors of the soil are the best judges of what is for the advantage of the kingdom.

JOHNATHAN SWIFT
Letter to Alexander Pope, 1721

'The sale of crown lands'

In every great monarchy of Europe the sale of the crown lands would produce a very large sum of money, which, if applied to the payment of the public debts, would deliver from mortgage a much greater revenue than any which those lands have ever afforded to the crown ... When the crown lands had become private property, they would, in the course of a few years, become well-improved and well-cultivated ... the revenue which the crown derives from the duties of customs and excise, would necessarily increase with the revenue and consumption of the people.

ADAM SMITH
Inquiry into the Nature and Causes of the Wealth of Nations, 1776

'The secure possession of a bleak rock'

Give a man the secure possession of a bleak rock, and he will turn it into a garden; give him a nine years' lease of garden and he will convert it into a desert.

ARTHUR YOUNG
Travels in France, 1787

'The light of intelligence spreads'

The value attached to the privileges of birth decreased in the exact proportion in which new paths were struck out to advancement ... as soon as land was held on any than a feudal tenure, and personal property began in its turn to counter influence and power, every improvement which was introduced in commerce or manufacture was a fresh element of the equality of conditions ... the divisions which once served mankind are lowered; property is divided, power is held in common, the light of intelligence spreads, and the capacities of all classes are equally cultivated; the State becomes democratic and the empire of democracy is slowly and peaceably introduced into the institutions and manners of the nation.

ALEXIS DE TOCQUEVILLE
Democracy in America, 1835

'The poor man's attachment to the tenements he holds'

... if ever household affections and loves are graceful things, they are graceful in the poor. The ties that bind the wealthy and the proud to home may be forged on earth, but those which link the poor man to his humble hearth are of the truer metal and bear the stamp of Heaven. The man of high descent may love the halls and lands of his inheritance as a part of himself: as trophies of his birth and power; his associations with them are associations of pride and wealth and triumph; the poor man's attachment to the tenements he holds, which strangers have held before, and may tomorrow occupy again, has a worthier root, struck deep into a purer soil.

CHARLES DICKENS
The Old Curiosity Shop, 1841
Of all the Victorian novelists Dickens was the only one fully to describe the situation, the hopes and the attitudes of the lower middle classes. His novels are full of clerks, shopkeepers, dressmakers, actors and midwives, and here he records the feelings of the Nubbles family to their poor, humble but decent home. Their attachment to it is just as powerful as a duke's to his vast estate.

'An Englishman's Home is his Castle'

At first with such discourse, and afterwards with conversation of a more general nature, did Mr Wemmick and I beguile the time and the road, until he gave me to understand that we had arrived in the district of Walworth.

It appeared to be a collection of back lanes, ditches, and little gardens, and to present the aspect of a rather dull retirement. Wemmick's house was a little wooden cottage in the midst of plots of garden, and the top of it was cut out and painted like a battery mounted with guns.

'My own doing,' said Wemmick. 'Looks pretty; don't it?'

I highly commended it. I think it was the smallest house I ever saw; with the queerest gothic windows (by far the greater part of them sham), and a gothic door, almost too small to get in at.

'That's a real flagstaff, you see,' said Wemmick, 'and on Sundays I run up a real flag. Then look here. After I have crossed this bridge, I hoist it up – so – and cut off the communication.'

The bridge was a plank, and it crossed a chasm about four feet wide and two deep. But it was very pleasant to see the pride with which he hoisted it up and made it fast; smiling as he did so, with a relish and not merely mechanically.

'At nine o'clock every night, Greenwich time,' said Wemmick, the gun fires. There he is, you see! And when you hear him go, I think you'll say he's a Stinger.'

The piece of ordnance referred to, was mounted in a separate fortress, constructed of lattice-work. It was protected from the weather by an ingenious little tarpaulin contrivance in the nature of an umbrella.

'Then, at the back,' said Wemmick, 'out of sight, so as not to impede the idea of fortifications – for it's a principle with me, if you have an idea, carry it out and keep it up – I don't know whether that's your opinion –'

I said, decidedly.

'– At the back, there's a pig, and there are fowls and rabbits; then, I knock together my own little frame, you see, and grow cucumbers; and you'll judge at supper what sort of a salad I can raise. So, sir,' said Wemmick, smiling again, but seriously too, as he shook his head, 'if you can suppose the little place besieged, it would hold out a devil of a time in point of provisions.' ...

Wemmick told me as he smoked a pipe that it had taken him a good many years to bring the property up to its present pitch of perfection.

'Is it your own, Mr Wemmick?'

'O yes,' said Wemmick, 'I have got hold of it, a bit at a time. It's a freehold, by George!'

'Is it, indeed? I hope Mr Jaggers admires it?'

'Never seen it,' said Wemmick. 'Never heard of it. Never seen the Aged. Never heard of him. No; the office is one thing, and private life is another. When I go into the office, I leave the Castle behind me, and when I come into the Castle, I leave the office behind me, If it's not in any way disagreeable to you, you'll oblige me by doing the same. I don't wish it professionally spoken about.'

CHARLES DICKENS
Great Expectations, 1860

'Property is Conservative'

'Plenty of sound Tories have made their fortune by trade ... Trade makes property, my good sir, and property is Conservative as they say now.'

GEORGE ELIOT
Felix Holt, The Radical, 1866

'A nation-wide property-owning democracy'

Long experience has taught us that to offer to the people any single panacea as the Socialists offer nationalization would be merely to delude ourselves and them. Life is not as simple as that. For the manifold and diverse problems that face us, manifold and diverse solutions must of necessity be required. But this I believe we can say: that there is one single principle that will unite all the solutions that we shall seek and propound. There is one principle underlying our approach to all these problems, a principle on which we stand in fundamental opposition to Socialism. The objective of Socialism is State ownership of all the means of production, distribution and exchange. Our objective is a nation-wide property-owning democracy. These objectives are fundamentally opposed. Whereas the Socialist purpose is the concentration of ownership in the hands of the State, ours is the distribution of ownership over the widest practicable number of individuals.

Both parties believe in a form of capitalism; but, whereas our opponents believe in State capitalism, we believe in the widest measure of individual capitalism. I believe this to be a fundamental principle of political philosophy. Man should be master of his environment and not its slave. That is what freedom means. It is precisely in the conception of ownership that man achieves mastery over his environment. Upon the institution of property depends the fulfilment of individual personality and the maintenance of individual liberty.

ANTHONY EDEN
Conservative Party Conference, 3 October, 1946

'A natural right of the family'

Secondly, private property is a natural right of the family, and generally of the subordinate group . . . Conservatives . . . refuse to treat either the State or the individual as absolute. Human souls, as they see it, exist as individuals, but as individuals forming part not merely of a political community but of various groups, of which the most important is the family. The perpetuation of these groups – families, local communities, voluntary associations – is a prime object of Conservative policy; Conservatives also regard it as essential to their perpetuation that groups and individuals should be able to possess and bequeath private property, including, if need be, considerable fortunes.

In particular, although Conservatives are prepared to concede the necessity of a graduated death duty as a means of keeping wealth fairly distributed, they are unable to understand the idea that men should be entitled to make fortunes for themselves but not be free to bequeath them to others when they die. They are convinced that to deprive them of this is to deprive them of one of the rights to which human beings are property entitled as such to aspire . . .

QUINTIN HOGG, VISCOUNT HAILSHAM
The Case for Conservatism, 1947

'The strongest force . . . is property'

The majority, the public man, the common man, the State, the spirit of the age – the many headed, many named monster knows that the strongest force opposed to him is property. Our great-grandparents used to speak of a modest inherited fortune as 'an independence'. Property enabled a man to perform unremunerative public services, to practise the arts, to defy his rulers. The State destroys private property in three ways; first, by literally robbing the widow and orphan by confiscating bequests; secondly, and more insidiously, by so taxing earned incomes that saving is impossible – in most trades and professions in most countries a man is allowed to enjoy a considerable part of his earnings if he squanders it on travel and entertaining; thrift alone is penalized; thirdly, the State has the power to debase the coinage, a process euphemistically called 'inflation' which in simple terms means paying the majority more than they earn.

EVELYN WAUGH
'The Private Man', 1962

'The inviolability of property'

This, I take it, is the reason that the Church and the University as institutions have almost invariably stood as strongly reactionary against any innovations which threaten the intrenched rights of property. It is not at bottom the greed of possession that moves them – though this motive also may have entered into the attitude of their governors, as into all the theories and practices of men – nor are we justified in casting into their teeth the reproach that they who profess to stand for spiritual things are in their corporate capacity the most tenacious upholders of worldly privilege. They are guided by an instinctive feeling that in this mixed and mortal state of our existence, the safety and usefulness of the institutions they control are finally bound up with the inviolability of property which has been devoted to unworldly pursuits, and removed from the control of popular passions and hasty legislation. They are the jealous guardians of that respite from material labour which they hold in fee for those who are by character destined more specifically to be the creators and transmitters of the world's intellectual and spiritual heritage. Nor does the need of privilege end with institutions. One shudders to think of the bleak pall of anxiety and the rage of internecine materialism that would fall upon society were the laws so altered as to transfer the predominant rights from property acquired to the labour by which it is produced. For *if property is secure, it may be the means to an end, whereas if it is insecure it will be the end itself.*

PAUL ELMER MORE

'Wealth cascading down the generations'

We can now see the lifeblood of ownership – of wealth – running through the veins of the country. Nearly four million more families own homes. And eight million people more own shares. And four and a half million people now have personal pensions.

But this revolution is still not complete. In the 1990s we must carry it further. We must extend savings and ownership in every form. And we now have the chance to make enduring change. For people in their middle years are inheriting homes, businesses, farms on a scale never before seen. The pioneers of the property-owning democracy are the parents of the capital-owning democracy to come.

We Conservatives have always passed our values on, from generation to generation. I believe that personal prosperity should follow the same course. I want to see wealth cascading down the generations. We do not see each generation starting out anew, with the past cut off and the future ignored.

So, in the next Parliament I believe that we must go much further in encouraging every family to save and to own. To extend every family's ability to pass on something to their children, to build up something of their own – for their own.

JOHN MAJOR
Conservative Party Conference, October 1991

6

'We Live in a Community of Individuals'

Property and individual freedom are two of the cornerstones of Conservatism, but they are not sufficient in themselves. The ownership of property carries with it obligations and is more than merely selfish enjoyment. The exercise of free choice is natural and right but it also implies that the views, feelings, interests and welfare of others must also be taken into account.

The obligation of the individual to the wider community in which he works, lives and plays has been a constant theme for conservative-minded thinkers from St Thomas Aquinas through Adam Smith, Burke and Disraeli to Churchill and Keith Joseph. Some have been inspired and guided by the moral injunction to love their neighbour. Others, by the practical consideration that people's security, independence and welfare depend upon their social relationships with their neighbours.

Disraeli declared in a bold over-simplification, 'power has only one duty – to secure the social welfare of the people'. Baldwin spoke of the need to 'combine for service'; Leo Amery of the common cause; and I outlined the need to reconcile the interests of the individual and those of the society in which he lives when I spoke of each one of us living in a 'community of individuals'.

Speaking to the Welsh conference in 1991, John Major said that his sort of Toryism was 'based on the liberal free market but sensitive to individual needs' and that its aim was to produce 'a nation that is sure in its aims and at ease with itself'.

'The common welfare of the community'

Whoever promotes the common welfare of the community promotes his own welfare at the same time: and this for two reasons. First, because individual well-being cannot exist without the welfare of the family, or city, or realm. Valerius Maximus says of the Romans of old that, 'They preferred rather to be poor men in a rich empire, than rich men in a poor empire.' Secondly, because man, being part of the family, or of the city, it is right that he should consider his personal well-being in the light of what prudence advises with regard to the common welfare. For the good disposition of any part must be determined by its relationship to the whole. For, as St Augustine says in the *Confessions*: 'All parts are base which do not fit or harmonise with their whole.'

ST THOMAS AQUINAS

'Public want and private wealth abound'

Now nothing can be more certain than this, that national luxury and national poverty may, in time, establish national prostitution. Besides this, it is to be considered, that the immense wealth of particular men is a circumstance which always attends national poverty, and is in a great measure and cause of it. We may apply already to our country thus much at least of that which Salust makes Cato say of the state of Rome; I wish we could apply no more, '*Habemus luxuriam, atque avaritiam, publicè egestatem, privatim opulentiam*; luxury and avarice, public want and private wealth abound.' Now, as public want, or general poverty, for in that sense I take it here, will lay numbers of men open to the attacks of corruption; so private wealth will have the same effect, especially where luxury prevails, on some of those who do not feel the public want; for there is imaginary as well as real poverty.

HENRY, VISCOUNT BOLINGBROKE, 1735

In the late seventeenth and eighteenth centuries the Country Party, the predecessor of the Tories, had a contempt for the monied interests in the court and city, and particularly the speculation and stockjobbing which created the South Sea Bubble. Jonathan Swift rounded on those 'whose whole fortunes lie in funds and stocks: so that power, which according to the old maxim, was used to follow land, is now gone over to money . . . Through the contrivance and cunning of stockjobbers, there has been brought in such a complication of knavery and cozenage, such a mystery of iniquity . . . as were never known in any age or country of the world.'

'Society is, indeed, a contract'

Society is, indeed, a contract. Subordinate contracts for objects of mere occasional interest may be dissolved at pleasure; but the state ought not to be considered as nothing better than a partnership agreement in a trade of pepper and coffee, calico or tobacco, or some other such low concern, to be taken up for a little temporary interest, and to be dissolved by the fancy of the parties. It is to be looked on with other reverence; because it is not a partnership in things subservient only to the gross animal existence of a temporary and perishable nature. It is a partnership in all science, a partnership in all art, a partnership in every virtue and in all perfection. As the ends of such a partnership cannot be obtained in many generations, it becomes a partnership not only between those who are living, but between those who are living, those who are dead, and those who are to be born. Each contract of each particular state is but a clause in the great primeval contract of eternal society, linking the lower with the higher natures, connecting the visible and invisible world, according to a fixed compact sanctioned by the inviolable oath which holds all physical and all moral natures each in their appointed place. This law is not subject to the will of those who, by an obligation above them, and infinitely superior, are bound to submit their will to that law.

EDMUND BURKE

'The true test'

A decent provision for the poor is the true test of civilization.

SAMUEL JOHNSON, 1770

Distribution of Wealth

What improved the circumstances of the greater part can never be regarded as an inconveniency to the whole. No society can surely be flourishing and happy, of which the far greater part of the members are poor and miserable.

ADAM SMITH

An Inquiry into the Nature and Causes of the Wealth of Nations, 1776

'Sometimes remembered with expressions of good will'

In relinquishing power I shall leave a name severely censured I fear by many who on public grounds deeply regret the severance of party ties, deeply regret that severance, not from interested or personal motives, but from the firm conviction that fidelity to party engagements – the existence and maintenance of a great party – constitutes a powerful instrument of government. I shall surrender power severely censured also by others, who from no interested motives, adhere to the principle of protection, considering the maintenance of it to be essential to the welfare and interests of the country; I shall leave a name execrated by every monopolist who, from less honourable motives, clamours for protection because it conduces to his own individual benefit; but it may be that I shall leave a name sometimes remembered with expressions of good will in the abodes of those whose lot it is to labour, and to earn their daily bread by the sweat of their brow, when they shall recruit their exhausted strength with abundant and untaxed food, the sweeter because it is no longer leavened by a sense of injustice.

ROBERT PEEL, 29 June 1846

By 1845 Peel had decided that the Corn Laws, one of the great arches of Conservatism supporting the landed gentry, had to be repealed. He was persuaded to do this by the potato famine in Ireland, the high level of unemployment, the poor state of manufacturing industry and commerce, and the low living standards of the working classes, the principle cause being that the price of bread was too high. Even behind the tariff wall, English farmers had not been able to produce sufficient grain to meet the market's demand. Peel accepted the economic case which had been vigorously promoted across the nation by the Anti-Corn Law League. But the clinching argument for him was that repeal was necessary in order to avoid disruption, dissension and even revolt. If any of these things happened then the British Constitution was at risk.

The interests of the landowning aristocracy were best secured from radical assault by bending to the clamour for repeal. Free trade helped to create the great prosperity of mid- and later Victorian England, and Peel's change of policy can be given the credit for that. However, it was devastating for the Conservative Party. It was out of office for nearly thirty years, not winning a majority again until 1874. Some of the most bitter attacks on Peel were made by Disraeli, who believed that he had betrayed basic Conservative principles and interests. It became Disraeli's duty, and his inspiration, to pick up the pieces and to refashion a Conservative Party that could win popular support. In all of this great turmoil the ageing Duke of Wellington expressed one of the abiding sentiments of Toryism when he declared: 'A good government of the country is more important than the Corn Laws or any other consideration'.

'The social welfare of the people'

The Tory Party has its origin in great principles and in noble instincts;
it sympathises with the lowly, it looks up to the Most High. It can
count its heroes and its martyrs; they have met in its behalf plunder,
prescription, and death. Nor when it finally yielded to the iron progress
of oligarchical supremacy, was its catastrophe inglorious. Its genius
was vindicated in golden sentences and with fervent arguments of
impassioned logic by St John; and breathed in the intrepid eloquence
and patriot soul of William Wyndham. Even now it is not dead but
sleepeth; and in an age of political materialism, of confused purposes
and perplexed intelligence, that aspires only to wealth because it has no
other accomplishment, as men rifle cargoes on the verge of shipwreck,
Toryism will yet arise from the tomb over which Bolingbroke shed his
last tear, to bring back strength to the Crown, liberty to the Subject,
and to announce that power has only one duty – to secure the social
welfare of the PEOPLE.

BENJAMIN DISRAELI
Sybil, or The Two Nations, 1845

'The "Tory Democracy" may yet exist'

Some of Lord Beaconsfield's phrases will bear any amount of micro-
scopic examination. Speaking at Manchester in 1871, by the alteration
of a letter in a quotation from the Vulgate, he revealed the policy which
ought to guide Tory leaders at the present time – Sanitas sanitatum,
omnia sanitas. Such was the quotation in which a careful mind will
discover a scheme of social progress and reform of dimensions so large
and wide-spreading that many volumes would not suffice to explain its
details. By it is shadowed forth, and in it is embraced, a social revolution which, passing by and diverting attention from wild longings for
organic change, commences with the little peddling boards of health
which occupy and delight the local government department, comprises
Lord Salisbury's plans for the amelioration of the dwellings of the
poor, carries with it Lord Carnarvon's idea of compulsory National
Insurance, includes Sir Wilfred Lawson's temperance propaganda, preserves and reclaims commons and open spaces favoured by Mr Bryce,
constructs peoples' parks, collects and opens to the masses museums,
libraries, art galleries, does not disdain the public washhouses of Mr

Jesse Collings. Public and private thrift must animate the whole, for it is from public thrift that the funds for these largesses can be drawn and it is by private thrift alone that their results can be utilized and appreciated. The expression – Tory Democracy – has excited the wonder of some, the alarm of others and great and bitter ridicule from the Radical Party. But the 'Tory Democracy' may yet exist; the elements for its composition only require to be collected and the labour may some day possibly be effected by the man, whoever he may be, upon whom the mantle of Elijah has descended.

RANDOLPH CHURCHILL
Fortnightly Review, 1883

'With no help from governments'

Kindliness, sympathy with the underdog, love of home! Are not these all characteristics of the ordinary Englishman that you know? He is a strong individualist in this, that he does not want to mould himself into any common mould, to be like everybody else; he likes to develop his own individuality. And yet he can combine for service. Some of the best things in this country have originated among our own common people with no help from governments – friendly society work, our trade unions, our hospitals and our education before the State took it in hand.

STANLEY BALDWIN, 1933

'The individuals it has in mind are also citizens'

Conservatism recognizes that individual effort, the individual desire to excel, the will for individual achievement and recognition will always remain the indispensable vitamins of human society. But the individuals it has in mind are also citizens. The qualities of cooperation, of public duty, of willingness to sacrifice personal interest and even life itself for the common cause are essential elements in the individuality which we would strive to foster.

LEO AMERY
Ashridge Journal, 1943

'The ladder and the queue'

The difference between our outlook and the Socialist outlook on life is the difference between the ladder and the queue. We are for the ladder. Let all try their best to climb. They are for the queue. Let each wait in his place till his turn comes. But, we ask, 'What happens if anyone slips out of his place in the queue?' Ah!' say the Socialists, 'Our officials – and we have plenty of them – come and put him back in it, or perhaps put him lower down to teach the others'. And then they come back at us and say 'We have told you what happens if anyone slips out of the queue, but what is your answer to what happens if anyone slips off the ladder?' Our reply is 'We shall have a good net and the finest social ambulance service in the world'. This is of course only a snapshot of a large controversy.

   WINSTON CHURCHILL, 8 October, 1951

'The aristocrat's special obligation'

As the inheritor of an estate, it is an aristocrat's special obligation to maintain and to pass it on. He does not regard what belongs to him as his own to do what he wills with but as a bequest of which he is, for his lifetime, the custodian, just as his father and grandfather were before him. And this sense of having a duty to perpetuate something that is impossible to create deliberately and easy to destroy, distinguishes the attitude of an aristocrat. He has an air of leisure, and the refinement that goes with leisure because his job of custodianship releases him from the whirl of his contemporary world and allows him to be indifferent to the demands of the moment. An aristocrat consequently has none of the brusqueness that characterises the man whose job it is to turn out something for here and now. But on the other hand an aristocrat does not feel free as an ordinary gentleman might to retire from the world. His job as custodian obliges him to play an active role in public life.

   SHIRLEY ROBIN LETWIN
   The Gentleman in Trollope, 1982

'The Victorians' moral and physical capital'

The Victorian age has been very badly treated in socialist propaganda. It was an age of constant and constructive endeavour in which the desire to improve the lot of the ordinary person was a powerful factor. We who are largely living off the Victorians' moral and physical capital can hardly afford to denigrate them.

MARGARET THATCHER, 1977

'Regulating competitiveness'

A society of autonomous individuals is the natural condition of mankind. That is not to say that such a society should never be transformed into something different, but merely that those who suggest such a transformation have a duty to produce some proper and cogent reason for it. This is because individuals are prior to societies and have rights independent of them. The idea of the state of nature, so beloved of eighteenth-century political theorists, is a historical myth, but like many myths it expresses an important truth which is not clearly expressed in any other way: that men have certain characteristics which are 'natural' in the sense that they have those characteristics whether they live under governments or not.

Men are so constituted that it is natural to them to pursue private rather than public ends. This is a simple matter of observation. The duty of governments is to accommodate themselves to this immutable fact about human nature. Their object (and one must assume the original purpose for which they were created) is merely to avoid the inconveniences which attend the uncontrolled pursuit by private individuals of private ends. In the absence of government men would have certain ambitions (such as the acquisition of wealth for themselves) which are natural to their humanity. They still have those ambitions when they come to live under governments. It is no part of a government's function to disapprove of those ambitions or to seek to change or frustrate them, for it owes its existence to them. Men have a natural right to their ambitions because it was not for the purpose of abolishing competitiveness that they submitted to government; it was for the purpose of regulating competitiveness and preventing it from taking violent, fraudulent or anti-social forms. It is in fact only the inconveniences which arise from the existence of numerous and conflicting rights, which make government a sensible solution.

KEITH JOSEPH AND ANTHONY SUMPTION, 1979

'From Doom to Hope'

The overall picture presented in the Report is grim, and even the prospects are described as 'bleak'. No Jewish contribution could be more valuable than to help turn despair into hope, resignation into confidence that – given determination, patience, perseverance and faith in the infinite capacity of man to prevail over adversity – the new ghettos will be transformed as were the old and the growing wealth of the nation will increasingly be shared by all through shifting the emphasis from rights to duties and from having a good time to making the times good.

IMMANUEL JAKOBOVITS, Chief Rabbi, 1986

In 1986 the Church of England published a report of the Archbishop of
Canterbury's Commission on Urban Priority Areas. This analysed the decay in the
inner cities and concluded that it was due to socio-economic factors and that it was
primarily up to the state to intervene. The role of the individual was played down.
This provoked the Chief Rabbi to issue his response which emphasized the crucial
role of individuals in the improvement of their own lot. I once heard Margaret
Thatcher say that 'there are only two great people in the world – the Pope and the
Chief Rabbi'.

'There is no such thing as society'

I think we've been through a period where too many people have been given to understand that if they have a problem, it's the government's job to cope with it. 'I have a problem, I'll get a grant.' 'I'm homeless, the government must house me.' They're casting their problem on society. And, you know, there is no such thing as society. There are individual men and women, and there are families. And no government can do anything except through people, and people must look to themselves first. It's our duty to look after ourselves and then, also, to look after our neighbour. People have got the entitlements too much in mind, without the obligations. There's no such thing as entitlement, unless someone has first met an obligation.

MARGARET THATCHER

Interview in *Woman's Own*, 1987

There is of course such a thing as society, though a dozen people would have a
dozen different definitions. Mrs Thatcher was attacking the idolatry of society,
which leads to less liberty for the individual. The interests of society must be seen
to prevail not just in the 'big things' like war or peace but in the 'little things' like
choosing a school for your own children or joining, or not joining, a trade union.
But society, however defined, owes its very existence and draws its strength from
the individuals who create it, modify it, respond to it or give it a push.

'A community of individuals'

I do not think there is any reason to apologize for the increased scope we have given for what might be called acquisitive individualism. Those who already have much should not look down upon the desire to own of those who do not . . . I do not accept that this drive for self-improvement is selfish. However, I do recognize that there is another side to the coin of economic individualism. That other side is social responsibility. Those who succeed have obligations above and beyond that of celebrating their own success.

While individuals are the basis of our society, the fact that we live together interdependently means that we live in a community of individuals. Many of the best things in life flow from the individual's drive for self realization. But at the same time we all live together in families, groups and communities. The responsible individual does not believe that his involvement with others is limited only to paying taxes and that's an end to the matter. The responsible individual is a concerned citizen, an active citizen, who by bringing his individual skills into play within a community role enhances the life of that community.

KENNETH BAKER
Bow Group annual dinner, 1987

British people are very charitable. Margaret Thatcher's government increased significantly the tax incentives for charitable gifts from both individuals and companies and quadrupled the tax relief claimed by charities. Some £5,000 million is given by individuals to charities each year. There is also a vast army of volunteers working for bodies ranging from Action against Allergy to the Zen Foundation. A survey in 1991 revealed that over half the population aged over eighteen had taken part in some voluntary activity in the previous year. All this spontaneous activity is geared to helping other people and the volunteers come from all ages and all backgrounds.

'A nation that is sure in its aims and at ease with itself'

Our distinctive Toryism is the polar opposite of Socialism. It rejects their policies based on envy. It rejects their attitudes which foment class division. For our belief – our Tory belief – grows from the commonsense instincts of the British. From their fair-mindedness, their sense of what is right and their sense of obligations to other people. It builds on the instinctive friendliness of our people. It seeks to unite, and not to divide. I want no barriers in my Party. And no barriers in our country either.

I want our Tory approach to strike a common chord with all generations – a Toryism based on the liberal free market but sensitive to individual needs. A Toryism that stands for a stable way of life rooted in decency. For the breaking open of closed doors in our society, whatever or wherever they may be. For a culture of generosity, public and private; respect for the contributions and opinions of others; and pride in our great national institutions. For making it easier for everyone to build up something to call their own and to pass it on to their children and those after them. For all those values that, as I believe, go to create a nation that is sure in its aims and at ease with itself. We want a Toryism that encourages and does not threaten. That is as relevant in the high-rise housing estate as by the village pond.

JOHN MAJOR
Welsh Conservative Party conference, 1991

'We serve One Nation best . . .'

We serve One Nation best by policies which recognise the changed pattern of work and encourage it; by insisting that the management structure of corporate business should be accountable; by monetary and fiscal management of impeccable soundness; by social and tax policies that promote investment, saving and capital accumulation; by ensuring that the major social tasks of government are performed efficiently; by mobilising the full resources of capitalism to build the infrastructure of our future society.

We conserve One Nation from hostile forces by better policies for fighting crime; by strengthening society's institutions for protecting itself; by reinforcing local and community involvement with a high sense of civic responsibility and of family values; and by rejecting the over-permissive codes of the anti-society left.

We keep our Nation as One by valuing and preserving the Union in all its diversity; by insisting that no part of the kingdom is subordinate or, in some demeaning way, dependent. We need never to forget that all regions, all areas, all nations within the nation, need each other and are part of a vital, confident society.

Above all, we prepare One Nation for future challenges by highlighting the international context in which our society now lives and by setting out, with candour and courage, the burdens to be shouldered if we want to live in a stable world order and contribute to its well-being.

DAVID HOWELL (editor)
'One Nation 2000', 1992

'Our shared historic culture'

Conservative thought at its best conveys the mutual dependence between the community and the free market. Each is enriched by the other. It is the point at which modern conservatism comes close to the most sophisticated liberalism

This preoccupation with linking communities and markets is part of a continuing Conservative concern with national integration. Disraeli's two nations, Salisbury's fears of national disintegration, the One Nation Group, John Major's opportunity society – all address the question of how to ensure that all British citizens feel that they participate in national life.

It is a fine point of political judgement, indeed of political principle, how much to expect us to share with our fellow citizens. Socialists are too ambitious: their egalitarianism was shown … to be wrong in principle as well as destructive in practice. Nor can one expect any longer, if one ever could, uniformity of belief to weld us into one moral community – the nation as a monastic order writ large. Those extreme communitarians, like socialists, demand too much. We have to rub along together on these islands and that requires tolerance of diversity.

It is also wrong to demand too little – the libertarian error. Without shared loyalties to institutions we lose any basis of legitimacy for the state. Our shared historic culture is the most powerful force for national integration. Education can give everyone and anyone access to our literary and historical tradition. It is a sad irony that those progressive thinkers so keen to criticize Thatcherite individualism and the privatization of industry – where it makes obvious sense – have themselves encouraged the privatization of our culture. Look at the changes in a typical school curriculum over the past thirty years and one can see the fracturing of our literary tradition as the trivial and the meretricious jostle alongside the great. Similarly, a sense of the shape of our history has been lost, to be replaced by a miscellany of themes and special subjects. No longer can we be confident that someone emerging from our schools will have come across the novels of Charles Dickens or know who Winston Churchill was. As Prince Charles rightly observed, that is indeed cultural disinheritance. It is real deprivation. The battle for educational standards is perhaps the most important single battle for a Conservative to fight.

DAVID WILLETTS
Modern Conservatism, 1992

7

'Stronger Support for the Family'

The family is the bulwark of society. Its strength derives from the loyalty it creates, the personal relationships, the love, the unity, and the prospect of continuity into the future. Not all families are happy, not all families live together, but the great majority do. Although divorce has become easier and more common, the popularity of marriage remains undiminished. Those who do separate often want to re-marry.

So, in spite of the pressures which undermine the family and in spite of the chatter of the permissive society, and in spite of the more relaxed social mores of today, the family still remains the pivot of personal affection. As early as the fourteenth century Chaucer rejoiced in the 'ease and prosperous joys of man and wife'. Edmund Burke reminded us that wider, public associations and affections all start with the familiar, the immediate, the local, with the family. John Galsworthy in The Forsyte Saga *celebrated the high, Victorian summer of family solidarity.*

More recently, Roger Scruton, Chris Patten and Margaret Thatcher have all spoken of the importance of the cohesion that stems from the family. The support for the family, in every possible way, should be in linchpin of Conservative policy. The family is the first and most effective unit of social welfare; the obligations it creates are readily shouldered, the love which it generates is shared, the problems it encounters are mutually solved, and the loyalty which it engenders is forged to survive the greatest pressure.

Ferdinand Mount in his admirable study of 1982 reminded us that many institutions and ideologies have been very cool about the family – the Church, communism, fascism – since the family represents a separate source of loyalty. This loyalty transcends political ideology and therefore is subversive of the authority derived from it. That is the source of the family's enduring strength.

'The ease, the prosperous joys of man and wife'

She took a servant when she took a lord,
A lord in marriage in a love renewed
By service, lordship set in servitude;
In servitude? Why no, but far above
Since he had both his lady and his love.
His lady certainly, his wife no less,
To which the law of love will answer 'yes'.
　So in the happiness that they had planned
He took his wife home to his native land
With joyful ease and reached his castle there
By Penmarch Point, not far from Finisterre,
And there they lived in amity unharried.
　Who can recount, unless he has been married,
The ease, the prosperous joys of man and wife?

GEOFFREY CHAUCER
'The Franklin's Tale' in *The Canterbury Tales*, 1387, trans. Nevill Coghill

'The joys of marriage'

The joys of marriage are the heaven on earth,
Life's paradise, great princess, the soul's quiet,
Sinews of concord, earthly immortality,
Eternity of pleasures; no restoratives
Like to a constant woman.

JOHN FORD, 1633

'Half a Man'

A man who is not married is half a man.

SAMUEL JOHNSON

'We begin our public affections in our families'

No man ever was attached by a sense of pride, partiality, or real affection, to a description of square measurement. He never will glory in belonging to the Chequer no. 71, or to any other badge-ticket. We begin our public affections in our families. No cold relation is a zealous citizen. We pass on to our neighbours and our habitual provincial connections. These are inns and resting places. Such divisions of our country as have been forced by habit and not by a sudden jerk of authority, are so many little images of the great country in which the heart found something which it could fill. The love to the whole is not extinguished by this subordinate partiality. Perhaps it is a sort of elemental training to those higher and more large regards, by which alone men come to be affected, as with their own concern, in the prosperity of a kingdom . . .

EDMUND BURKE

Reflections on the Revolution in France, 1790

'Then all the Cratchit family drew round the hearth'

Then up rose Mrs Cratchit, Cratchit's wife, dressed out but poorly in a twice-turned gown, but brave in ribbons, which are cheap and make a goodly show for sixpence; and she laid the cloth, assisted by Belinda Cratchit, second of her daughters, also brave in ribbons; while Master Peter Cratchit plunged a fork into the saucepan of potatoes, and getting the corners of his monstrous shirt-collar (Bob's private property, conferred upon his son and heir in honour of the day) into his mouth, rejoiced to find himself so gallantly attired, and yearned to show his linen in the fashionable Parks. And now two smaller Cratchits, boy and girl, came tearing in, screaming that outside the baker's they had smelt the goose, and known it for their own; and basking in luxurious thoughts of sage-and-onion, these young Cratchits danced about the table, and exalted Master Peter Cratchit to the skies, while he (not proud, although his collars nearly choked him) blew the fire, until the slow potatoes bubbling up, knocked loudly at the saucepan-lid to be let out and peeled.

'What has ever got your precious father then,' said Mrs Cratchit. 'And your brother, Tiny Tim! And Martha warn't as late last Christmas Day by half-an-hour!' . . .

At last the dinner was all done, the cloth was cleared, the hearth swept, and the fire made up. The compound in the jug being tasted and considered perfect, apples and oranges were put upon the table, and a shovel-full of chesnuts on the fire. Then all the Cratchit family drew round the hearth, in what Bob Cratchit called a circle, meaning half a one; and at Bob Cratchit's elbow stood the family display of glass; two tumblers, and a custard-cup without a handle.

These held the hot stuff from the jug, however, as well as golden goblets would have done; and Bob served it out with beaming looks, while the chestnuts on the fire sputtered and crackled noisily. Then Bob proposed:

'A Merry Christmas to us all, my dears. God bless us!'

Which all the family re-echoed.

'God bless us every one!' said Tiny Tim, the last of all.

He sat very close to his father's side, upon his little stool. Bob held his withered little hand in his, as if he loved the child, and wished to keep him by his side, and dreaded that he might be taken from him.

CHARLES DICKENS

A Christmas Carol, 1843

I have included this famous passage from A *Christmas Carol* to show how important the family was in Victorian England. It is easy to sneer at its romantic sentimentality, but Dickens was not just describing an ideal. For many in his vast popular audience the family was the very heart of their existence, enabling them to cope with poverty and care for its weakest members.

'At Home' at Old Jolyon's

Those privileged to be present at a family festival of the Forsytes have seen that charming and instructive sight – an upper middle-class family in full plumage. But whatsoever of these favoured persons has possessed the gift of psychological analysis (a talent without monetary value and properly ignored by the Forsytes) has witnessed a spectacle, not only delightful in itself, but illustrative of an obscure human problem. In plainer words, he has gleaned from a gathering of this family – no branch of which had a liking for the other, between no three members of whom existed anything worthy of the name of sympathy – evidence of that mysterious concrete tenacity which renders a family so formidable a unit of society, so clear a reproduction of society in miniature. He has been admitted to a vision of the dim roads of social progress, has understood something of patriarchal life, of the swarmings of savage hordes, of the rise and fall of nations. He is like one who, having watched a tree grow from its planting – a paragon of tenacity, insulation, and success, amidst the deaths of a hundred other plants less fibrous, sappy, and persistent – one day will see it flour-

ishing with bland, full foliage, in an almost repugnant prosperity, at the
summit of its efflorescence.

JOHN GALSWORTHY
The Man of Property, 1906
This is the first paragraph from *The Forsyte Saga*, set in the high Victorian
afternoon of 1886. The Forsyte family is gathered at the home of its patriarch at
Stanhope Gate.

A PRAYER FOR MY DAUGHTER

May she become a flourishing hidden tree
That all her thoughts may like the linnet be,
And have no business but dispensing round
Their magnanimities of sound,
Nor but in merriment begin a chase,
Nor but in merriment a quarrel.
O may she live like some green laurel
Rooted in one dear perpetual place.

My mind, because the minds that I have loved,
The sort of beauty that I have approved,
Prosper but little, has dried up of late,
Yet knows that to be choked with hate
May well be of all evil chances chief.
If there's no hatred in a mind
Assault and battery of the wind
Can never tear the linnet from the leaf.

An intellectual hatred is the worst,
So let her think opinions are accursed.
Have I not seen the loveliest woman born
Out of the mouth of Plenty's horn,
Because of her opinionated mind
Barter that horn and every good
By quiet natures understood
For an old bellows full of angry wind?

Considering that, all hatred driven hence,
The soul recovers radical innocence
And learns at last that it is self-delighting,
Self-appeasing, self-affrighting,

And that its own sweet will is Heaven's will;
She can, though every face should scowl
And every windy quarter howl
Or every bellows burst, be happy still.

And may her bridegroom bring her to a house
Where all's accustomed, ceremonious;
For arrogance and hatred are the wares
Peddled in the thoroughfares.
How but in custom and in ceremony
Are innocence and beauty born?
Ceremony's a name for the rich horn,
And custom for the spreading laurel tree.

    W. B. YEATS, 1919

'Do we then want to break marriage?'

It is marriage, perhaps, which had given man the best of his freedom, given him his little kingdom of his own within the big kingdom of the State ... It is a true freedom because it is a true fulfilment, for man, woman and children. Do we then want to break marriage? If we do break it, it means we all fall to a far greater extent under the direct sway of the State.

    D. H. LAWRENCE, 1932

'The prime focus of leisure, and the origin of self-respect'

The family is the prime focus of leisure, and the origin of self-respect, being the first institution through which the social world is perceived. It is also autonomous; it is a form of life which has no aim besides itself. What is achieved through family union could not be achieved in some other way. The family is therefore instinct with concrete values, providing each of its participants with an unending source of rational objectives, which cannot be specified in advance but which arise from the realities of family life. The child who saves his pocket money in order to make a gift to his mother acts under the first impulse of rational conduct, acting towards an end the reality of which is more vivid to him than anything he might abstractly understand. Thus he makes his mark in the family, learns the 'ways of freedom', discovering himself and another through the act of love . . .

It matters enormously to parents that their children should be something, and not just anything. It is natural to seek preferment and security
for them, and to be pleased when they acquire it. It is also natural to wish
to pass on to them every attribute that might survive one's own
departure. The principle of legacy – whereby a household outlasts its
members – is therefore a consequence of family love. So too is the
principle of hereditary privilege. This is not confined to a particular
class. It is as much a desire of the labourer to work for the advantage of
his child (rather than anyone else's), as it is a desire of the landed
aristocrat. Massive legal interference in legacy and hereditary right
constitutes a direct affront to the securest of social feelings. It is therefore
impossible for those affected by it to be persuaded of its legitimacy. In
this matter conservative politics directly supports and stems from a
fundamental social bond. It seeks to conserve social continuity, so that
people may envisage generations which stretch before and after them.
Without that vision much of the motive for procreation is lost, and the
child himself becomes an accident, an anxiety, and a reminder of one's
isolation. The parent at rest with his child has a dominant desire, which
is this: what I am and what I value, I here pass on. The complexity and
consolation of this thought has never been better captured than in the
passage of *Ulysses*, sometimes known as 'Ithaca', in which Bloom
projects towards Stephen the image of himself as father. Reflect on these
things, and you will see that, however vociferously men may declare
their attachment to other ideologies, in their most solemn and silent
innervations they are naturally conservative.

ROGER SCRUTON
The Meaning of Conservatism, 1980

'A little tame and bloodless'

The family is a subversive organisation. In fact, it is the ultimate and only
consistently subversive organisation. Only the family has continued
throughout history and still continues to undermine the State. The
family is the enduring permanent enemy of all hierarchies, churches and
ideologies. Not only dictators, bishops and commissars but also humble
parish priests and café intellectuals find themselves repeatedly coming
up against the stony hostility of the family and its determination to resist
interference to the last . . .

*

Yet it remains true that the dominant force in the Western world is the desire of the urban working class to fulfil its own aspirations. And among the first of those aspirations, most intimate and ancient, is the desire for equality, privacy and independence *in marriage*. Why is it that this desire for the independence of marriage should continue to look stronger than the desire for personal independence – which is so often said to be the dominant trend of our times? Why do people still wish to submerge, at least partially, their personalities in marriage and devote a great part of their lives, perhaps the major part, to 'working at' this battered old form of human relationship?

It can only be said, in the most hesitant fashion possible, that it may be because marriage still seems to be the most *interesting* enterprise which most of us come across. With all its tediums and horrors, it has both more variety and more continuity than any other commitment we can make. Its time-scale is far grander; there are still marriages alive which are older than the Bolshevik Revolution. Its passions, both of love and hatred, are more intense. Its outcomes – children, grandchildren, heirlooms of flesh and blood – stretch away over the horizon; they are the only identifiable achievements with most of us are likely to leave behind us, even if, like many achievements, they are liable to be flawed and only partially within our control. Marriage and the family make other experiences, both pleasant and unpleasant, seem a little tame and bloodless. And it is difficult to resist the conclusion that a way of living which is both so intense and so enduring must somehow come naturally to us, that it is part of being human.

FERDINAND MOUNT

The Subversive Family, 1982

These are the opening and concluding paragraphs of Ferdinand Mount's admirable study, *The Subversive Family*. He shows that the family over the centuries has formed a unit of freedom and independence which has been resented by the Church, communism, Hitler, 'advanced' thinkers and social engineers. But its attraction has survived them all since it represents the hopes of ordinary people.

'Stronger support for the family is the linchpin'

To re-allocate resources, which are at present skewed against families with children, in order to assist them, does not remove responsibilities from families, it increases them. It expects more of parents, not less. But it helps them to do more too. Bringing children into the world and bringing them up is the most valuable and rewarding thing that most of us ever do. It is an important job and, of course, it is a job for both parents. There is no assumption that it is only a woman's job or that it is the only fulfilling work that a woman can ever carry out. More married women, thanks to sensible changes in social attitudes, improved education and the gadget-assisted elimination of some of the drudgery of housework, will want to work in the future and will be able to work. Technological developments may help them to combine work with their role as mothers, and changes in personnel practices (the provision of paternity leave for instance) should also assist. Nevertheless, the mother's role is vital in a family and in its social policies a government should demonstrate the priority that it attaches to it.

Stronger support for the family is the linchpin of any policy for encouraging community care, which involves sharing the responsibilities assumed by the Welfare State, not off-loading them. Community care means above all care by the family and that has very often meant care by women. Community care and a more pluralist approach to welfare also entails greater help for voluntary organisations, which tap such a rich source of individual energy and initiative.

Our aim must be a welfare society, based on support for the family, a society in which the existing institutions of the Welfare State will play a central part – in the case of our health services, *the* central part. There is no case for dismantling the Welfare State; when they function well, its services help to bind the community together and to support rather than weigh down the economic life of the nation. Yet we need more variety in welfare if we are to have higher standards, and we need more diversity in the financing of welfare if we are to extend provision. Private health insurance and occupational pension schemes should be encouraged as additional contributions to a welfare society, not attacked as threats to the integrity of the Welfare State.

CHRIS PATTEN
'The Tory Case', 1983

'We believe in open doors'

Conservatives believe in choice, and their view of the importance of the individual within the law underlies the Conservative Party's commitment to equal opportunities for women. We believe in open doors; many that were once barred to women are now plainly open, but some, though unlocked, still need a good shove to demonstrate to our daughters that women do have a vast range of futures waiting for them. Indeed you can say that women have a potentially greater range than men, for one of our commitments is to ensure that those doors marked 'Home Management' and 'Childcare' stay open to all – men as well as women – as important options in our choices for life. Too often nowadays these options are made to look less significant, and the skills required less praiseworthy, than the high-earning lifestyles of big city business.

I believe, with the Government, and most Conservatives, that in the interests of justice and the nation's need, all doors in the world of work should be open to women on equal terms with men. I also believe that in response to women's own wishes, and the needs of their families and children, it must be possible for women to spend as much time as they choose as 'Household Managers', returning to work when or if their responsibilities permit; and that tax, training and social security systems should support and facilitate, not hinder, this vital flexibility.

MARY BAKER
'Opening Doors for Women', 1987

'It is on the family that we in government build our own policies'

What is certain, however, is that any set of social and economic arrangements which is not founded on the acceptance of individual responsibility will do nothing but harm. We are all responsible for our own actions. We cannot blame society if we disobey the law. We simply cannot delegate the exercise of mercy and generosity to others.

The politicians and other secular powers should strive, by their measures, to bring out the good in people and to fight down the bad: but they can't create the one or abolish the other. They can only see that the laws encourage the best instincts and convictions of the people, instincts and convictions which I am convinced are more deeply rooted than is often supposed.

This is nowhere more evident than in the basic ties of the family which are at the heart of our society and are the very nursery of civic virtue. It is on the family that we in government build our own policies for welfare, education and care. You recall that Timothy was warned by St Paul that anyone who neglects to provide for his own house (meaning his own family) has disowned the faith and is 'worse than an infidel'.

MARGARET THATCHER
Speech to the General Assembly of the Church of Scotland, 21 May 1988

8

'I am a Defender of the Middle Class'

Aristotle was the first political writer to understand that if a society was to be resilient and resourceful it needed to be based on a strong middle class. Government by an aristocracy, or an élite however it might be formed, becomes self-regarding and out of touch. Government by the proletariat is usually revolutionary rather than evolutionary in origin, leading to single-party rule and dictatorship. This in turn leads to corruption, with the dispensation of privilege in the hands of the party.

The existence of a middle class provides a stratum of society which values the acquisition of education and wealth as keys to independence and social mobility. The middle class comprises the professional, the entrepreneur and the salaried. For most members of the middle class, their aspiration is to be comfortable rather than rich. Having achieved this state, middle-class members of society can afford to look beyond material wants. They involve themselves in 'quality-of-life' issues and cultural pursuits. They form the backbone of voluntary organizations, and seek public office where the fulfilment of duties and obligations counter-balances the material benefits they derive from society. While the middle class does not wield the collective power which the organized working class can mobilize, they nevertheless have influence by virtue of being able to articulate their concerns. Despite its numerical inferiority, the middle class is the class from which society draws most of its leaders. So when the middle class is disturbed by events or policies, political parties move swiftly to reassure it.

Conservatism has never relied for electoral success on any single group or class. If it had, it would have been superseded and forefeited its claim to be a national party. The Labour Party, on the other hand, has unashamedly proclaimed itself the spokesman of the working class. One of the ironies of British politics, however, is that a large number of working-class voters do support the Conservatives, indeed without them the Conservative Party would never have been elected to office in recent years. The alignment of class and party in Britain is not clear cut.

The appeal of the Conservatives has always been to allow people from whatever background to advance through their own efforts. This meritocratic approach means that some will get ahead, advance and prosper but others may fare less well. Socialists do not believe in this approach. While they may share with Conservatives a belief in equality of opportunity, their policies are aimed at achieving equality of outcome. For the socialist, justice requires an equal distribution of the world's goods. To a Conservative that is not only unfair, but unrealistic. Socialism creates a society of bleak uniformity which is inherently unstable, since it pays no heed to man's aspirations. Conservatives recognize the instincts and desires in human nature which mean that the fortunes of some move up and the fortunes of others move down. It is only through such social mobility that an organic and vigorous society emerges: one that reflects the ebb and flow of life and yet enables progress to unfold in an orderly way.

'The steadiest element'

First we must grasp a principle which is universally applicable to them all: it is essential that that part of the population which desires the maintenance of the constitution should be larger than that which does not.

But at all times a legislator ought to endeavour to attach the middle section of the population firmly to the constitution. If he is framing laws oligarchical in character, he should have the middle class always in view; if democratic, he should again make them attractive to the middle class. Wherever the number of the middle class is larger than a combination of the two extremes, or even than one only, then there is a good chance of permanence for the constitution. There is no danger of rich and poor making common cause against *them*; for neither will want to be subservient to the other, and if they are looking for a compromise, they will not find any better than the middle-class polity which they have already ...

The middle class is also the steadiest element, the least eager for change. They neither covet, like the poor, the possessions of others, nor do others covet theirs, as the poor covet those of the rich. So they live less risky lives, not scheming and not being schemed against. Phocylides's wish was therefore justified when he wrote 'Those in the middle have many advantages; that is where I wish to be in society.'

ARISTOTLE
Politics, Book IV, *c.* 335 BC

'Power, authority and distinction'

You do not imagine, that I wish to confine power, authority, and distinction to blood, and names, and titles. No, Sir. There is no qualification for government, but virtue and wisdom, actual or presumptive. Wherever they are actually found, they have, in whatever state, condition, profession or trade, the passport of Heaven to human place and honour. Woe to the country which would madly and impiously reject the service of the talents and virtues, civil, military, or religious, that are given to grace and to serve it; and would condemn to obscurity every thing formed to diffuse lustre and glory around a state. Woe to that country too, that passing into the opposite extreme, considers a low education, a mean contracted view of things, a sordid

mercenary occupation, as a preferable title to command. Every thing
ought to be open; but not indifferently to every man. No rotation; no
appointment by lot; no mode of election operating in the spirit of
sortition or rotation, can be generally good in a government conversant
in extensive objects. Because they have no tendency, direct or indirect,
to select the man with a view to the duty, or to accommodate the one to
the other, I do not hesitate to say, that the road to eminence and power,
from obscure condition, ought not to be made too easy, nor a thing too
much of course. If rare merit be the rarest of all rare things, it ought to
pass through some sort of probation. The temple of honour ought to be
seated on an eminence. If it be open through virtue, let it be remembered too, that virtue is never tried but by some difficulty, and some
struggle.

EDMUND BURKE
Reflections on the Revolution in France, 1790

'The master-spring of public prosperity'

If no man could hope to rise or fear to fall in society; if industry did not
bring its own reward, and indolence its punishment; we could not hope
to see that animated activity in bettering our own condition which now
forms the master-spring of public prosperity.

THOMAS MALTHUS

'Why a poor man may be a Conservative'

I will state some of the reasons why a poor man may be an Operative
Conservative. I am very well aware that a man may be joined to a
'Radical Association,' to the 'Working Man's Association,' and to a
'Political Union,' and all will be right and square; but only let a man be
a member of an Operative Conservative Society, why astonishment is
at once excited, and the exclamation made, 'I cannot for the world see
why a man is to be a Conservative Operative.'

The First reason why a poor man may be a Conservative, is this; that
he rightly and properly and justly appreciates all those great blessings
and advantages which, as an Englishman, he enjoys, and which have
accrued to him from living under that invaluable constitution which is
the pride of his country and the glory of all lands.

Secondly. That the attempts which are now making by men of all castes, and of all creeds; by men of all religion, and men of no religion; by men of all principles, and by men of no principle, to root up the Constitution under pretence of improving it, will lead ultimately to anarchy and national confusion, and consequently to the prostration of that beautiful structure.

Thirdly. The members of these Societies, being convinced that, should 'the British Constitution fall, truth and reason and the cause of liberty would fall with it; and they who were buried in its ruins would be happier than those who survived it.' I say, being convinced of this important truth, they feel it to be their paramount duty to rally round the Constitution of their country, and if they can by possibility do any good to its cause, even in the most humble way, they cheerfully offer the sacrifice upon its sacred altar.

Fourthly. They are opposed to all those dogmas which are trumpeted forth by a certain class of political empiries, viz. Vote by Ballot, Household Suffrage, and Annual Parliaments, &c., believing that the adoption of these measures would, so far from tending to produce the real welfare of the country, lead to a train of national evils the most woful and lasting in their consequences.

Fifthly. They believe that the principles of Conservatism are founded upon reason, justice, truth, revelation, and sound loyalty; and that, in their general tendencies and operations, they not only contribute largely to the maintenance and preservation of all our great Institutions, but essentially aid in security to all classes of society that degree of security and happiness which forms the basis of a great and mighty empire.

WILLIAM PAUL
A History of the Origin and Progress of Operative Conservative Societies, 1839

Two Nations

'Well society may be in its infancy,' said Egremont slightly smiling; 'but, say what you will, our Queen reigns over the greatest nation that ever existed.'

'Which nation?' asked the younger stranger, 'for she reigns over two.'

The stranger paused; Egremont was silent but looked inquiringly.

'Yes,' resumed the younger stranger after a moment's interval. 'Two nations between whom there is no intercourse and no sympathy; who are as ignorant of each other's habits, thoughts, and feelings as if they were dwellers in different zones or inhabitants of different planets; who are formed by a different breeding, and fed by a different food, are ordered by different manners, and are not governed by the same laws.'

'You speak of – ' said Egremont hesitatingly.

'THE RICH AND THE POOR.'

BENJAMIN DISRAELI

Sybil, 1845

In this famous passage the hero, Egremont, is shown the existence of two nations in England by a Chartist agitator. The scene is set in the ruins of an old abbey at sunset.

'The palace is not safe'

The palace is not safe when the cottage is not happy.

BENJAMIN DISRAELI

Speech in Lady Londonderry's grounds, 1848

Disraeli's romantic vision of the aristocracy and the working classes coming together through an identity of interest went back to the paternalistic attitudes of earlier centuries. After his death *The Times* in a memorable phrase said that Disraeli perceived 'the conservative working man as the sculptor perceives the angel prisoned in a block of marble'.

'The novel features under which despotism may appear'

I think, then, that the species of oppression by which democratic nations are menaced is unlike anything that ever before existed in the world; our contemporaries will find no prototype of it in their memories. I seek in vain for an expression that will accurately convey the whole of the idea I have formed of it; the old words *despotism* and *tyranny* are inappropriate; the thing itself is new, and since I cannot name, I must attempt to define it.

I seek to trace the novel features under which despotism may appear in the world. The first thing that strikes the observation is an innumerable multitude of men, all equal and all alike incessantly endeavouring to procure the petty and paltry pleasures with which they glut their lives. Each of them living apart, is as a stranger to the fate of all the rest; his children and his private friends constitute to him the whole of mankind. As for the rest of his fellow citizens, he is close to them, but he does not see them; he touches them but he does not feel them; he exists only in himself and for himself alone; and it his kindred still remain to him, he may be said at any rate to have lost his country.

Above this race of men stands an immense and tutelary power, which takes upon itself alone to secure their gratifications and to watch over their fate. That power is absolute, minute, regular, provident, and mild. It would be like the authority of a parent if, like that authority, its object was to prepare men for manhood, but it seeks, on the contrary, to keep them in perpetual childhood; it is well content that the people should rejoice, provided that they think of nothing but rejoicing. For their happiness such a government willingly labors, but it chooses to be the sole agent and the only arbiter of their necessities, facilitates their pleasures, manages their principal concerns, directs their industry, regulates the descent of property, and subdivides their inheritances; what remains, but to spare them all the care of thinking and all the trouble of living?

Thus it every day renders the exercise of the free agency of man less useful and less frequent; it circumscribes the will within a narrower range and gradually robs a man of all the uses of himself. The principle of equality has prepared men for these things; it has predisposed them to endure them and often to look on them as benefits.

ALEXIS DE TOCQUEVILLE, 1850

'You cannot'

You cannot strengthen the weak by weakening the strong.
You cannot bring about prosperity by discouraging thrift.
You cannot help the wage earner by pulling down the wage payer.
You cannot further the brotherhood of man by encouraging class hatred.
You cannot help the poor by destroying the rich.
You cannot keep out of trouble by spending more than you earn.
You cannot build character and courage by taking away man's initiative and independence.
You cannot help men permanently by doing for them what they could and should do for themselves.

ABRAHAM LINCOLN

'When everyone is somebodee'

There lived a King, as I've been told,
In the wonder-working days of old,
When hearts were twice as good as gold,
 And twenty times as mellow.
Good-temper triumphed in his face,
And in his heart he found a place
For all the erring human race
 And every wretched fellow.
When he had Rhenish wine to drink
It made him very sad to think
That some, at junket or at jink,
 Must be content with toddy.
He wished all men as rich as he
(And he was rich as rich could be),
So to the top of every tree
 Promoted everybody.

  Lord Chancellors were cheap
 as sprats,
And Bishops in their shovel hats
Were plentiful as tabby cats –
 In point of fact, too many.
Ambassadors cropped up like hay,
Prime Ministers and such as they
Grew like asparagus in May,
 And Dukes were three a penny.
On every side Field Marshals gleamed,
Small beer were Lords Lieutenant deemed,
With Admirals the ocean teemed
 All round his wide dominions.
And Party Leaders you might meet
In twos and threes in every street,
Maintaining, with no little heat,
 Their various opinions.

> That King, although no one
> 　　denies
> His heart was of abnormal size,
> Yet he'd have acted otherwise
> 　　If he had been acuter.
> The end is easily foretold,
> When every blessed thing you hold
> Is made of silver, or of gold,
> 　　You long for simple pewter.
> When you have nothing else to wear
> But cloth of gold and satins rare,
> For cloth of gold you cease to care –
> 　　Up goes the price of shoddy.
> In short, whoever you may be,
> To this conclusion you'll agree,
> When everyone is somebodee,
> 　　Then no one's anybody!

W. S. GILBERT
The Gondoliers, 1889

'Matter of life or death'

We are now come, or are coming fast, to a time when Labour laws will
be made by the Labour interest for the advantage of Labour. The
regulation of all the conditions of labour by the State, controlled and
guided by the Labour vote, appears to be the idea aimed at ...
Personally I can discern no cause for alarm in this prospect and I
believe that on this point you and I are in perfect agreement. Labour in
his modern movement has against it the prejudices of property, the
resources of capital, and all the numerous forces – social, professional
and journalist – which those prejudices and resources can influence. It
is our business as Tory politicians to uphold the Constitution. If under
the Constitution as it now exists, and as we wish to see it preserved, the
Labour interest finds that it can obtain its objects and secure its own
advantage, then that interest will be reconciled to the Constitution, will
find faith in it and will maintain it. But if it should unfortunately occur
that the Constitutional party, to which you and I belong, are deaf to
hear and slow to meet the demands of Labour, are stubborn in opposition to those demands and are persistent in the habit of ranging

themselves in unreasoning and short-sighted support of all the present rights of property and capital, the result may be that the Labour interest may identify what it will take to be defects in the Constitutional party with the Constitution itself, and in a moment of indiscriminate impulse may use its power to sweep both away. This view of affairs, I submit, is worthy of attention at a time when it is a matter of life or death to the Constitutional party to enlist in the support of the Parliamentary Union of the United Kingdom a majority of the votes of the masses of Labour.

LORD RANDOLPH CHURCHILL
Letter to the Liberal-Unionist candidate for Tyneside, 1892

'What is middle class morality?'

DOOLITTLE: Dont say that, Governor. Dont look at it that way. What am I, Governors both? I ask you, what am I? I'm one of the undeserving poor: thats what I am. Think of what that means to a man. It means that hes up agen middle class morality all the time. If theres anything going and I put in for a bit of it, it's always the same story: 'Youre undeserving; so you cant have it.' But my needs is as great as the most deserving widow's that ever got money out of six different charities in one week for the death of the same husband. I don't need less than a deserving man: I need more. I don't eat less hearty than him; and I drink a lot more. I want a bit of amusement, cause I'm a thinking man. I want cheerfulness and a song and a band when I feel low. Well, they charge me just the same for everything as they charge the deserving. What is middle class morality? Just an excuse for never giving me anything. Therefore, I ask you, as two gentlemen, not to play that game on me. I'm playing straight with you. I aint pretending to be deserving. I'm undeserving; and I mean to go on being undeserving. I like it; and thats the truth. Will you take advantage of a man's nature to do him out of the price of his own daughter what hes brought up and fed and clothed by the sweat of his brow until shes growed big enough to be interesting to you two gentlemen? Is five pounds unreasonable? I put it to you; and I leave it to you.

HIGGINS (*Rising, and going over to Pickering*) Pickering: if we were to take this man in hand for three months, he could choose between a seat in the Cabinet and a popular pulpit in Wales.

PICKERING: What do you say to that, Doolittle?

DOOLITTLE: Not me, Governor, thank you kindly. Ive heard all the preachers and all the prime ministers – for I'm a thinking man and game for politics or religion or social reform same as all the other amusements – and I tell you it's a dog's life anyway you look at it. Undeserving poverty is my line. Taking one station in society with another, it's – it's – well, it's the only one that has any ginger in it, to my taste.

G. B. SHAW
Pygmalion, 1912

This is an engaging defence of the undeserving poor by the dustman appropriately called Doolittle. He went so far as to 'sell' his daughter.

'The custom in our little epoch'

It is the custom in our little epoch to sneer at the middle classes. Cockney artists profess to find the bourgeoisie dull; as if artists had any business to find anything dull. Decadents talk contemptuously of its conventions and its set tasks; it never occurs to them that conventions and set tasks are the very way to keep that greenness in the grass and that redness in the roses – which they have lost for ever. Stevenson in his incomparable 'Lantern Bearers,' describes the ecstasy of a schoolboy in the mere fact of buttoning a dark lantern under a dark greatcoat. If you wish for that ecstasy of the schoolboy, you must have the boy; but you must also have the school. Strict opportunities and defined hours are the very outline of that enjoyment.

G. K. CHESTERTON

'I don't understand English titles'

I don't understand English titles,' she said.

'No?' I said.

'No,' she said. 'There's nothing I enjoy more than curling up with a good English book, but the titles always puzzle me. That New York paper called you the Earl of Havershot. Is an Earl the same as a Duke?'

'Not quite. Dukes are a bit higher up.'

'Is it the same as Viscount?'

'No. Viscounts are a bit lower down. We Earls rather sneer at Viscounts. One is pretty haughty with them, poor devils.'

'What is your wife? A Countess?'

'I haven't got a wife. If I had she would be a Countess.'
A sort of far-away look came into her eyes.
'The Countess of Havershot,' she murmured.
'That's right. The Countess of Havershot.'
'What is Havershot? The place where you live?'
'No. I don't quite know where the Havershot comes in. The family doss-house is at Biddleford, in Norfolk.'
'Is it a very lovely place?'
'Quite a goodish sort of shack.'
'Battlements?'
'Lots of battlements.'
'And deer?'
'Several deer.'
'I love deer.'
'Me, too. I've met some very decent deer.'
P. G. WODEHOUSE
Laughing Gas, 1936

'The working classes and the middle classes are drawing together'

The effect of all this is a general softening of manners. It is enhanced by the fact that modern industrial methods tend always to demand less muscular effort and therefore to leave people with more energy when their day's work is done. Many workers in the light industries are less truly manual labourers than is a doctor or a grocer. In tastes, habits, manners and outlook the working class and the middle class are drawing together. The unjust distinctions remain, but the real differences diminish. The old-style 'proletarian' – collarless, unshaven and with muscles warped by heavy labour – still exists, but he is constantly decreasing in numbers; he only predominates in the heavy-industry areas of the north of England.

After 1918 there began to appear something that had never existed in England before: people of indeterminate social class. In 1910 every human being in these islands could be 'placed' in an instant by his clothes, manners and accent. That is no longer the case. Above all, it is not the case in the new townships that have developed as a result of cheap motor cars and the southward shifts of industry. The place to look for the germs of the future England is in light-industry areas and along the arterial roads. In Slough, Dagenham, Barnet, Letchworth, Hayes – everywhere, indeed, on the outskirts of great towns the old pattern is gradually changing into something new. In those vast new wildernesses of glass and brick the sharp distinctions of the older kind of town, with its slums and mansions, or of the country, with its manor-houses and squalid cottages, no longer exist. There are wide gradations of income, but it is the same kind of life that is being lived at different levels, in labour-saving flats or council houses, along the concrete roads and in the naked democracy of the swimming-pools. It is a rather restless, cultureless life, centring round tinned food, *Picture Post*, the radio and the internal combustion engine. It is a civilization in which children grow up with an intimate knowledge of magnetoes and in complete ignorance of the Bible. To that civilisation belong the people who are most at home in and most definitely *of* the modern world, the technicians and the higher-paid skilled workers, the airmen and their mechanics, the radio experts, film producers, popular journalists and industrial chemists. They are the indeterminate stratum at which the older class distinctions are beginning to break down.

GEORGE ORWELL

The Lion and the Unicorn: Socialism and the English Genius, 1941

Orwell recognized that the class structure of Britain was changing and changing quickly. The beneficiary was not the Labour Party as he predicted but the Conservatives. Of the five towns he mentions, only the Ford plant at Dagenham kept the seat for Labour in 1992. The Conservatives were able to appeal to the emerging non-class society. Orwell rightly mentioned the significance of *Picture Post* as a stimulant to social change, and if he had not succumbed to consumption and had lived into the age of the Sunday colour magazine supplements he would have witnessed their impact upon the promotion of middle-class ambitions and desires for clothes, cars, holidays, houses and living styles. The Sunday colour supplements have done more to reinforce Conservative values and ideas than the papers' political writers and leaders.

'The life of the English Gentleman'

But it will be appropriate, by way of concluding this initial portrait of the gentleman, to emphasize once more the fundamental ethical difference which sets him apart from the aristocrat. The aristocrat, then, is concerned to demonstrate his status by consumption, possession and display; the gentleman, while he knows that his position requires of him dignity and a solid style of living, sets his store on performance and

not on show. To the aristocrat, badges, trappings, banquets and titles
are the true ends of his pride: to the gentleman such ornaments serve
only to lend seemliness to his office and so to ensure that he will be the
more readily and faithfully assisted in discharging it. The aristocrat
avoids the menial task because he sees it as distasteful, the gentleman
because it is unworthy: the aristocrat spurns business because he is, as
he thinks, above money, the gentleman because, once he has a mere
sufficiency, he is indifferent to it ... I trust that one point at least has
gone home: the life of the English Gentleman is centred on one purpose
– to recognize and to honour his obligation and his trust.

SIMON RAVEN
The English Gentleman, 1961

'I am myself passionately a defender of the middle class'

I am myself passionately a defender of the middle class and of the
professional class into which I was born and of which I have been a
member all my life. I do not believe myself to be a snob in the social
sense, although I would prefer to be thought one than to fall into the
inverted snobbery which is so popular nowadays. But I will maintain to
my last gasp the right of the middle class, and of the professional class,
to its own way of life, its own standards of living, its right to spend its
money on the education of its own children in its own way often at very
considerable sacrifice and always at considerable saving to the public,
and the right to spend its money on private medicine. It seems to me
that all these are as legitimate a use of one's spending income as buying
a package holiday at Ibiza or owning a sports car, and with the average
male weekly wage standing at more than £40 (that is more than £2,000
a year), and miners earning up to and above £100 (that is £5,000 a
year), I see absolutely no reason why we should be grudged the liberty
we demand, and, although I would never wish the Conservative Party
to be a class party, I see the liberties of my own class bound up with the
liberties of other minorities; those who do not wish to strike, those
who do not wish to join a particular union, or any union, those who
prefer to remain self-employed, those who farm, those who fish, those
who can own small businesses, or shops, those who do not wish to pay
the political contribution, those who wish to own their own homes, or
those who wish to let their homes to others for a brief period without
losing the power to recover them. In other words my conception of

democracy is not just majority rule, but diversity in unity, and the rights of minority groups, racial, religious, class, occupational, cultural, to be themselves, and to contribute to the nation in their own way.

QUINN HOGG, VISCOUNT HAILSHAM
'Conservative Philosophy', 1974

'An unrepentant bourgeois'

... this egalitarian drive increases the pressure, already very severe, on our middle class. The full effect on our culture, largely based on the middle class, has not been felt yet, but many of us are feeling gloomy about our prospects.

I write here as an unrepentant bourgeois, knowing very well that the art and thought of Western Europe have come mostly not from aristocrats, peasants and workers but from the so often despised bourgeoisie.

J. B. PRIESTLEY
Sunday Telegraph, 1975

'We are all unequal'

Some Socialists seem to believe that people should be numbers in a State computer. We believe they should be individuals. We are all unequal. No one, thank heavens, is quite like anyone else, however much the Socialists may pretend otherwise. We believe that everyone has the right to be unequal. But to us, every human being is equally important. Engineers, miners, manual workers, shop assistants, farmworkers, postmen, housewives – these are the essential foundations of our society, and without them there would be no nation. But there are others with special gifts who should also have their chance, because if the adventurers who strike out in new directions in science, technology, medicine, commerce, and industry are hobbled, there can be no advance. The spirit of envy can destroy: it can never build. Everyone must be allowed to develop in the way he chooses the abilities he knows he has within him – and she knows she has within her.

MARGARET THATCHER
Conservative Party Conference, 1975

'Inequality is an unavoidable feature'

The 'social structure' is a subject about which it is necessary to speak carefully. For Burke, who inserted it into modern thinking, it meant Monarchy, Aristocracy, Church and People; for us it means something very much more complicated. It means all the gradations of classes that exist in a modern society, including a far larger middle class than Burke had conceived of, a more powerful and less Christian intelligentsia than he thought desirable and a division, which scarcely existed in his mind, between the lower-middle classes and an immense, self-conscious working class beneath them. It includes the conception that taxation should not prevent responsibility being rewarded, provided that that does not entail penalizing those who have wealth without assignable social responsibility. It includes a system of law which makes it possible to maintain a variety of educational systems, to own, accumulate speak, publish and so on.

To put this in terms of inequality is to adopt a socialist analysis. But, since inequality is an unavoidable feature, it is best to meet the analysis head on and agree that the Conservative conception of a social structure not only assumes that marked inequalities are inevitable but also declines to justify them because their inevitability makes justification unnecessary.

MAURICE COWLING
Conservative Essays, 1978

9

'Utopias are not for us'

*Conservatives are deeply suspicious of grandiose and idealistic pro-
grammes that seek to change the face of the world. They are naturally
sceptical of such policies for two reasons. First, they share a belief,
derived from much Christian thought, that man is imperfect and that
human nature is fallible, and this creates a certain sense of humility.
Secondly, they have seen too many sweeping programmes of reform,
too many great movements for social improvement, lead to chaos and
leave a country in a worse position.*

*Fanatics down the ages from Savonarola to Robespierre, from Lenin
to Hitler, have sought to impose their brand of Utopian ideas upon
eager disciples and poor subjects alike. But such men of destiny usually
find that they have to rule through the use of terror and they succeed
only in plunging their people into untold misery and suffering.*

*This does not mean that Conservatives have no ideals and no hopes
for a better world. Quintin Hogg vehemently rejected that when he
wrote, 'A depressing creed? A negative creed? No! A Holy Gospel! All
the great evils of our time have come from men who mocked and
exploited human misery by pretending that good government, that is
government according to their way of thinking, could offer Utopia'.*

*Seventy years earlier James Fitzjames Stephens, the most significant
Conservative philosopher of the late nineteenth century, warned
against 'a moral Don Quixote' who was always liable to sacrifice
himself and his neighbours.*

*The Conservative way is much more down-to-earth, relying more
upon common sense – the intelligent approach rather than the intellectual. When Tom Paine wrote* The Rights of Man *it was more readily
welcomed in France and America than in Britain. When a British*

person thinks of liberty he doesn't have a vision of a classic Roman matron swathed in majestic robes carrying a banner emblazoned with the word. He has a vision of being left alone in his own home, to get on with his own business, free from people telling him what to do, free from nosy parkers, free from officials of all kind and particularly tax-collectors. Macaulay put it well in his essay on Lord Bacon when he said 'an acre in Middlesex is better than a principality in Utopia'.

'Men are continually in competition for honour and dignity'

It is true, that certain living creatures, as Bees, and Ants, live sociably one with another, (which are therefore by *Aristotle* numbred amongst Politicall creatures); and yet have no other direction, than their particular judgements and appetites; nor speech, whereby one of them can signifie to another, what he thinks expedient for the common benefit: and therefore some man may perhaps desire to know, why Man-kind cannot do the same. To which I answer,

First, that men are continually in competition for Honour and Dignity, which these creatures are not; and consequently amongst men there ariseth on that ground, Envy and Hatred, and finally Warre; but amongst these not so.

Secondly, that amongst these creatures, the Common good differeth not from the Private; and being by nature enclined to their private, they procure thereby the common benefit. But man, whose Joy consisteth in comparing himselfe with other men, can relish nothing but what is eminent.

Thirdly, that these creatures having not (as man) the use of reason, do not see, nor think they see any fault, in the administration of their common businesse: whereas amongst men, there are very many, that thinke themselves wiser, and abler to govern the Publique, better than the rest; and these strive to reforme and innovate, one this way, another that way; and thereby bring it into Distraction and Civill warre.

Fourthly, that these creatures, though they have some use of voice, in making knowne to one another their desires, and other affections; yet they want that art of words, by which some men can represent to others, that which is Good, in the likeness of Evill; and 'Evill, in the likenesse of Good; and augment, or diminish the apparent greatness of Good and Evill; discontenting men, and troubling their Peace and their pleasure.

Fifthly, irrationall creatures cannot distinguish between *Injury and Dammage*; and therefore as long as they be at ease, they are not offended with their fellows: whereas Man is then most troublesome, when he is most at ease: for then it is that he loves to shew his Wisdome, and controule the Actions of them that governe the Common-wealth.

Lastly, the agreement of these creatures is Naturall; that of men, is by Covenant only, which is Artificiall: and therefore it is no wonder if there be somwhat else required (besides Covenant) to make their Agreement constant and lasting; which is a Common Power, to keep them in awe, and to direct their actions to the Common Benefit.

THOMAS HOBBES
Leviathan, 1651

'Every revolution contains in it something of evil'

The burthen of proof lies heavily on those who tear to pieces the whole frame and contexture of their country, that they could find no other way of settling a government fit to obtain its rational ends, except that which they have pursued by means unfavourable to all the present happiness of millions of people, and to the utter ruin of several hundreds of thousands. In their political arrangements, men have no right to put the well-being of the present generation wholly out of the question. Perhaps the only moral trust with any certainty in our hands, is the care of our own time. With regard to futurity, we are to treat it like a ward. We are not so to attempt an improvement of his fortune, as to put the capital of his estate to any hazard ... Without attempting therefore to define what never can be defined, the case of a revolution in government, this, I think, may be safely affirmed, that a sore and pressing evil is to be removed, and that a good, great in its amount, and unequivocal in its nature, must be probable almost to certainty, before the inestimable price of our own morals, and the well-being of a number of our fellow citizens, is paid for a revolution. If ever we ought to be economists even to parsimony, it is in the voluntary production of evil. Every revolution contains in it something of evil.

EDMUND BURKE
Appeal from the New to the Old Whigs, 1791

'The whole web and texture of human understanding and society'

Those who think they can *make a clear stage of it*, and frame a set of opinions on all subjects by an appeal to reason alone, and without the smallest intermixture of customs, imagination or passion, know just as little of themselves as they do of human nature ... custom, passion, imagination, insinuate themselves into and influence almost every judgment we pass or sentiment we indulge, and are a necessary help (as well as hindrance) to the human understanding; and that to attempt to refer every question to abstract truth and precise definition, without allowing for the frailty of prejudice, which is the unavoidable consequence of the frailty and imperfection of reason, would be to unravel the whole web and texture of human understanding and society. Such daring anatomists of morals and philosophy think that the whole beauty of the mind consists in the skeleton; cut away, without remorse, all sentiment, fancy, tastes, as superfluous excrescenses; and in their own eager, unfeeling pursuit of scientific truth and elementary principles, they 'murder to dissect'.

WILLIAM HAZLITT
'On Prejudice'

'Against all systems built on abstract rights'

Genius of Burke! forgive the pen seduced
By specious wonders, and too slow to tell
Of what the ingenious, what bewildered men,
Beginning to mistrust their boastful guides,
And wise men, willing to grow wiser, caught
Rapt auditors! from thy most eloquent tongue –
Now mute, for ever mute in the cold grave.
I see him, – old, but vigorous in age, –
Stand like an oak whose stag-horn branches start
Out of its leafy brow, the more to awe
The younger brethren of the grove. But some –
While he forewarns, denounces, launches forth,
Against all systems built on abstract rights,
Keen ridicule; the majesty proclaims
Of Institutes and Laws, hallowed by time;
Declares the vital power of social ties
Endeared by Custom; and with high disdain,
Exploding upstart Theory, insists
Upon the allegiance to which men are born –
Some – say at once a froward multitude –
Murmur (for truth is hated, where not loved)
As the winds fret within the Aeolian cave,
Galled by their monarch's chain. The times were big

With ominous change, which, night by night, provoked
Keen struggles, and black clouds of passion raised;
But memorable moments intervened,
When Wisdom, like the Goddess from Jove's brain,
Broke forth in armour of resplendent words,
Startling the Synod. Could a youth, and one
In ancient story versed, whose breast had heaved
Under the weight of classic eloquence,
Sit, see, and hear, unthankful, uninspired?
WILLIAM WORDSWORTH
The Prelude, 1850

'The man who works from himself outwards'

The man who works from himself outwards, whose conduct is governed by ordinary motives, and who acts with a view to his own advantage and the advantage of those who are connected with himself in definite, assignable ways, produces in the ordinary course of things much more happiness to others (if that is the great object of life) than a moral Don Quixote who is always liable to sacrifice himself and his neighbours. When you have to deal with a man who expects pay and allowances, and is willing to give a fair day's work for it as long as the arrangement suits him, you know where you are. Deal with such a man fairly, and in particular cases, if he is a man of spirit and courage, he will deal with you not only fairly but generously. Earn his gratitude by kindness and justice, and he will in many cases give you what no money could buy or pay for. On the other hand, a man who has a disinterested love for the human race – that is to say, who has got a fixed idea about some way of providing for the management of the concerns of mankind – is an unaccountable person with whom it is difficult to deal upon any well-known and recognized principles, and who is capable of making his love for men in general the ground of all sorts of violence against men in particular.

JAMES FITZJAMES STEPHEN
Liberty, Equality, Fraternity, 1873
Stephen's classic work of 1873 challenged the assumption that democracy necessarily increased justice and humanity and he questioned the effectiveness of government intervention.

THE GODS OF THE COPYBOOK HEADINGS

As I pass through my incarnations in every age and race,
I make my proper prostrations to the Gods of the Market-Place.
Peering through reverent fingers I watch them flourish and fall,
And the Gods of the Copybook Headings, I notice, outlast them all.

We were living in trees when they met us. They showed us each in turn
That Water would certainly wet us, as Fire would certainly burn:
But we found them lacking in Uplift, Vision and Breadth of Mind,
So we left them to teach the Gorillas while we followed the March of
Mankind . . .

With the Hopes that our World is built on they were utterly out of
touch,
They denied that the Moon was Stilton; they denied she was even
Dutch.
They denied that Wishes were Horses; they denied that a Pig had
Wings.
So we worshipped the Gods of the Market Who promised these beauti-
ful things . . .

Then the Gods of the Market tumbled, and their smooth-tongued
wizards withdrew,
And the hearts of the meanest were humbled and began to believe it
was true
That All is not Gold that Glitters, and Two and Two make Four –
And the Gods of the Copybook Headings limped up to explain it once
more.

As it will be in the future, it was at the birth of Man –
There are only four things certain since Social Progress began:-
That the Dog returns to his Vomit and the Sow returns to her Mire,
And the burnt Fool's bandaged finger goes wabbling back to the Fire;

And that after this is accomplished, and the brave new world begins
When all men are paid for existing and no man must pay for his sins,
As surely as Water will wet us, as surely as Fire will burn,
The Gods of the Copybook Headings with terror and slaughter return!
RUDYARD KIPLING, 1919

'Respect for the established fact'

Their strength, politically speaking, lies in a recognition of expediency, complemented by respect for the established fact. One of the facts particularly clear to them is the suitability to their minds, their tempers, their habits, of a system of polity which has been established by the slow effect of generations within this sea-girt realm. They have nothing to do with ideals: they never trouble themselves to think about the Rights of Man. If you talk to them (long enough) about the rights of the shopman, or the ploughman, or the cat's-meat-man, they will lend ear, and, when the facts of any such case have been examined, they will find a way of dealing with them. This characteristic of theirs they call Common Sense. To them, all things considered, it has been of vast service; one may even say that the rest of the world has profited by it not a little. That Uncommon Sense might now and then have stood them in better stead is nothing to the point. The Englishman deals with things as they are, and first and foremost accepts his own being.

GEORGE GISSING

The Private Papers of Henry Ryecroft, 1903

'Utopia never arrives'

Although he had no direct connexion with any political party, Kipling was a Conservative, a thing that does not exist nowadays. Those who now call themselves Conservatives are either Liberals, Fascists or the accomplices of Fascists. He identified himself with the ruling power and not with the opposition. In a gifted writer this seems to us strange and even disgusting, but it did have the advantage of giving Kipling a certain grip on reality. The ruling power is always faced with the question, 'In such and such circumstances, what would you *do*?', whereas the opposition is not obliged to take responsibility or make any real decisions. Where it is a permanent and pensioned opposition, as in England, the quality of its thought deteriorates accordingly. Moreover, anyone who starts out with a pessimistic, reactionary view of life tends to be justified by events, for Utopia never arrives and 'the gods of the copybook headings', as Kipling himself put it, always return. Kipling sold out to the British governing class, not financially but emotionally. This warped his political judgement, for the British ruling class were not what he imagined, and it led him into abysses of folly and snobbery, but he gained a corresponding advantage from having at least tried to imagine what action and responsibility are like. It is a great thing in his favour that he is not witty, not 'daring', has no wish to *épater les bourgeois*. He dealt largely in platitudes, and since we live in a world of platitudes, much of what he said sticks. Even his worst follies seem less shallow and less irritating than the 'enlightened' utterances of the same period, such as Wilde's epigrams or the collection of cracker-mottoes at the end of *Man and Superman*.

GEORGE ORWELL
Rudyard Kipling, 1942

'The most a politician can do'

The Conservative contends that the most a politician can do is to ensure that some, and these by no means the most important, conditions in which the good life can exist are present, and, more important still, to prevent fools or knaves from setting up conditions which make any approach to the good life impossible except for solitaries or authorities. A depressing creed? A negative creed? No! A Holy Gospel! All the great evils of our time have come from men who mocked and exploited human misery by pretending that good government, that is government according to their way of thinking, could offer Utopia.

QUINTIN HOGG, VISCOUNT HAILSHAM
The Case for Conservativism, 1947

'The application of force and the threat of it'

The great dividing line in British politics has always been between those who regard politics as supremely important and those who conceive it to be the handmaid of religion, art, science and society. The Left are in the first category, Conservatives are in the second. The Left find it easy to love politics because they do not understand what it is. They have never grasped the meaning of the classic definition of politics as the science of the application of public force. A politician is a man whose business it is to manipulate as justly and humanely as he can the most powerful instrument of torture and destruction which human ingenuity has invented, the sovereign State. He is not paid to exhort, like a moralist, or to imagine, like a poet, but to govern; and government is the application of force and the threat of it to human beings. The motives upon which he operates are necessarily the lowest in human nature, the fear of pain and the hope of material reward. When he legislates he is not prescribing a remedy but performing a surgical operation. His words are important only because they are backed by law courts, armies police forces and prisons. Every political act is performed with the hangman in the background.

T. E. UTLEY
Essays in Conservatism, 1949

'A conversation, not an argument'

In politics, then, every enterprise is a consequential enterprise, the pursuit, not of a dream, or of a general principle, but of an intimation. What we have to do with is something less imposing than logical implications or necessary consequences: but if the intimations of a tradition of behaviour are less dignified or more elusive than these, they are not on that account less important. Of course, there is no piece of mistake-proof apparatus by means of which we can elicit the intimation most worthwhile pursuing; and not only do we often make gross errors of judgment in this matter, but also the total effect of a desire satisfied is so little to be forecast, that our activity of amendment is often found to lead us where we would not go. Moreover, the whole enterprise is liable at any moment to be perverted by the incursion of an approximation to empiricism in the pursuit of power. These are imperfections which can never be eliminated. But it is to be believed that our mistakes will be less frequent and less disastrous, and our achievements more manageable, if we escape the illusion that politics can ever be anything more than the pursuit of intimations; a conversation, not an argument.

MICHAEL OAKESHOTT, 1962

'Grudging toleration of the Conservative Party'

Growing older, I have lost the need to be political, which means, in this country, the need to be left. I am driven into grudging toleration of the Conservative Party because it is the party of non-politics, of resistance to politics. I have seen how many of the evils of life – failure, loneliness, fear, boredom, inability to communicate – are ineradicable by political means, and that attempts so to eradicate them are disastrous. The ideal of the brotherhood of man, the building of the Just City, is one that cannot be discarded without lifelong feelings of disappointment and loss. But, if we are to live in the real world, discard it we must. Its very nobility makes the results of its breakdown doubly horrifying, and it breaks down, as it always will, not by some external agency but because it cannot work.

KINGSLEY AMIS

'The foundations of Conservatism'

Scepticism and empiricism are the foundations of Conservatism: scepticism of all human ideas and all human endeavour, and the determina- . tion to look at things as they are. Of course the scepticism often hardens into orthodoxy. Principles and institutions are claimed to be immutable, part of the sacred inheritance in whose defence suicide would be preferable to ignoble surrender. This was a common attitude in 1911. And empiricism often degenerates into, so to speak, post-empiricism: looking at things as they were instead of as they are.

At its highest level the conflict between scepticism and orthodoxy might be dramatised as a conflict between the two greatest conservative philosophers, Hume and Burke. Hume, believing that 'all general maxims in politics ought to be established with great caution', was sceptical about everything, in favour of moderation in all things, averse to last ditches, empirical without curb. Burke shared Hume's suspicion of general political truths and knew change to be inevitable. But his reverence for Britain, her history, her constitution, and his Whig overlords, sometimes on crucial issues ossified his prejudices into dogma and made the finished product of his thought inconsistent with its basic conceptions. Thus he defended the eighteenth century representative system in opposition to Pitt's attempts at reform, and insisted that peace never could and never should be made with the revolutionary government in France. Burke's occasional dogmatism was Whiggish, and there has often been a deal of Whiggery in the old guard's perennial attempts to prevent the Conservative party following the path of empiricism, a path which frequently leads disconcertingly close to the headquarters of the other side.

IAN GILMOUR
The Body Politic, 1969

'Utopias are not for us'

What general political attitudes do we need to carry through our economic and other policies to success? We do not want to counter dogma with dogma and offer a mirror right-wing image to that of the doctrinaire left. One of the most important themes of Conservative philosophy has always been its rejection of Utopias and its insistence that politics is an empirical activity in which there cannot be absolutes about what is either possible or desirable. Utopias are not for us.

That of course does not imply that Conservatives have no political objectives other than the attainment and preservation of office. As a party we may be short on dogma but we are long on values. One of those values is a recognition of the variety of human nature and of human beings and an appreciation of the need for political flexibility. Burke's is the classic statement of the Conservative position: 'Circumstances (which with some gentlemen pass for nothing) give in reality to every political principle its distinguishing colour and discriminating effect. The circumstances are what render every civil and political scheme beneficial or noxious to mankind.' Nowhere do circumstances change more swiftly or unpredictably than in the realm of economics. The strategy of the government will have to be pursued resolutely and over a long period if it is to succeed, but we must as a party avoid the danger of elevating our economic priorities into absolute moral principles from which it is impossible to deviate or to develop in any circumstances. We need in other words a stabilisation programme without which there can be no hope for the stimulation of the private sector.

NORMAN ST JOHN STEVAS
Tory Reform Group, Conservative Party Conference, 1979

'A belief in the imperfection of human nature'

Conservatism in both its forms, religious and secular, rests on a belief in the imperfection of human nature. This imperfection is both intellectual and moral. The consequence of men's intellectual imperfection is that they should not conduct their political affairs under the impulsion of large, abstract projects of change arrived at by individual thinkers working in isolation from the practical realities of political life. They should be guided rather by the accumulated political wisdom of the community. The consequence of men's moral imperfection is that men, acting on their own uncontrolled impulses, will on the whole act badly, however elevated their professed intentions may be. They need, therefore, the restraint of customary and established laws and institutions, of an objective and impersonal barrier to the dangerous extravagance of subjective, personal impulse. But of the two imperfections it is the intellectual one that is specifically emphasized by conservatism. Government of any kind has always been seen as a remedy for sin. The specifically conservative attitude to government sees it also as a remedy for men's intellectual defects.

ANTHONY QUINTON
The Politics of Imperfection

'Out of the crooked timber of humanity'

But, in the end, it is not a matter of purely subjective judgement: it is dictated by the forms of life of the society to which one belongs, a society among other societies, with values held in common, whether or not they are in conflict, by the majority of mankind throughout recorded history. There are, if not universal values, at any rate a minimum without which societies could scarcely survive. Few today would wish to defend slavery or ritual murder or Nazi gas chambers or the torture of human beings for the sake of pleasure or profit or even political good – or the duty of children to denounce their parents, which the French and Russian revolutions demanded, or mindless killing. There is no justification for compromise on this. But on the other hand, the search for perfection does seem to me a recipe for bloodshed, no better even if it is demanded by the sincerest of idealists, the purest of heart. No more rigorous moralist than Immanuel Kant has ever lived, but even he said, in a moment of illumination, 'Out of the crooked timber of humanity no straight thing was ever made.' To force people into the neat uniforms demanded by dogmatically believed-in schemes is almost always the road to inhumanity. We can only do what we can: but that we must do, against difficulties.

Of course social or political collisions will take place; the mere conflict of positive values alone makes this unavoidable. Yet they can, I believe, be minimized by promoting and preserving an uneasy equilibrium, which is constantly threatened and in constant need of repair – that alone, I repeat, is the precondition for decent societies and morally acceptable behaviour, otherwise we are bound to lose our way. A little dull, as a solution, you will say? Not the stuff of which calls to heroic action by inspired leaders are made? Yet if there is some truth in this view, perhaps that is sufficient. An eminent American philosopher of our day once said, 'There is no *a priori* reason for supposing that the truth, when it is discovered, will necessarily prove interesting.' It may be enough if it is truth, or even an approximation of it; consequently I do not feel apologetic for advancing this.

SIR ISAIAH BERLIN
The Crooked Timber of Humanity, 1990

10

'We have to be Moralists all the Time'

It has been said that the Church of England is the Conservative Party at prayer. There are certain similarities between these two bodies. Both have few basic texts and such as there are have evolved. The 1662 Prayer Book had no single author or single intention; it emerged from practice, usage, controversy and struggle. Both are suspicious of excessive emotion, prefer observance and attendance to evangelical fervour, and tend to be reserved and undemonstrative as well as quietly resolute that things are best left to go on as they are.

Of course Conservatives have no monopoly of Christian observance. The Liberal Party has attracted many Methodists, Baptists and chapel-goers. The Labour Party always had a strain of Christian socialism which was so well represented in the House of Commons by Eric Heffer and movingly expressed in his last speech just before he died. But religion today plays a less prominent part in politics than it did in the nineteenth century.

Conservative thinkers down the centuries have recognized the importance of religious values both for individuals and for the nation. Many measures of reform in the nineteenth century – the abolition of slavery, the prison reforms, the extension of nursing, and the salvation of fallen women owed a great deal to Christian teaching. Moreover the Conservative approach has always recognized man's imperfection and his need for resources outside himself. People cannot exist in a spiritual vacuum, even though many have ceased to have any religious belief and no longer attend church regularly. Politicians in particular do need a moral framework from which they can develop their ideas and policies, and for me, humanism is inadequate and insubstantial. I believe it is still important for our whole society to be guided and inspired by religious belief and the moral teachings derived from it.

'The mean between the two extremes'

It hath been the wisdom of the Church of *England*, ever since the first compiling of her Publick Liturgy, to keep the mean between the two extremes, of too much stiffness in refusing, and of too much easiness in admitting any variation from it. For, as on the one side, common experience sheweth, that where a chance hath been made of things advisedly established (no evident necessity so requiring) sundry inconveniences have thereupon ensued; and those many times more and greater than the evils, that were intended to be remedied by such change: So on the other side, the particular Forms of Divine Worship, and the Rites and Ceremonies appointed to be used therein, being things in their own nature indifferent, and alterable, and so acknowledged; it is but reasonable, that upon weighty and important considerations, according to the various exigency of times and occasions, such changes and Alterations should be made there in, as to those that are in place of Authority should from time to time seem either necessary or expedient. Accordingly we find, that in the Reigns of several Princes of blessed memory since the Reformation, the Church, upon just and weighty considerations her thereunto moving, hath yielded to make such Alterations in some particulars, as in their respective times were thought convenient: yet so, as the main body and Essentials of it (as well in the chiefest Materials, as in the frame and order thereof) have still continued the same unto this day, and do yet stand firm and unshaken, notwithstanding all the vain attempts and impetuous assaults made against it, by such men as are given to change, and have always discovered a great regard to their own private fancies and interests, than to that duty they owe to the Publick.

Preface to *The Book of Common Prayer*, 1662

'We have to be moralists all the time'

Whether the aim is to be useful or happy, the first requisite is the religious and moral knowledge of right and wrong ... we have to be moralists all the time ... we are geometricians and physiologists only by chance.

SAMUEL JOHNSON

'We have obligations to mankind at large'

We have obligations to mankind at large, which are not in consequence of any special voluntary pact. They arise from the relation of man to man, and the relation of man to God, which relations are not matters of choice. On the contrary, the force of all the pacts which we enter into with any particular person, or number of persons amongst mankind, depends upon those prior obligations. In some cases the subordinate relations are voluntary, in others they are necessary – but the duties are all compulsive. When we marry, the choice is voluntary, but the duties are not a matter of choice ... Parents may not be consenting to their moral relation; but consenting or not, they are bound to a long train of burdensome duties towards those with whom they have never made a convention of any sort.

EDMUND BURKE
An Appeal from the New to the Old Whigs, 1791

'The centre of gravity in a realm'

I respect the talents of many, and the motives and character of some, among you too sincerely to court the scorn which I anticipate. But neither shall the fear of it prevent me from declaring aloud, and as a truth which I hold it the disgrace and calamity of a professed statesman not to know and acknowledge, that a permanent, nationalised, learned order, a national clerisy or Church is an essential element of a rightly constituted nation, without which it wants the best security alike for its permanence and its progression ... But it is duty and wisdom to aim at making as many as possible soberly and steadily religious; inasmuch as the morality which the State requires in its citizens for its own wellbeing and ideal immortality, and without reference to their spiritual interest as individuals, can only exist for the people in the form of religion. But the existence of a true philosophy, or the power and habit of contemplating particulars in the unity and fontal mirror of the idea, – this in the rulers and teachers of a nation is indispensable to a sound state of religion in all classes. In fine, religion, true or false, is and ever has been the centre of gravity in a realm, to which all other things must and will accommodate themselves.

SAMUEL TAYLOR COLERIDGE
On the Constitution of Church and State, 1830

'In one tide, deep rolling, full and free'

MILDENHALL, WILTS

Ah let me enter, once again, the pew
Where the child nodded as the sermon grew;
Scene of soft slumbers! I remember now
The chiding finger; and the frowning brow
Of stern reprovers, when the ardent June
Flung through the glowing aisles the drowsy noon;
Till closed the learn'd harangue, with solemn look
Arose the chaunter of the sacred book –
The parish clerk (death-silenced) far-famed then
And justly, for his long and loud – Amen!
Rich was his tone, and his exulting eye
Glanced to the ready choir, enthroned on high,
Nor glanced in vain; the simple hearted throng
Lifted their voices, and dissolved in song;
Till in one tide, deep rolling, full and free
Rung through the echoing pile, old England's psalmody.

N. T. CARRINGTON 1830

Of all the churches which remain almost untouched by the Victorians, the loveliest I know is Mildenhall, near Marlborough. It stands in the Kennet water meadows, a simple four-square affair: three-storeyed tower, nave, aisles either side and a chancel. But as you approach it there are signs of the past – clear glass panes, patched and flaking outside walls looking like an old water colour. And then the inside! You walk into the church of a Jane Austen novel, into a forest of magnificent oak joinery, an ocean of box pews stretching shoulder high all over the church. Each is carved with decorations in a Strawberry Hill Gothick manner. The doors and sides of the pews take a graceful curve either side of the font and another curve above them is made by the elegant west gallery. Norman pillars just raise their sculptured heads above the woodwork of the aisles. Two huge pulpits stand, one each side of the chancel arch. The old stone floors remain, the long cream-washed walls, the stone arch mouldings, picked out subtly white to form a pale contrast. The chancel, as it should be, is richest of all – panelled, with elaborate-carved pews for the squarson and his family, a carved canopy hanging over the Commandment board behind the

altar, delicately carved communion rails in the Chippendale style. Even
the red leather kneelers at these rails and the scarlet service books are
the same date – 1816.

JOHN BETJEMAN, 1954

'Speak of original sin or not as you please'

Speak or fail to speak of God as you think right, but the fact that men
are deeply moved by ideas about power, wisdom, and goodness, on a
superhuman scale which they rather apprehend than comprehend, is
certain. Speak of original sin or not as you please, but the fact that all
men are in some respects and at some times both weak and wicked,
that they do the ill they would not do, and shun the good they would
pursue is no less certain. To describe this state of things as a 'miserable
bondage' is, to say the least, an intelligible way of speaking. Calvin's
theory was that in order to escape from this bondage men must be true
to the better part of their nature, keep in proper subjection its baser
elements, and look up to God as the source of the only valuable kind of
freedom – freedom to be good and wise . . .

I believe that many men are bad, a vast majority of men indifferent,
and many good, and that the great mass of indifferent people sway this
way or that according to circumstances, one of the most important of
which circumstances is the predominance for the time being of the bad
or good.

JAMES FITZJAMES STEPHEN
Liberty, Equality, Fraternity, 1873

'Our national faith'

If we preserved our national faith it mattered not in the end what
catastrophes might overtake us, we should rise again from every defeat
with renewed vigour and renewed power of usefulness and greatness.
But if it were destroyed we should fall inevitably and never rise again.

LORD HUGH CECIL

Conservatism, 1912

Lord Hugh Cecil (1869–1956) was the youngest son of Robert Cecil, Marquess of
Salisbury, the Conservative Prime Minister. His abiding preoccupation was
Christian teaching and he could well have gone into the Church. Instead he became
an MP in 1895 and was still talking about Christian teaching in the House of

Lords' debate on R. A. Butler's Education Bill on D-Day in 1944.

He was Churchill's best man in 1908 but led a group of MPs in the Parliamentary Bill crisis that attacked Asquith and the Liberals quite viciously in the House. He was a man of high principle; an elegant writer but indolent, with a capacity to interest rather than to persuade.

In his book *Conservatism*, written for the Home University Library in 1912, he argued that the basis of Conservatism was Christian values and the liberty that came from free will. Christ, he averred, was not a socialist, since there is no reference to State control in the New Testament! But at the same time he condemned the economics of *laisser-faire* – 'the competitive system is certainly not a Christian system'.

'The very idea of unselfishness is voluntary'

The mere transference of material wealth from one pocket to another is a thing which Christianity ignores as indifferent if done by just means, and rebukes as dishonest if done by unjust. For the State, therefore, to come down with the hand of power and take from one set of people and give to another, is to act in a manner altogether remote from the teaching of such parables as Dives and Lazarus or the Good Samaritan. We can see this vividly if we suppose the Good Samaritan to act as the State is sometimes urged to act. Suppose that instead of relieving the distressed man at his own cost, he had run after the Priest and the Levite and by compulsion constrained them to come back and minister with *their* oil and *their* wine to the sufferings of the afflicted. Suppose he had required them to set the poor man upon *their* beast of burden and to take him to the inn, and had finally forced from each of them one of the two pence which were necessary to pay the cost of entertainment. Does any one suppose that the Good Samaritan would, after such acts, have been held up as the type of the love of a Christian to his neighbour? Clearly, reflections however just on the prevalence of luxury, on the abundance of expenditure on purely selfish objects, on the painful contrasts between the extremes of riches and the extremes of poverty, furnish from the Christian point of view not even the slightest ground to justify the compulsory transfer of property from rich to poor. Christian self-sacrifice is altogether wanting in such a transfer. The State sacrifices nothing; and the rich are merely victims of confiscation. They are impoverished but still selfish; for compulsion can be no remedy for selfishness. The very idea of unselfishness is voluntary. Like mercy, its quality is not strained. Compulsory unselfishness is an absurdity, a contradiction in terms.

LORD HUGH CECIL
Religion and Politics

'The action of religion'

We are surrounded, crowded, embarrassed by social questions ... the sole hope of solving these great problems is by the action of religion.

ROBERT CECIL, MARQUESS OF SALISBURY
On the East London Church Fund, 1896

Salisbury was a devout and practising Christian. He introduced free elementary schooling in 1891, convinced that a grounding in Christian principles was essential for working-class children, and that there was 'no agency so efficient for this education as the Church of Christ.'

'Support'

Ah you, my dear Clemmy, are like a great pillar: you support the church from the inside. But I am like a flying buttress: I support the church from the outside.

WINSTON CHURCHILL
This was Churchill's reply to his wife when he was chided for not going to church regularly.

'More than one road to Heaven'

Nothing is more essential to Conservatism that the idea of historical relativity. Though the Conservative Party is a Christian Party, and indeed because it is a Christian Party, it does not hold that Scripture or a rational observation of the universe entitles anyone to claim divine authority for any particular political constitution. The basis of Richard Hooker's *Ecclesiastical Polity*, the great apology for the Anglican Reformation and the first treatise on political Conservatism, is the view that even in matters of ecclesiastical government there is more than one road to heaven.

T. E. UTLEY
Essays in Conservatism, 1949

CHURCH OF ENGLAND THOUGHTS OCCASIONED BY
HEARING THE BELLS OF MAGDALEN TOWER FROM THE
BOTANIC GARDEN, OXFORD, ON ST MARY MAGDALEN DAY

I see the urn against the yew,
   The sunlit urn of sculptured stone,
I see its shapely shadow fall
On this enormous garden wall
   Which makes a kingdom of its own:

A grassy kingdom sweet to view
   With tiger lilies still in flower
And beds of umbelliferæ
Ranged in Linnaean symmetry,
   All in the sound of Magdalen tower.

A multiplicity of bells,
   A changing cadence, rich and deep
Swung from those pinnacles on high
To fill the trees and flood the sky
   And rock the sailing clouds to sleep.

A Church of England sound, it tells
   Of 'moderate' worship, God and State.
Where mattins congregations go
Conservative and good and slow
   To elevations of the plate.

And loud through resin-scented chines
   And purple rhododendrons roll'd,
I hear the bells for Eucharist
From churches blue with incense mist
   Where reredoses twinkle gold.

Chapels-of-ease by railway lines
   And humble streets and smells of gas!
I hear your plantive ting-tangs call
From many a gabled western wall
   To Morning Prayer or Holy Mass.

In country churches old and pale
   I hear the changes smoothly rung

And watch the coloured sallies fly
From rugged hands to rafters high
  As round and back the bells are swung.

Before the spell begin to fall,
  Before the bells have lost their power,
Before the grassy kingdom fade
And Oxford traffic roar invade,
  I thank the bells of Magdalen Tower.
    JOHN BETJEMAN, 1954
I could not resist including this lovely poem as I spent three happy years at
Magdalen listening to those same bells.

CHURCH GOING

Once I am sure there's nothing going on
I step inside, letting the door thud shut.
Another church: matting, seats, and stone,
And little books; sprawlings of flowers, cut
For Sunday, brownish now; some brass and stuff
Up at the holy end; the small neat organ;
And a tense, musty, unignorable silence,
Brewed God knows how long. Hatless, I take off
My cycle-clips in awkward reverence,

Move forward, run my hand around the font.
From where I stand, the roof looks almost new –
Cleaned, or restored? Someone would know: I don't.
Mounting the lectern, I peruse a few
Hectoring large-scale verses, and pronounce
'Here endeth' much more loudly than I'd meant.
The echoes snigger briefly. Back at the door
I sign the book, donate an Irish sixpence,
Reflect the place was not worth stopping for.

Yet stop I did: in fact I often do,
And always end much at a loss like this,
Wondering what to look for; wondering, too,
When churches fall completely out of use
What we shall turn them into, if we shall keep

A few cathedrals chronically on show,
Their parchment, plate and pyx in locked cases,
And let the rest rent-free to rain and sheep.
Shall we avoid them as unlucky places?

Or, after dark, will dubious women come
To make their children touch a particular stone;
Pick simples for a cancer; or on some
Advised night see walking a dead one?
Power of some sort or other will go on
In games, in riddles, seemingly at random;
But superstition, like belief, must die,
And what remains when disbelief has gone?
Grass, weedy pavement, brambles, buttress, sky,

A shape less recognisable each week,
A purpose more obscure. I wonder who
Will be the last, the very last, to seek
This place for what it was; one of the crew
That tap and jot and know what rood-lofts were?
Some ruin-bibber, randy for antique,
Or Christmas-addict, counting on a whiff
Of gown-and-bands and organ-pipes and myrrh?
Or will he be my representative,

Bored, uninformed, knowing the ghostly silt
Dispersed, yet tending to this cross of ground
Through suburb scrub because it held unsplit
So long and equably what since is found
Only in separation – marriage, and birth.
And death, and thoughts of these – for which was built
This special shell? For, though I've no idea
What this accoutred frowsty barn is worth.
It pleases me to stand in silence here;

A serious house on serious earth it is.
In whose blent air all our compulsions meet,
Are recognised, and robed as destinies
And that much never can be obsolete.
Since someone will forever be surprising
A hunger in himself to be more serious.

And gravitating with it to this ground.
Which, he once heard, was proper to grow wise in,
If only that so many dead lie round.

PHILIP LARKIN, 1954

Decency

If you don't believe in God, all you have to believe in is decency ...
decency is very good. Better decent than indecent. But I don't think it's
enough.

HAROLD MACMILLAN

ANGLO-CATHOLIC CONGRESSES

We, who remember the Faith, the grey-headed ones,
  Of those Anglo-Catholic Congresses swinging along,
Who heard the South Coast salvo of incense-guns
  And surged to the Albert Hall in our thousands strong
  With 'extreme' colonial bishops leading in song;

We, who remember, look back to the blossoming May-time
  On ghosts of servers and thurifers after Mass,
The slapping of backs, the flapping of cosssocks, the play-time,
  A game of Grandmother's Steps on the vicarage grass –
  'Father, a little more sherry. I'll fill your glass.'

We recall the triumph, that Sunday after Ascension,
  When our Protestant suffragan suffered himself to be coped –
The SYA and the Scheme for Church Extension –
  The new diocesan's not as 'sound' as we'd hoped,
  And Kensit threatens and has Sam Gurney poped?

Yet, under the Travers baroque, in a limewashed whiteness,
  The fiddle-back vestments a-glitter with morning rays,
Our Lady's image, in multiple-candled brightness,
  The bells and banners – those were the waking days
  When Faith was taught and fanned to a golden blaze.

JOHN BETJEMAN, 1966

'Pioneers of good works'

But it is not, as a matter of fact, in its corporate witness that I find the activity of the spirit most convincing. It is the contact between the spirit and the individual which seems to me to show the most spectacular results. How much of what is now taken for granted in what is good in society owes its original inspiration to a consciously Christian motivation, even where the work has been subsequently overtaken, and taken over, by the apparatus of the modern state. Wilberforce was motivated by Christianity when he set about his campaign to end the slave trade. Florence Nightingale's original motivation was Christian, and the source of her expertise when she first sought to revive the almost forgotten craft of nursing was a teaching order of nuns where the art had been kept alive. Our whole system of education, public and private, our network of hospitals, our social security system itself, have each a clear origin in Christian foundations and whatever can be said against much of the theorization, and much of the practice which they embodied, the motivation which underlay them was good and, in origin at least, the practice was disinterested. The Christians have been pioneers of good works throughout their history. They have been the originators, and secular society has largely caught up with their efforts, made good their deficiencies of scale, and corrected their faults. No one who has studied the ancient world can get very far without being horror-struck with the hurricane of libido, lust, cruelty and greed of which Jung spoke, and those of us who have an increasing contact with the post-Christian society in which we live are disturbed to find the very same features reproducing themselves under widely differing political systems, in almost exact proportions as the spirit ceases to be cultivated, and the life of the spirit lived.

QUINTIN HOGG, VISCOUNT HALISHAM
The Door wherein I Went, 1975

'A central animating belief'

The power of religion can also be seen in the lives and characters of nations. The life of nations without a central animating belief is a decay. Indeed nations form themselves around thoughts or ideas, which have their own life-cycle. These ideas are essentially religious in character, though they are not always religious in expression. A nation

which has no such idea, or has lost confidence in its idea, is empty
inside; like a hollow tree it can continue to stand, and can even put out
fresh leaves in spring, but it will not stand the storm.

WILLIAM REES-MOGG
An Humbler Heaven, 1977

'At best trivial and at worst hypocritical'

In the developed western nations the politicization of Christianity is
already very advanced. It takes the form of identifying Christian teachings with the moral outlook and political ideas of liberalism. Christians
themselves, of course, only believe that they are endorsing agreed
moral truths – providing a religious foundation for the higher principles which liberalism promotes. They see such concepts as democratic
pluralism, equality, individualist Human Rights, the freedom to choose
values, and so forth, as basic expressions of Christianity, the modern
applications of the moral precepts of Christ. But to an external obser-
ver, or to non-liberals, their commitment to these principles looks like
ordinary political preference. To Marxists, the fundamental principles
of liberalism, together with their religious backing, are merely for-
malized expressions of class ideology. Criticisms of capitalism – which
are now the staple matter of much Christian social commentary (but
criticisms which leave the basis of the social system undisturbed)
appear at best trivial, at worst hypocritical. To those who are sceptical
of all versions of Christian politics, including conservative ones – and
this is my own position – the present identification of Christianity with
western bourgeois liberalism seems an unnecessary consecration of a
highly relative and unstable set of values, the more unsatisfactory
because it is generally done unconsciously. Liberalism actually
occupies a very narrow band in the possible spectrum of political
theories. To regard it as the distillation of Christian wisdom, as the
contemporary repository of a timeless faith, is, to say the least, a
short-term view. But related by class and cultural preference to the
educated élites whose endorsement of liberal values they so faithfully
reproduce, the leaders of the western churches seem completely
unaware of how partial their political vision actually is.

E. NORMAN
Christianity and the World Order, 1979

FOR CANON BROWN, WHO LIKES CONTEMPORARY SPEECH

Do not imagine, Canon Brown,
That when the chips are really down
It will be folk like you who speak
So plain, while we are sham antique.
Do you know, arrogant old fool,
(That's modern, mate, so keep your cool)
It is you who are antiquarian
And we who think that san ne fairy-ann
Whether the words are old or new
But only, what work they can do?
What work can you do, idle lump?
While you defile the parish pump
Some of us like our water clean
And like to use words we can *mean.*
And so did Cranmer, who had to cook
For standing by his common book.
Write me a Book of Common Prayer
That is not made up of hot air
With words that are as plain as this
And, oh boy! that will take the piss
Out of those who wrote Series 3
And (I confess it) out of me.

C. H. SISSON, 1979

In the winter of 1979 the debate over the use of the Cranmer liturgy as opposed to the modern English version Series 3 came to a head. A pro-Cranmer petition was signed by 600 well-known people and a Canon Brown from Devizes wrote to the *Guardian*, saying that such matters should be left to the Church. This so incensed the poet C. H. Sisson that he wrote this poem and travelled to Devizes to pin it, like a latter-day Luther, to the door of Canon Brown's church. Alas, the organist found it first and took it down. But it should not be lost to posterity.

'The foundations on which our house has been built'

The importance of our schools in transmitting, and so preserving, our moral inheritance cannot be over-estimated. They play a co-ordinate role with the family in this vital task, on the successful discharge of which so much of our future depends. The educational system remains the foundation of the civilization of the dialogue which differentiates free and responsible men from animals on the one hand and criminals on the other. Wolves don't discuss the merits of hunting in packs, and guns never argue.

Such is the case for giving a high priority to the teaching of moral values in schools, but we cannot stop there and are driven on to raise other questions: where do these values come from? On what ultimately do they rest? The answer is religion. To say this is not to deny the contribution of secularism and rationalism to morality. Much less does it reject the proposition – supported by the facts – that morality can exist without religion. But it is to assert that within the British tradition morality has drawn its inspiration, its strength and its sanctions much more from Christianity than from the Enlightenment. It could, of course, have been otherwise: the *philosophes* might have been our prophets, and Hinduism or Mohammedanism might have been our spiritual inspiration (and one day may be), but in fact they have not been so. Christianity is the soil in which the roots of our morality have been planted. Cut them off from this and the morality is likely to die.

Freedom, democracy and morality in Britain are all three heavily indebted to Christian insights. Of course, good theology is no guarantee of good government – otherwise Roman Catholics would be placed in a nice dilemma by the history of the Papal States. Yet Christianity has provided the individual with a profound sense of his own worth. It has given him an alternative source of authority by which to judge and delimit the authority of the state. At the same time, by recognizing the reality of man's sinfulness as well as his dynamic towards virtue, it has contributed to the creation of those institutional and constitutional checks which protect him from the abuse of naked power. On this view the British office of the Leader of the Opposition, which takes into the constitution itself the principle of resistance to government, is a very Christian institution. As Reinhold Niebuhr has put it: 'Man's capacity for justice makes democracy possible; but man's inclination to injustice makes democracy necessary.'

The case for the teaching of religion in our schools is not, then, primarily a theological one – although theology and its adherents may provide some useful ancillary troops – but cultural, historical and social Christianity has got into the foundations on which our house has been built, and it cannot be taken out without a grave risk of the house falling down.

NORMAN ST JOHN STEVAS
Religious and Moral Values in School, 1984

Relevance of Bible Principles to Political Life

May I also say a few words about my personal belief in the relevance of Christianity to public policy – to the things that are Caesar's?

The Old Testament lays down in Exodus the Ten Commandments as given to Moses, the injunction to Leviticus to love our neighbour as ourselves and generally the importance of observing a strict code of law. The New Testament is a record of the Incarnation, the teachings of Christ and the establishment of the Kingdom of God. Again we have the emphasis on loving our neighbour as ourselves and on 'Do-as-you would-be-done-by'.

I believe that by taking together these key elements from the Old and New Testaments, we gain a view of the universe, a proper attitude to work, and principles to shape economic and social life. We are told we must work and use our talents to create wealth. 'If a man will not work he shall not eat' wrote St Paul to the Thessalonians. Indeed, abundance rather than poverty has a legitimacy which derives from the very nature of the Creation. Nevertheless, the Tenth Commandment – 'Thou shalt not covet' – recognizes that making money and owning things could become selfish activities. But it is not the creation of wealth that is wrong but the love of money for its own sake. The spiritual dimension comes in deciding what one does with the wealth.

How could we respond to the many calls for help, or invest in the future, or support the wonderful artists and craftsmen whose work also glorifies God, unless we had first worked hard and used our talents to create the necessary wealth? And remember the woman with the alabaster jar of ointment.

MARGARET THATCHER
Speech to the General Assembly of the Church of Scotland, 21 May 1988

'Christianity should not be interpreted as a political manifesto'

It seems to me that the Church's vision of civil society, and of the forces and factors which make for its vitality, is impoverished by the centrality which is being attached to State action. A vital civil society is one which conceives itself as a moral community, certainly: this is of the heart and essence of the Catholic tradition. But at the same time civil society derives its vitality from the energies, initiatives, and responsible choices of the myriad of individuals and families which compose it. If one of the marks of a civil society is cohesion, another is spontaneity: and a strong civil society is one in which cohesion is spontaneous.

In my view Christianity should not be interpreted as a political manifesto for putting secular matters right, or as a blueprint for social policy. It sets out the path that mankind must take to get to heaven. It deals with the corruption of human nature and how by experiencing grace we can find salvation. I have already accepted that the Church has a vital concern about secular matters – the Second Commandment. I would hope, however, that political or social assertions made by churchmen would be clearly derived from Christian doctrine and not just from a fashionable analysis of contemporary views. Your particular authority, and you have authority, derives from your understanding of Christian doctrine. It also helps you to measure the particular problems of our time against a long historical perspective. We are but the most recent members of the living body of Christ.

I recognize therefore that the Churches necessarily comment on secular matters that bear upon their pastoral role. But by the same token Government will be bound to hold views about the moral development of society. Individuals and families are in the frontline of responsibility, but the fact is that it is to Government that people so often turn to deal with the consequences of crime, drug abuse, Aids, child abuse, divorce, the breakdown of the family. It follows therefore that Government is justified in taking a view on the moral aspects of these matters and developing policies to deal with them.

KENNETH BAKER
Address to the Church of England Synod, 1989

11

'The Limitation of Government'

The essence of liberty is to be allowed to get on with the business of one's own life without the looming presence of Big Brother looking over one's shoulder, intrusive, threatening and punitive. The British do not like being pushed around or taking orders, or having their lives dictated by some remote authority. They believe that the Government should do those things which only a government can do; to keep peace abroad, to maintain public order at home, to see that justice is enforced and the needy are properly looked after, and that public services really do serve the public. Politicians should curb the itch to interfere and innovate too much, an itch brought on by the grandiose hope that they can order people's lives better than they can themselves.

Conservatives prefer the small-scale, more familiar and more human forms of organization. The village and the parish are places with which people can identify. This is much easier in the country than the town. A city like London, though its inhabitants may well call themselves Londoners, only really functions and survives because it is composed of a mass of small communities each with their particular local interests; the cleanliness of their parks, the safety of their streets and the quality of their schools. Chesterton, champion of the Napoleon of Notting Hill, is a surer guide than H. G. Wells advocating the planned hygienic megalopolis. Burke, in a classic phrase, said that 'to love the little platoon we belong to in society, is the first principle of public affections'.

Dr Johnson thundered that 'a Tory does not wish to give more real power to Government'. Lord Salisbury at the end of the nineteenth century said much the same, and in the twentieth century Isaiah Berlin concluded that 'the desire not be impinged upon, to be left to one's self, has been a mark of high civilization.' Margaret Thatcher crisply restated this in 1979: 'My goal was, and is, not the extension but limitation of Government'.

'The great chessboard of human society'

The man of system ... seems to imagine that he can arrange the different members of a great society with as much ease as the hand arranges the different pieces upon a chessboard. He does not consider that the pieces upon the chessboard have no other principle of motion besides that which the hand impresses upon them; but that, in the great chessboard of human society, every single piece has a principle of motion of its own, altogether different from that which the legislature might choose to impress upon it. If those two principles coincide and act in the same direction, the game of human society will go on easily and harmoniously, and is very likely to be happy and successful. If they are opposite or different, the game will go on miserably and the society must be at all times in the highest degree of disorder.

ADAM SMITH
Law, Legislation and Liberty, 1780

'A Tory does not wish to give more real power to Government'

One day, when I told him that I was a zealous Tory, but not enough 'according to knowledge,' and should be obliged to him for 'a reason,' he was so candid, and expressed himself so well, that I begged of him to repeat what he had said, and I wrote down as follows:

OF TORY AND WHIG.

A wise Tory and a wise Whig, I believe, will agree. Their principles are the same, though their modes of thinking are different. A high Tory makes government unintelligible: it is lost in the clouds. A violent Whig makes it impracticable: he is for allowing so much liberty to every man, that there is not power enough to govern any man. The prejudice of the Tory is for establishment; the prejudice of the Whig is for innovation. A Tory does not wish to give more real power to Government; but that Government should have more reverence. Then they differ as to the Church. The Tory is not for giving more legal power to the Clergy, but wishes they should have a considerable influence, founded on the opinion of mankind; the Whig is for limiting and watching them with a narrow jealousy.

SAMUEL JOHNSON

'To love the little platoon'

To be attached to the subdivision, to love the little platoon we belong
to in society, is the first principle (the germ as it were) of public
affections. It is the first link in the series by which we proceed towards
a love to our country, and to mankind.

EDMUND BURKE
Reflections on the Revolution in France, 1790

'A restless desire of governing too much'

It is one of the finest problems in legislation, and what has often
engaged my thoughts whilst I followed that profession. 'What the state
ought to take upon itself to direct by the public wisdom, and what it
ought to leave, with as little interference as possible, to individual
discretion'. Nothing, certainly, can be laid down on the subject that
will not admit of exceptions, many permanent, some occasional. But
the clearest line of distinction, which I could draw, whilst I had my
chalk to draw any line, was this; that the state ought to confine itself to
what regards the state, or the creatures of the state, namely, the
exterior establishment of its religion; its magistracy; its revenue; its
military force by sea and land; the corporations that owe their existence to its fiat; in a word, to everything that is *truly and properly*
public, to the public peace, to the public safety, to the public order, to
the public prosperity. In its preventive police it ought to be sparing of
its efforts, and to employ means, rather few, unfrequent, and strong,
than many, and frequent, and, of course, as they multiply their puny
politic race, and dwindle, small and feeble ... as [statesmen] descend
from the state to a province, from a province to a parish, and from a
parish to a private house, they go on accelerated in their fall. They
cannot do the lower duty; and, in proportion as they try it, they will
certainly fail in the higher. They ought to know the different depart-
ments of things; what belongs to laws, and what manners alone can
regulate. To these, great politicians may give a leaning, but they cannot
give a law.

   ... the leading vice of the French monarchy ... was ... a restless
desire of governing too much. The hand of authority was seen in
everything, and in every place. All, therefore, that happened amiss in
the course even of domestic affairs, was attributed to the government;

and as it always happens in this kind of officious universal interference, what began in odious power, ended always, I may say without an exception, in contemptible imbecility.

EDMUND BURKE
Thoughts and Penalties on Scarcity

Minding one's own Business

'If everybody minded their own business,' the Duchess said in a hoarse growl, 'the world would go round a deal faster than it does.'

LEWIS CARROLL
Alice in Wonderland, 1865

No higher than a Policeman

I rank myself no higher in the scheme of things than a policeman – whose utility would disappear if there were no criminals.

ROBERT CECIL, MARQUESS OF SALISBURY

Liberty: a Definition

Liberty consists in the power of doing what others disapprove of.

LORD HUGH CECIL

'Overwhelming concentrations of power'

What, then, are the characteristics of our society in respect of which we consider ourselves to enjoy freedom and in default of which we would not be free in our sense of the word? But first, it must be observed that the freedom we enjoy is not composed of a number of independent characteristics of our society which in aggregate make up our liberty. Liberties, it is true, may be distinguished, and some may be more general or more settled and mature than others, but the freedom which the English libertarian knows and values lies in a coherence of mutually supporting liberties, each of which amplifies the whole and none of which stands alone. It springs neither from the separation of church and state, nor from the rule of law, nor from private property, nor from parliamentary government, nor from the writ of *habeas corpus*, nor from the independence of the judiciary, nor from any one of the thousand other devices and arrangements characteristic of our society, but from what each signifies and represents, namely, the absence from our society of overwhelming concentrations of power. This is the most general condition of our freedom, so general that all other conditions may be seen to be comprised within it. It appears, first, in a diffusion of authority between past, present and future. Our society is ruled by none of these exclusively. And we should consider a society governed wholly by its past, or its present, or its future to suffer under a despotism of superstition which forbids freedom. The politics of our society are a conversation in which past, present and future each has a voice; and though one or other of them may on occasion properly prevail, none permanently dominates, and on this account we are free. Further, with us power is dispersed along all the multitude of interests and organizations of interest which comprise our society. We do not fear or seek to suppress diversity of interest, but we consider our freedom to be imperfect so long as the dispersal of power among them is incomplete, and to be threatened if any one interest or combination of interests, even though it may be the interest of a majority, acquires extraordinary power. Similarly, the conduct of government in our society involves a sharing of power, not only between the recognized organs of government, but also between the Administration and the Opposition. In short, we consider ourselves to be free because no one in our society is allowed unlimited power – no leader, faction, party or 'class', no majority, no government, church, corporation, trade or professional association or trade union. The secret of its freedom is that it is composed of a multitude of organizations in the constitution of the best of which is reproduced that diffusion of power which is characteristic of the whole.

MICHAEL OAKESHOTT

Rationalism in Politics, 1962

This is one of the most eloquent expressions since the war of the instinctive attitudes of a conservative.

'If only politicians and scientists were lazier'

Most of the world's troubles seem to come from people who are too busy. If only politicians and scientists were lazier, how much happier we should all be. The lazy man is preserved from the commission of almost all the nastier crimes, and many of the motives which make us sacrifice to toil the innocent enjoyment of leisure, are among the most ignoble – pride, avarice, emulation, vainglory and the appetite for power over others.

EVELYN WAUGH
The Seven Deadly Sins, 1962

'The desire not to be impinged upon'

There seems to be scarcely any discussion of individual liberty as a conscious political ideal (as opposed to its actual existence) in the ancient world. Condorcet has already remarked that the notion of individual rights is absent from the legal conceptions of the Romans and Greeks, this seems to hold equally of the Jewish, Chinese, and all other ancient civilizations that have since come to light. The domination of this ideal has been the exception rather than the rule, even in the recent history of the West. Nor has liberty in this sense often formed a rallying cry for the great masses of mankind. The desire not to be impinged upon, to be left to oneself, has been a mark of high civilization both on the part of individuals and communities. The sense of privacy itself, of the area of personal relationships as something sacred in its own right, derives from a conception of freedom which, for all its religious roots, is scarcely older, in its developed state, than the Renaissance or the Reformation. Yet its decline would mark the death of a civilization, of an entire moral outlook.

ISAIAH BERLIN
Four Essays on Liberty, 1959

'Not the extension but the limitation of government'

When you stood in the contest for the leadership of the party in November 1974, did you see yourself as standing for something that was different from what the previous leader, Mr Heath, had represented?
I felt, and the Conservatives who elected me presumably felt, that the next leader of the party must clearly stand up against the direction in which the country had been moving under both previous governments. We had moved too far towards a society controlled by government, too far towards what wasn't, and isn't, my idea of a society that can flourish.

We all talk today about social morality, social justice, social responsibility. We'll only get those things when you have a high proportion of individuals of worth and responsibility. My goal was, and is, not the extension but the limitation of government; the goal of the Labour Party is all-pervasiveness of government. At the time of the leadership contest which began in November 1974 we were coming to a stage when there really wasn't a party which was clearly standing for the limitation of government.

Limitation of government doesn't make for a weak government – don't make that mistake. If you've got the role of government clearly set out, then it means very strong government *in that role*. Very strong indeed. You weaken government if you try to spread it over so wide a range that you're not powerful where you *should* be because you've got into areas where you *shouldn't* be. And we had gone far too intimately into too much detail, and we were thinking, almost, of having not just Phase Three or Phase Four of an incomes policy but of Phase 34!

Everything was getting so rigid, something had to be done about it, and it was time the Conservative Party said what it was. What the Conservative Party offers today is a really completely different idea about the role of government, and that idea, I think, represents one of these big changes of direction which sometimes occur in politics.

MARGARET THATCHER
Interviewed by Kenneth Harris, 1979

'Helping people to help themselves'

We want to work *with* the grain of human nature, helping people to help themselves – and others. This is the way to restore that self-reliance and self-confidence which are the basis of personal responsibility and national success.

Attempting to do too much, politicians have failed to do those things which *should* be done. This has damaged the country and the authority of government. We must concentrate on what should be the priorities of *any* government.

Conservative Party Manifesto, 1979

'From the hub of the wheel towards the rim'

One thing we have learnt over the last years is that the smaller unit is more personal and more identifiable, more human, and more effective than the larger unit. The responsible government is one which creates, as we have done, structures for the involvement of the responsible citizen.

The task for Government in the years ahead is to pass more power from the hub of the wheel towards the rim. Socialism remains committed to the hub, the central control, the power of direction. Conservatism is much more about the rim of the wheel, where there is activity in smaller groups, where there is greater spontaneity, more independence, and more chance for individual activity. We have set out down this road on education, and I am confident that there will be a strong response from the active, committed citizens, the parents and the local community to the opportunities we are offering.

There have been times, and there still are times, when political leaders' faith in what individuals can do for themselves is greater than the faith those individuals have. There is a fine balance to be struck between expecting too much of our people and their perception of whether they can achieve what is expected of them. Even electorates can fight shy of freedoms and responsibilities if they have become so conditioned to State dependence that anything else seems unthinkable.

KENNETH BAKER
Bow Group Annual Dinner, 1988

'From the role of manager to the role of enabler'

Finally the role I have described for a local politician is not merely one which should promote better local government, it is also one which should make the role of local councillor – particularly a Conservative councillor – more rewarding and fulfilling than it is now. His role will shift from the role of manager to the role of enabler and decider of local priorities, always conscious of what his decisions will cost his charge-payers. As the monopoly position of local authorities in many areas is challenged, so councillors will less and less be in a position where they can be manipulated by the power of monopoly unions. It will be both in their interests and in the interests of the workforce to put high standards and good service to the public above everything else. In that sense the politician's role will be much more political.

NICHOLAS RIDLEY, 1989

12

'The Man of Conservative Temperament'

As Conservatism has no set dogma and no list of things which Conservatives must support, I have tried in this chapter to give examples of the conservative temperament – those modes of thought and attitudes which characterize people of a conservative disposition.

The chapters on tradition and change contain several examples of a conservative temperament. In this chapter I have highlighted the specific qualities of restraint and steadiness – a still centre of calm. In the seventeenth century, Halifax in his Character of a Trimmer *wrote of the man who did not veer or lurch from one side of the boat to another but remained calmly in the middle. In the early nineteenth century, Talleyrand warned people not to be over-zealous – 'Surtout pas trop de zèle' – a fault he never suffered from himself. In 1856 Walter Bagehot observed that the human race would be much wiser, 'If we had been readier to sit quiet'.*

These are all warnings to the busy politician who is always on the look-out for an immediate solution to the many problems that beset him. Michael Oakeshott identifies most precisely the particular qualities that mark out a conservative: 'He prefers small and limited innovations to large and indefinite'. He has a sense of proportion which allows him to take a measured and considered view. His approach is sometimes criticized as too negative and close to being a justification of torpor. But, it is far too subtle to be merely negative. It has a positive side – it is cautious not supine, reflective not languid, modest not grandiose.

'If the boat went even'

If men are together in a boat, and one part of the company would weigh it down on one side, another would make it lean as much to the contrary; it happeneth there is a third opinion of those, who conceive it would do as well, if the boat went even without endangering the passengers. Now it is hard to imagine by what figure in language, or by what rule in sense, this cometh to be a fault, and it is much more a wonder it should be thought a heresy.

GEORGE SAVILE, MARQUESS OF HALIFAX
The Character of a Trimmer, 1688

ELEGY
WRITTEN IN A COUNTRY CHURCH-YARD

The curfew tolls the knell of parting day,
　The lowing herd wind slowly o'er the lea,
The ploughman homeward plods his weary way,
　And leaves the world to darkness, and to me.

Now fades the glimmering landscape on the sight,
　And all the air a solemn stillness holds,
Save where the beetle wheels his droning flight,
　And drowsy tinklings lull the distant folds:

Save that from yonder ivy-mantled tower
　The moping owl does to the moon complain
Of such as, wandering near her secret bower,
　Molest her ancient solitary reign.

Beneath those rugged elms, that yew-tree's shade,
　Where heaves the turf in many a mouldering heap,
Each in his narrow cell for ever laid,
　The rude Forefathers of the hamlet sleep.

The breezy call of incense-breathing morn,
　The swallow twittering from the straw-built shed,
The cock's shrill clarion, or the echoing horn,
　No more shall rouse them from their lowly bed.

For them no more the blazing hearth shall burn,
   Or busy housewife ply her evening care:
No children run to lisp their sire's return,
   Or climb his knees the envied kiss to share.

Oft did the harvest to their sickle yield,
   Their furrow oft the stubborn glebe has broke;
How jocund did they drive their team afield!
   How bow'd the woods beneath their sturdy stroke!

Let not Ambition mock their useful toil,
   Their homely joys, and destiny obscure,
Nor Grandeur hear with a disdainful smile
   The short and simple annals of the Poor.

The boast of heraldry, the pomp of power,
   And all that beauty, all that wealth e'er gave,
Awaits alike th' inevitable hour:
   The paths of glory lead but to the grave.

Nor you, ye Proud, impute to these the fault
   If Memory o'er their tomb no trophies raise,
Where through the long-drawn aisle and fretted vault
The pealing anthem swells the note of praise.

Can storied urn or animated bust
   Back to its mansion call the fleeting breath?
Can Honour's voice provoke the silent dust,
   Or Flattery soothe the dull cold ear of Death?

Perhaps in this neglected spot is laid
   Some heart once pregnant with celestial fire;
Hands, that the rod of empire might have sway'd,
   Or waked to ecstasy the living lyre:

But Knowledge to their eyes her ample page
   Rich with the spoils of time, did ne'er unroll;
Chill Penury repress'd their noble rage,
   And froze the genial current of the soul.

Full many a gem of purest ray serene
   The dark unfathom'd caves of ocean bear:
Full many a flower is born to blush unseen,
   And waste its sweetness on the desert air.

Some village-Hampden, that with dauntless breast
  The little tyrant of his fields withstood,
Some mute inglorious Milton here may rest,
  Some Cromwell, guiltless of his country's blood.

Th' applause of list'ning senates to command,
  The threats of pain and ruin to despise,
To scatter plenty o'er a smiling land,
  And read their history in a nation's eyes,

Their lot forbad: nor circumscribed alone
  Their growing virtues, but their crimes confined;
Forbad to wade through slaughter to a throne,
  And shut the gates of mercy on mankind,

The struggling pangs of conscious truth to hide.
  To quench the blushes of ingenuous shame,
Or heap the shrine of Luxury and Pride
  With incense kindled at the Muse's flame.

Far from the madding crowd's ignoble strife,
  Their sober wishes never learn'd to stray;
Along the cool sequester'd vale of life
  They kept the noiseless tenour of their way.
  THOMAS GRAY, 1751

'A steady course of wisdom and virtue'

We are afraid to put men to live and trade each on his own private
stock of reason; because we suspect that this stock in each man is
small, and the individuals would do better to avail themselves of the
general bank and capital of nations, and of ages. Many of our men of
speculation, instead of exploding general prejudices, employ their sagacity to discover the latent wisdom which prevails in them. If they find
what they seek, and they seldom fail, they think it more wise to
continue the prejudice, with the reason involved, than to cast away the
coat of prejudice, and to leave nothing but the naked reason; because
prejudice, with its reason, has a motive to give action to that reason,
and an affection which will give it permanence. Prejudice is of ready
application in the emergency; it previously engages the mind in a
steady course of wisdom and virtue, and does not leave the man

hesitating in the moment of decision, sceptical, puzzled, and unresol-
ved. Prejudice renders a man's virtue his habit; and not a series of
unconnected acts. Through just prejudice, his duty becomes a part of
his nature.

ＥDMUND BURKE, 1790

'Publish . . .'

Publish and be damned.

ARTHUR WELLESLEY, DUKE OF WELLINGTON

Courage – 'visage de fer'

On Waterloo Day, 18 June 1832, a mob lay in wait for the Duke while
he was sitting to Pistrucci at the Mint. They greeted him as he emerged
with such apt slogans as 'Bonaparte for ever!' and, refusing to be
shaken off, gave him the longest five-mile ride of his life. There were
critical moments when he sighted loose paving-stones and then a
loaded coal-cart. 'Here's the artillery coming up', he joked, 'we must
look out.' But the mob were too intent on their quarry to notice the
coal-cart and by now he had acquired a small bodyguard to save him
from being dragged from his horse. Two Chelsea Pensioners had
offered their services. 'Then keep close to me now', he said, ordering
them to stand with their backs against his stirrups whenever his horse
was stopped. A magistrate and some police joined his escort, a man in a
buggy protected his rear, and after failing to give the mob the slip by a
diversion through Lincoln's Inn, he reached clubland to find the worst
was over. The men in the bay-windows marvelled at the set face
looking straight ahead. A 'visage de fer' was one's only choice, as he
told Mrs Arbuthnot two months later, apropos of life in general. They
said that the iron mask had slipped a little when an apothecary with
whom he had had dealings rushed out of Surgeon's Hall shouting
'Waterloo, Waterloo!' and he himself admitted being touched by the
many women who waved their handkerchiefs from upper windows
and implored him to come indoors. But he would not stop. 'If I were to
get in, in what manner was I to get out again?' At last he reached
Apsley House, and turning to Lord St Germans, who had joined him
outside the United Services Club, raised his hat: 'An odd day to choose.
Good morning!' Each window of Apsley House had its own iron

shutter, behind which the broken glass of October 1831 had not been replaced. The glass was mended in time for the Waterloo Banquet of 1833, but the Duke retained the shutters and to the end of his life was apt to raise his hat ironically and point towards them if a crowd began cheering him.

ELIZABETH LONGFORD
Wellington, Pillar of State, 1972

The Definition of a Gentleman

It is almost a definition of a gentleman to say he is one who never inflicts pain ... If he engages in controversy of any kind, his disciplined intellect preserves him from the blundering discourtesy of better, perhaps, but less educated minds, who, like blunt weapons, tear and hack instead of cutting clean, who mistake the point in argument, waste their strength on trifles, misconceive their adversary and leave the question more involved than they find it. He may be right or wrong in his opinion, but he is too clear-headed to be unjust: he is as simple as he is forcible, and as brief as he is decisive. Nowhere shall we find greater candour, consideration, indulgence: he throws himself into the minds of his opponents, he accounts for their mistakes. He knows the weakness of human reason as well as its strength, its provinces and its limits. If he be an unbeliever, he will be too profound and large-minded to ridicule religion or to act against it; he is too wise to be a dogmatist or fanatic in his infidelity. He respects piety and devotion; he even supports institutions as venerable, beautiful, or useful, to which he does not assent: he honours the ministers of religion, and it contents him to decline its mysteries without assailing or denouncing them. He is a friend of religious toleration; and that, not only because his philosophy has taught him to look on all forms of faith with an impartial eye, but also from the gentleness and effeminacy of feeling which is the attendant on civilization.

CARDINAL J. H. NEWMAN
The Idea of a University, 1873

'Readier to sit quiet'

Pascal said that most of the evils of life arose from 'man's being unable to sit still in a room'; and, though I do not go to that length, it is certain that we should have been a far wiser race than we are if we had been readier to sit quiet – we should have known much better the way in which it was best to act when we came to act. The rise of physical science, the first great body of practical truth provable to all men, exemplifies this in the plainest way. If it had not been for quiet people, who sat still and studied the sections of the cone, if other quiet people had not sat still and studied the theory of infinitesimals, or other quiet people had not sat still and worked out the doctrine of chances, the most 'dreamy moonshine', as the purely practical mind would consider, of all human pursuits; if 'idle stargazers' had not watched long and carefully the motions of the heavenly bodies – our modern astronomy would have been impossible; and without our astronomy 'our ships, our colonies, our seamen', all which makes modern life, modern life could not have existed. Ages of sedentary, quiet, thinking people were required before that noisy existence began; and without those pale preliminary students it never could have been brought into being.

WALTER BAGEHOT
Physics and Politics, 1876

'Going to the dogs'

I have for so many years entertained a firm conviction that we are going to the dogs that I have got quite accustomed to the expectation.

ROBERT CECIL, MARQUESS OF SALISBURY

'It's a terrible business to make up one's mind'

I'm not for Free Trade, and I'm not for Protection;
I approve of them both, and to both have objection.
In going through life, I continually find
It's a terrible business to make up one's mind.
And it's always the best in political fray
To take up the line of the Vicar of Bray.

So, in spite of all comments, reproaches, and predictions,
I firmly adhere to Unsettled Convictions.

SIR WILFRED LAWSON, 1904

In 1903 the Tory Party was split between the Imperial Protectionists led by Joseph
Chamberlain and the Free Traders. Poor Balfour had to try to keep his party
together but he couldn't paper over the cracks. This squib from the opposition was
near the mark for Balfour, one of whose works was entitled *Defence of Philosophic
Doubt*.

'Facing it – always facing it – that's the way to get through'

A hollow echoing noise, like that of a shout rolling in a rocky chasm,
approached the ship and went away again. The last star, blurred,
enlarged, as if returning to the fiery mist of its beginning, struggled with
the colossal depth of blackness hanging over the ship – and went out.

'Now for it!' muttered Captain MacWhirr. 'Mr. Jukes.'

'Here, sir.'

The two men were growing indistinct to each other.

'We must trust her to go through it and come out on the other side.
That's plain and straight. There's no room for Captain Wilson's storm-
strategy here.'

'No, sir.'

'She will be smothered and swept again for hours,' mumbled the
Captain. 'There's not much left by this time above deck for the sea to
take away – unless you or me.'

'Both, sir,' whispered Jukes breathlessly.

'You are always meeting trouble half way, Jukes,' Captain MacWhirr
remonstrated quaintly. 'Though it's a fact that the second mate is no
good. D'ye hear, Mr. Jukes? You would be left alone if . . .'

Captain MacWhirr interrupted himself, and Jukes, glancing on all
sides, remained silent.

'Don't you be put out by anything,' the Captain continued, mumbling
rather fast. 'Keep her facing it. They may say what they like, but the
heaviest seas run with the wind. Facing it – always facing it – that's the
way to get through. You are a young sailor. Face it. That's enough for
any man. Keep a cool head.'

'Yes, sir,' said Jukes, with a flutter of the heart.

In the next few seconds the Captain spoke to the engine-room and got
an answer.

For some reason Jukes experienced an access of confidence, a sensation that came from outside like a warm breath, and made him feel equal to every demand. The distant muttering of the darkness stole into his ears. He noted it unmoved, out of that sudden belief in himself as a man safe in a shirt of mail would watch a point . . .

Captain MacWhirr was trying to do up the top button of his oilskin coat with unwonted haste. The hurricane, with its power to madden the seas, to sink ships, to uproot trees, to overturn strong walls and dash the very birds of the air to the ground, had found this taciturn man in its path, and, doing its utmost, had managed to wring out a few words. Before the renewed wrath of winds swooped on his ship, Captain MacWhirr was moved to declare, in a tone of vexation, as it were: 'I wouldn't like to lose her.'

He was spared that annoyance.

JOSEPH CONRAD
Typhoon, 1903

Captain MacWhirr was ordinary, responsive, taciturn and short, with just enough imagination to carry him through each successive day. He is tested to the ultimate when his ship is hit by a typhoon. His steady, undramatic leadership saves the ship, the crew and the passengers.

'Invulnerable to the strength of facts'

He stood there for all the parentage of his kind, for men and women by no means clever or amusing, but whose very existence is based upon honest faith, and upon the instinct of courage. I don't mean military courage, or civil courage, or any special kind of courage. I mean just that inborn ability to look temptations straight in the face, – a readiness unintellectual enough, goodness knows, but without a pose, – a power of resistance, don't you see, ungracious if you like, but priceless – an unthinking and blessed stiffness before the outward and inward terrors, before the might of nature and the seductive corruption of men – backed by a faith invulnerable to the strength of facts, to the contagion of example, to the solicitation of ideas. Hang ideas! They are tramps, vagabonds, knocking at the back door of your mind, each taking a little of your substance, each carrying away some crumb of that belief in a few simple notions you must cling to if you want to live decently and would like to die easy!

JOSEPH CONRAD
Lord Jim, 1905

'We stand for the removal of suspicion'

For two years past, in the face of great difficulties ... I have striven to
consolidate and to breathe a living force into my great Party ... I want
my Party today to make a gesture to the country [of peace] and to say
to them: 'We have our majority; we believe in the justice of the Bill
which has been brought in today, but we are going to withdraw our
hand, and we are not going to push our political advantage home at a
time like this. Suspicion which has prevented stability in Europe is the
one poison which is preventing stability at home, and we offer the
country today this. We, at any rate, are not going to fire the first shot.
We stand for peace. We stand for the removal of suspicion in the
country. We want to create an atmosphere, a new atmosphere in a new
Parliament for a new age, in which the people can come together ...'

Although I know that there are those who work for different ends
from most of us in this House, yet there are many in all ranks and all
parties who will re-echo my prayer. 'Give peace in our time, O Lord.'

STANLEY BALDWIN, 1927

This was considered to be one of Baldwin's most effective speeches in the House of
Commons. A Conservative backbencher's private bill was to require members of
trade unions to 'contract in' to the political levy. This had been official party policy
and it would have dealt a deadly blow to the Labour Party, whose finances and
capacity to fight elections depended upon the enforced TU political levy. Baldwin
decided to assert his authority as leader of the party and opposed the bill for,
characteristically, he felt such a measure was an act of vindictiveness. Churchill
was surprised by this action, commenting, 'I had no idea he could show such
power. He has never done it before. The whole Conservative Party turned round
and obeyed without one single mutineer.'

'The prerogative of the harlot'

The papers conducted by Lord Rothermere and Lord Beaverbrook are
not newspapers in the ordinary acceptance of the term. They are
engines of propaganda for the constantly changing policies, desires,
personal wishes, personal likes and dislikes of two men. What are their
methods? Their methods are direct falsehood, misrepresentation, half-
truths, the alteration of the speaker's meaning by publishing a sentence
apart from the context, such as you see in those leaflets handed out
outside the doors of this hall: suppression and editorial criticism of
speeches which are not reported in the paper. These are methods hated

alike by the public, by the whole of the rest of the press ... What the proprietorship of these papers is aiming at is power, and power without responsibility – the prerogative of the harlot throughout the ages.

STANLEY BALDWIN, 1930

In 1930 Beaverbrook, who owned the *Daily Express*, and Rothermere, who owned the *Daily Mail*, campaigned to remove Baldwin from the leadership of the Tory Party over the issue of Imperial Preference, and in the Westminster by-election they put up their own candidate against the official Tory, Duff Cooper. This occasioned Baldwin's most famous comment, which may have been penned by his cousin Rudyard Kipling.

'A cultivation of the spontaneous'

The virtues possessed by the British people possessed in a higher degree than most other people, excepting only a few of the smaller nations, like the Swiss and the Dutch, were independence and self-reliance, individual initiative and local responsibility, the successful reliance on voluntary activity, non-interference with one's neighbour and tolerance of the different and queer, respect for custom and tradition, and a healthy suspicion of power and authority. British strength, British character, and British achievements are to a great extent the result of a cultivation of the spontaneous. But almost all the traditions and institutions in which British moral genius has found its most characteristic expression, and which in turn have moulded the national character and the whole moral climate of England, are those which the progress of collectivism and its inherently centralistic tendencies are progressively destroying.

F. A. HAYEK
The Road to Serfdom, 1944

'Small and limited innovations'

From all this the man of conservative temperament draws some appropriate conclusions. First, innovation entails certain loss and possible gain, therefore, the onus of proof, to show that the proposed change may be expected to be on the whole beneficial, rests with the would-be innovator. Secondly, he believes that the more closely an innovation resembles growth (that is, the more clearly it is intimated in and not merely imposed upon the situation) the less likely it is to result in a preponderance of loss. Thirdly, he thinks that an innovation which is a response to some specific defect, one designed to redress some specific disequilibrium, is more desirable than one which springs from a notion of a generally improved condition of human circumstances, and is far more desirable than one generated by a vision of perfection. Consequently, he prefers small and limited innovations to large and indefinite. Fourthly, he favours a slow rather than a rapid pace, and pauses to observe current consequences and make appropriate adjustments. And lastly, he believes the occasion to be important; and, other things being equal, he considers the most favourable occasion for innovation to be when the projected change is most likely to be limited to what is intended and least likely to be corrupted by undesired and unmanageable consequences.

MICHAEL OAKESHOTT
Rationalism in Politics, 1962

'The man of conservative temperament'

The disposition to be conservative is, then, warm and positive in respect of enjoyment, and correspondingly cool and critical in respect of change and innovation: these two inclinations support and elucidate one another. The man of conservative temperament believes that a known good is not lightly to be surrendered for an unknown better. He is not in love with what is dangerous and difficult; he is unadventurous; he has no impulse to sail uncharted seas; for him there is no magic in being lost, bewildered or shipwrecked. If he is forced to navigate the unknown, he sees virtue in heaving the lead every inch of the way. What others plausibly identify as timidity, he recognizes in himself as rational prudence, what others interpret as inactivity, he recognizes as a disposition to enjoy rather than to exploit. He is cautious, and he is disposed to indicate his assent or dissent, not in absolute, but in graduated terms. He eyes the situation in terms of its propensity to disrupt the familiarity of the features of his world ...

A storm which sweeps away a copse and transforms a favourite view, the death of friends, the sleep of friendship, the desuetude of customs of behaviour, the retirement of a favourite clown, involuntary exile, reversals of fortune, the loss of abilities enjoyed and their replacement by others — these are changes, none perhaps without its compensations, which the man of conservative temperament unavoidably regrets.

MICHAEL OAKESHOTT
Rationalism in Politics, 1962

DOGGEREL BY A SENIOR CITIZEN

for Robert Lederer

Our earth in 1969
Is not the planet I call mine,
The world, I mean, that gives me strength
To hold off chaos at arm's length.

My Eden landscapes and their climes
Are constructs from Edwardian times,
When bath-rooms took up lots of space,
And, before eating, one said Grace.

The automobile, the aeroplane,
Are useful gadgets, but profane:
The enginry of which I dream
Is moved by water or by steam.

Reason requires that I approve
The light-bulb which I cannot love:
To me more reverence-commanding
A fish-tail burner on the landing.

My family ghosts I fought and routed,
Their values, though, I never doubted:
I thought their Protestant Work-Ethic
Both practical and sympathetic.

When couples played or sang duets,
It was immoral to have debts:
I shall continue till I die
To pay in cash for what I buy.

The Book of Common Prayer we knew
Was that of 1662:
Though with-it sermons may be well,
Liturgical reforms are hell.

Sex was, of course – it always is –
The most enticing of mysteries,
But news-stands did not yet supply
Manichaean pornography.

Then Speech was mannerly, an Art,
Like learning not to belch or fart:
I cannot settle which is worse,
The Anti-Novel or Free Verse.

Nor are those Ph.D's my kith,
Who dig the symbol and the myth:
I count myself a man of letters
Who writes, or hopes to, for his betters.

Dare any call Permissiveness
An educational success?
Saner those class-rooms which I sat in,
Compelled to study Greek and Latin.

Though I suspect the term is crap,
If there *is* a Generation Gap,
Who is to blame? Those, old or young,
Who will not learn their Mother-Tongue.

But Love, at least, is not a state
Either *en vogue* or out-of-date,
And I've true friends, I will allow,
To talk and eat with here and now.

Me alienated? Bosh! It's just
As a sworn citizen who must
Skirmish with it that I feel
Most at home with what is Real.
        W. H. AUDEN

'He got on his bike'

The figure of three million unemployed has been mentioned many times. It is an appalling total. Whether it is measured in economic terms of costs in benefits paid, wages not earned, taxes not paid, goods not produced, or in the equally vital terms of social pressures, the human misery, the frustration and indignity that come with the feelings of rejection and alienation as real job seekers are faced day after day with a fruitless search for work, we cannot ignore the price that unemployment today is exacting, and indeed, it is exacting it for the failures of the past.

Yes ... I know those problems. I grew up in the thirties with an unemployed father. He did not riot – he got on his bike and looked for work and he kept looking until he had found it.

NORMAN TEBBIT
Conservative Party Conference, 1981

'The essence of Toryism'

The essence of Toryism is that good government depends far more on men than measures, and that its peculiar and unique contribution is in the high quality of leaders it can be relied upon to produce.

PEREGRINE WORSTHORNE

'The core and fire-centre of conservatism'

The conservative principles *par excellence* are proportion and measure; self-expression through self-restraint; preservation through reform; humanism and classical balance; a fruitful nostalgia for the permanent beneath the flux; and a fruitful obsession for unbroken historic continuity. These principles together create freedom, a freedom built not on the quicksand of adolescent defiance but on the bedrock of ethics and law. ...

The core and fire-centre of conservatism, its emotional *élan*, is a humanist reverence for the dignity of the individual soul. This is incompatible with fascist or Stalinist collectivism; incompatible with a purely mechanistic view of man; incompatible with a purely economic view of history.

PETER VIERECK
Conservatism Revisited

13

'To me, England is the Country, and the Country is England'

The Tory Party is strongest in the country areas, as it has been over the centuries. This is partly because life in rural areas is more measured and less frantic than the 'madding crowd's ignoble strife'. The respect for Tory values is not born out of quaint romanticism, rather an understanding and love of that which endures in the countryside. Many town dwellers share this affinity with and affection for the countryside. So the Conservative Party's electoral prospects have never been harmed by its association with the shires.

Like the rhythm of nature and the cycle of the seasons, the Conservative approach demonstrates continuity and predictability.

Conservatives have never been simply a party to defend farming interests. That would be politically suicidal. The traditional love of the countryside has developed in the twentieth century into a desire to preserve as much of its remaining beauty as possible. Therefore, alongside the introduction of conservation measures, other steps have been taken to promote the active protection of the land by those who earn their living from it. This concern for Britain's natural heritage was eloquently expressed by Margaret Thatcher in a speech to the Royal Society in 1988, and repeated later that year at the Party Conference.

SWEET AUBURN

Sweet Auburn, loveliest village of the plain,
Where health and plenty cheered the labouring swain,
Where smiling spring its earliest visit paid,
And parting summer's lingering blooms delayed,
Dear lovely bowers of innocence and ease,
Seats of my youth, when every sport could please,
How often have I loitered o'er thy green,
Where humble happiness endeared each scene!
How often have I paused on every charm,
The sheltered cot, the cultivated farm,
The never failing brook, the busy mill,
The decent church that topped the neighbouring hill,
The hawthorn bush, with seats beneath the shade,
For talking age, and whispering lovers made!
How often have I blest the coming day,
When toil remitting lent its turn to play,
And all the village train from labour free
Led up their sports beneath the spreading tree,
While many a pastime circled in the shade,
The young contending as the old surveyed;
And many a gambol frolicked o'er the ground,
And slights of art and feats of strength went round;
And still as each repeated pleasure tired,
Succeeding sports the mirthful band inspired;
The dancing pair that simply sought renown
By holding out to tire each other down;
The swain mistrustless of his smutted face,
While secret laughter tittered round the place;
The bashful virgin's side-long looks of love,
The matron's glance that would those looks reprove!
These were thy charms, sweet village; sports like these,
With sweet succession taught even toil to please;
These round thy bowers their cheerful influence shed
These were thy charms – but all these charms are fled.
   Sweet smiling village, loveliest of the lawn,
Thy sports are fled, and all thy charms withdrawn;
Amidst thy bowers the tyrant's hand is seen
And desolation saddens all thy green:

One only master grasps the whole domain,
And half a tillage stints thy smiling plain;
No more thy glassy brook reflects the day,
But choked with sedges, works its weedy way;
Along thy glades, a solitary guest,
The hollow sounding bittern guards its nest;
Amidst thy desert walks the lapwing flies,
And tires their echoes with unvaried cries.
Sunk are thy bowers, in shapeless ruin all,
And the long grass o'ertops the mouldering wall;
And trembling, shrinking from the spoiler's hand,
Far, far away thy children leave the land.
　　Ill fares the land, to hastening ills a prey,
Where wealth accumulates and men decay:
Princes and lords may flourish, or may fade;
A breath can make them, as a breath has made;
But a bold peasantry, their country's pride,
When once destroyed, can never be supplied.
　　OLIVER GOLDSMITH, 1770

Goldsmith was a romantic who disliked the Whigs for their cant but he chided the
Tories if they did not live up to their duties.

'The nature and quality of all living things'

If the cultivators of the land be not, generally speaking, the most
virtuous and most happy of mankind, there must be something at work
in the community to counteract the operations of nature. This way of life
gives the best security for health and strength of body. It does not teach,
it necessarily produces early rising; constant forethought; constant
attention; and constant care of dumb animals. The nature and qualities
of all living things are known to country boys better than to philosophers. The seasons, the weather, the causes and effects of propagation,
in cultivation, in tillage, are all known from habit, from incessant
repetition of observation. The nature, the properties, the various uses, of
different soils and woods are familiar to the mind of country boys.
Riding, climbing, swimming, nothing comes amiss, and they are come,
and are not sought. Rural affairs leave not a day, not an hour, unoc-
cupied and without its cares, its promises, and its fruitions. The seasons,
which wait for no man; the weather, which is no respector of person,

and which will be what it will be, produce an habitual looking forward, and make the farmer provident, whatever might have been his natural disposition. The farmer's cares are pleasing cares. His misfortunes can seldom be more than lessons.

WILLIAM COBBETT
Quoted in *The Progress of a Ploughboy to a Seat in Parliament*, 1933

'The plain country gentleman'

The plain country gentleman, who, living on his own means, amongst his own people, becomes the natural protector of and referee between the farmer and the peasant, and in case of need the firmest asserter of their rights and his own against the aggression of the crown, or the independent and dauntless defender of the crown's rights against the innovations of political fanaticism.

SIR WALTER SCOTT
The Life of Napoleon, 1827

'This England'

This England, lay before Shakespeare as it lies before us all, with its green fields, and its long hedgerows, and its many trees, and its great towns, and its endless hamlets, and its motley society, and its long history, and its bold exploits, and its gathering power; and he saw that they were good. To him, perhaps, more than to any one else, has it been given to see, that they were a great unity, a great religious object; that if you could only descend to the inner life, to the deep things, to the secret principles of its noble vigour, to the essence of character, to what we know of Hamlet, and seem to fancy of Ophelia, we might so far as we are capable of so doing, understand the nature which God has made.

WALTER BAGEHOT
'Shakespeare the Individual', 1853

The liberals sometimes lay claim to Walter Bagehot (1826–1876). He was a prolific writer and journalist, editor of the *Economist*, constitutional historian and literary critic: one of those big Victorian minds. However, Norman St John Stevas, who edited fourteen volumes of Bagehot's writings, asserts that his interests, attitudes and cast of mind were essentially Conservative. He suspected restless change for change's sake and recognized the need for the stability that came from tradition.

THE GLORY OF THE GARDEN

Our England is a garden that is full of stately views,
Of borders, beds and shrubberies and lawns and avenues,
With statues on the terraces and peacocks strutting by;
But the Glory of the Garden lies in more than meets the eye.

For where the old thick laurels grow, along the thin red wall,
You find the tool- and potting-sheds which are the heart of all;
The cold-frames and the hot-houses, the dungpits and the tanks,
The rollers, carts and drain-pipes, with the barrows and the planks.

And there you'll see the gardeners, the men and 'prentice boys
Told off to do as they are bid and do it without noise;
For, except when seeds are planted and we shout to scare the birds
The Glory of the Garden it abideth not in words.

And some can pot begonias and some can bud a rose,
And some are hardly fit to trust with anything that grows;
But they can roll and trim the lawns and sift the sand and loam,
For the Glory of the Garden occupieth all who come.

Our England is a garden, and such gardens are not made
By singing: 'Oh, how beautiful!' and sitting in the shade,
While better men than we go out and start their working lives
At grubbing weeds from gravel-paths with broken dinner-knives.

There's not a pair of legs so thin, there's not a head so thick,
There's not a hand so weak and white, nor yet a heart so sick,
But it can find some needful job that's crying to be done,
For the Glory of the Garden glorifieth every one.

Then seek your job with thankfulness and work till further orders,
If it's only netting strawberries or killing slugs on borders;
And when your back stops aching and your hands begin to harden,
You will find yourself a partner in the Glory of the Garden.

Oh, Adam was a gardener, and God who made him sees
That half a proper gardener's work is done upon his knees,
So when your work is finished, you can wash your hands and pray
For the Glory of the Garden, that may not pass away!
And the Glory of the Garden it shall never pass away!
   RUDYARD KIPLING, *c.* 1918

'To me, England is the country, and the country is England'

To me, England is the country, and the country is England. And when I ask myself what I mean by England, when I think of England when I am abroad, England comes to me through my various senses – through the ear, through the eye, and through certain imperishable scents. I will tell you what they are, and there may be those among you who feel as I do.

The sounds of England, the tinkle of the hammer on the anvil in the country smithy, the corncrake on a dewy morning, the sound of the scythe against the whetstone, and the sight of a plough team coming over the brow of a hill, the sign that has been seen in England since England was a land, and may be seen in England long after the Empire has perished and every works in England has ceased to function, for centuries the one eternal sight of England. The wild anemones in the woods in April, the last load at night of hay being drawn down a lane as the twilight comes on, when you can scarcely distinguish the figures of the horses as they take it home to the farm, and above all, most subtle, most penetrating and most moving, the smell of wood smoke coming up in an autumn evening, or the smell of the scutch fires: that wood smoke that our ancestors, tens of thousands of years ago, must have caught on the air when they were coming home with the result of the day's forage, when they were still nomads, and when they were still roaming the forests and the plains of the continent of Europe. These things strike down into the very depths of our nature, and touch chords that go back to the beginning of time and the human race, but they are chords that with every year of our life sound a deeper note in our innermost being ... The love of these things is innate and inherent in our people. It makes for that love of home, one of the strongest features of our race, and it is that that makes our race seek its new home in the Dominions overseas, where they have room to see things like this that they can no more see at home. It is that power of making homes, almost peculiar to our people, and it is one of the sources of their greatness. They go overseas, and they take with them what they learned at home: love of justice, love of truth, and the broad humanity that are so characteristic of English people.

STANLEY BALDWIN
Speech to the Royal Society of St George, 1924

'English country life'

The point was that a thing like English country life does not spring up merely out of living in the country. It does not spring up in America, or for that matter in Asia or Africa or a great part of Europe. It is the perfect artistic expression of something English, just as the best American architecture is the expression of something American. But you will not find the first in anything called a village or the second in anything called a city. And if you let it perish, you are like men who should look on at the ruin of the last Greek god or the last Christian cathedral.

G. K. CHESTERTON, 1931

But not all aspects of the countryside ...

God save me from the Porkers,
    God save me from their sons,
Their noisy tweedy sisters
    Who follow with the guns,
The old and scheming mother,
    Their futures that she plann'd,
The ghastly younger brother
    Who married into land.

Their shots along the valley
    Draw blood out of the sky,
The wounded pheasants rally
    As hobnailed boots go by.
Where once the rabbit scampered
    The waiting copse is still
As Porker fat and pampered
    Comes puffing up the hill.

'A left and right! Well done, sir!
    They're falling in the road;
And here's your other gun, sir.'
    'Don't talk. You're here to load.'
He grabs his gun, not seeing
    A thing but birds in air,
And blows them out of being
    With self-indulgent stare.

Triumphant after shooting
   He still commands the scene,
His Land Rover comes hooting
   Beaters and dogs between.
Then dinner with a neighbour,
   It doesn't matter which,
Conservative or Labour,
   So long as he is rich.

A *faux-bonhomme* and dull as well,
   All pedigree and purse,
We must admit that, though he's hell,
   His womenfolk are worse.
Bright in their county gin sets
   They tug their ropes of pearls
And smooth their tailored twin sets
   And drop the names of earls.

Loud talks of meets and marriages
   And tax-evasion's heard
In many first-class carriages
   While servants travel third.
'My dear, I have to spoil them too –
   Or who would do the chores?
Well, here we are at Waterloo,
   I'll drop you at the Stores.'

God save me from the Porkers,
   The pathos of their lives,
The strange example that they set
   To new-rich farmers' wives
Glad to accept their bounty
   And worship from afar,
And think of them as county –
   County is what they are.
   JOHN BETJEMAN
   'County'

'When it supported the rural areas'

And to noble Lords who sit loyally, as I have done for so many years,
to support the Government, I would say that the Conservative Party
has always been strongest when it supported the rural areas. It had
terrible disasters after the Repeal period and the Corn Laws. Disraeli
made himself into a country squire and bought Hughenden, and they
all believed that he really was a country squire. As Prime Minister, the
great Lord Salisbury was a purely rural leader. We come with a great
jump to Baldwin and Mary Webb, and all that he talked about the
country and his magnificent speech on England at the St. George's Day
dinner – 'the scutch fires at night, when the forager comes home'. That
was true Conservative rural policy and philosophy. I believe that we
should not accept this clause. I feel, I am sorry to say, like Martin
Luther: '*Ich kann nicht anders.*' I can do no other. I ask noble Lords to
do no other.

R. A. BUTLER

House of Lords, 1980

In 1980 the Government decided to reduce the amount of assistance which a local
education authority could give for the free transport of children to school. This
bore down particularly on rural primary schools, and the measure was defeated in
the Lords by a combination of the Catholic Church, the farmers and the Tory
backwoodsmen. Rab Butler reminded the party of its traditional duty.

'All we have is a life tenancy'

Pride in these islands – our countryside, our seas and rivers – runs like
a thread through our history and literature. Sometimes, it seems a
perverse pride.

'Fog, fog, everywhere' begins one of Dickens's greatest novels. That
was still true in London when I first went to work there. But the Clean
Air Act of 1956 – passed by a Conservative Government – banished
smog from the air we breathe.

The Thames is now the cleanest metropolitan estuary in the world
and £4 billion is now being spent on the Mersey. I want to see the
industrial rivers of the North and Midlands – and of Europe – as clean
as the Thames. We have led Europe in banning the dumping of harmful
industrial waste in the North Sea.

Given our record, we are well placed to take the lead with other

Governments in practical efforts to protect the wider world. We will work with them to end the destruction of the world's forests. We shall direct more of our overseas aid to help poor countries to protect their trees and plant new ones. We will join with others to seek further protection of the ozone layer – that global skin which protects life itself from ultraviolet radiation. We will work to cut down the use of fossil fuels, a cause of both acid rain and the greenhouse effect. That means a policy for safe, sensible and balanced use of nuclear power.

It's we Conservatives who are not merely friends of the Earth – we are its guardians and trustees for generations to come. The core of Tory philosophy and for the case for protecting the environment are the same. No generation has a freehold on this earth. All we have is a life tenancy – with a full repairing lease. This Government intends to meet the terms of that lease in full.

MARGARET THATCHER
Conservative Party Conference, 1988

14

'Land of our Birth'

Conservatives have an instinctive pride in their country. That does not mean to say they have a monopoly of patriotic sentiment, or willingness to make sacrifices for Britain. Many others, following different political allegiances, have made similar sacrifices. But for the Tory, patriotism means a willingness to speak up unashamedly for his country even when the case may be weakest and when others are dodging about, looking for any reason to say nothing.

No country is perfect, but the Tory does not gloat over our national blemishes nor find exaggerated, often illusory, attractions in other countries. In Gilbert's list of people who never would be missed there's the idiot 'who praises every century but this and every country but his own'. The bien-pensant class is not new to Britain.

At the time when our national consciousness was emerging, Shakespeare wrote of:

> This happy breed of men, this little world,
> This precious stone set in the silver sea.

A century later Halifax said that his ideal politician 'would rather dye than see a spire of English Grass trampled down by a foreign trespasser'. And in the twentieth century, lest any should think that love of one's country has no longer an appeal, Churchill rallied Britons to resist that alien and vicious creed which threatened the freedom and democracy not only of our country but also of the world. In Tom Stoppard's play Travesties, the Englishman Carr rounds upon the Bolshevik for claiming that 'War is Capitalism with the gloves off', and in a splendid piece of invective bluntly retorts, 'I went to war because it was my duty, because my country needed me, and that's patriotism.'

'Deare countrey'

... Deare countrey! O! how dearely deare
Ought thy rembraunce and perpetuall band
Be to thy foster Childe, that from thy hand
Did commun breath and nouriture receave.
How brutish is it not to understand
How much to her we owe, that all us gave;
That gave unto us all what ever good we have.
    EDMUND SPENSER

'This England'

This royal throne of kings, this sceptred isle,
This earth of majesty, this seat of Mars,
This other Eden, demi-paradise,
This fortress built by Nature for herself
Against infection and the hand of war,
This happy breed of men, this little world,
This precious stone set in the silver sea,
Which serves it in the office of a wall,
Or as a moat defensive to a house;
Against the envy of less happier lands
This blessed plot, this earth, this realm, this England.
    WILLIAM SHAKESPEARE
    John of Gaunt in *Richard II, c.* 1595

'A Stalk of English Juice'

Our *Trimmer* is far from Idolatry in other things, in one thing only he
cometh near it, his Country is in some degree his Idol; he doth not
Worship the Sun, because 'tis not peculiar to us, it rambles about the
World, and is less kind to us than others; but for the Earth of England,
tho perhaps inferior to that of many places abroad, to him there is
Divinity in it, and he would rather dye than see a spire of *English* Grass
trampled down by a foreign trespasser: He thinketh there are a great
many of his mind, for all plants are apt to taste of the Soyl in which
they grow, and we that grow here have a Root that produceth in us a
Stalk of English Juice which is not to be changed by grafting or foreign

infusion; and I do not know whether any thing less will prevail than the Modern Experiment, by which the Blood of one Creature is transmitted into another; according to which, before the *French* blood can be let into our Bodies, every drop of our own must be drawn out of them.

GEORGE SAVILE, MARQUESS OF HALIFAX
The Character of a Trimmer, 1688

'A Patriot'

It ought to be deeply impressed on the minds of all who have voices in this national deliberation, that no man can deserve a seat in parliament who is not a PATRIOT. No other man will protect our rights, no other man can merit our confidence.

A Patriot is he whose public conduct is regulated by one single motive, the love of his country; who, as an agent in parliament, has for himself neither hope nor fear, neither kindness nor resentment, but refers every thing to the common interest.

That of five hundred men, such as this degenerate age affords, a majority can be found thus virtuously abstracted, who will affirm? Yet there is no good in despondence: vigilance and activity often effect more than was expected. Let us take a Patriot where we can meet him; and that we may not flatter ourselves by false appearances, distinguish those marks which are certain, from those which may deceive: for a man may have the external appearance of a Patriot, without the constituent qualities; as false coins have often lustre, tho' they want weight.

SAMUEL JOHNSON, 1774

THE CHILDREN'S SONG

Land of our Birth, we pledge to thee
Our love and toil in the years to be;
When we are grown and take our place,
As men and women with our race.

Father in Heaven who lovest all.
Oh help Thy children when they call;
That they may build from age to age,
An undefiled heritage.

Teach us to bear the yoke in youth,
With steadfastness and careful truth;
That, in our time, Thy Grace may give
The Truth whereby the Nations live.

Teach us to rule ourselves alway,
Controlled and cleanly night and day;
That we may bring, if need arise,
No maimed or worthless sacrifice.

Teach us to look in all our ends,
On Thee for judge, and not our friends;
That we, with Thee, may walk uncowed
By fear or favour of the crowd.

Teach us the Strength that cannot seek,
By deed or thought, to hurt the weak;
That, under Thee, we may possess
Man's strength to comfort man's distress.

Teach us Delight in simple things,
And Mirth that has no bitter springs;
Forgiveness free of evil done,
And Love to all men 'neath the sun!

Land of our Birth, our faith, our pride,
For whose dear sake our fathers died;
Our Motherland, we pledge to thee,
Head, heart, and hand through the years to be!
    RUDYARD KIPLING
    Puck of Pook's Hill, 1906

WHY ENGLAND IS CONSERVATIVE

I

Because of our dear Mother, the fair Past,
On whom twin Hope and Memory safely lean,
And from whose fostering wisdom none shall wean
Their love and faith, while love and faith shall last:
Mother of happy homes and Empire vast,
Of hamlets meek, and many a proud demesne,

Blue spires of cottage smoke 'mong woodlands green,
And comely altars where no stone is cast.
And shall we barter these for gaping Throne,
Dismantled towers, mean plots without a tree,
A herd of hinds too equal to be free,
Greedy of other's, jealous of their own,
And, where sweet Order now breathes cadenced tone,
Envy, and hate, and all uncharity?

II

Banish the fear! 'Twere infamy to yield
To folly what to force had been denied,
Or in the Senate quail before the tide
We should have stemmed and routed in the field.
What though no more we brandish sword and shield,
Reason's keen blade is ready at our side,
And manly brains, in wisdom panoplied,
Can foil the shafts that treacherous sophists wield.
The spirit of our fathers is not quelled.
With weapons valid even as those they bore,
Domain, Throne, Altar, still may be upheld,
So we disdain, as they disdained of yore,
The foreign froth that foams against our shore,
Only by its white cliffs to be repelled!

ALFRED AUSTIN

'And so is man rooted'

And then, I repeat, I was going home – to that home distant enough for all its hearthstones to be like one hearthstone, by which the humblest of us has the right to sit. We wander in our thousands over the face of the earth, the illustrious and the obscure, earning beyond the seas our fame, our money, or only a crust of bread; but it seems to me that for each of us going home must be like going to render an account . . .

Say what you like, to get its joy, to breathe its peace, to face its truth, one must return with a clear conscience. All this may seem to you sheer sentimentalism; and indeed very few of us have the will or the capacity to look consciously under the surface of familiar emotions. There are the girls we love, the men we look up to, the tenderness, the friendships, the opportunities, the pleasures! But the fact remains that you must touch your reward with clean hands, lest it turn to dead leaves, to thorns, in your grasp. I think it is the lonely, without a fireside or an affection they may call their own, those who return not to a dwelling but to the land itself, to meet its disembodied, eternal, and unchangeable spirit – it is those who understand best its severity, its saving power, the grace of its secular right to our fidelity, to our obedience. Yes! few of us understand, but we all feel it though, and I say *all* without exception, because those who do not feel do not count. Each blade of grass has its spot on earth whence it draws its life, its strength; and so is man rooted to the land from which he draws his faith together with his life.

JOSEPH CONRAD
Lord Jim, 1905

The Coronation of George V, 1910

It is to be doubted whether one person in that whole assembly had a clear thought in his head. Rather, words and their associations marched in a grand chain, giving hand to hand: England, Shakespeare, Elizabeth, London; Westminster, the docks, India, the Cutty Sark, England; England, Gloucestershire, John of Gaunt; Magna Carta, Cromwell, England.

VITA SACKVILLE-WEST

'I am moved by a feeling'

Loyalties to a county, a party, a constitution, a national sovereign, a tribal chief, a church, a race, a creed, are characteristic specimens of the class. They may be ill-directed: they often are. Nevertheless, it is such loyalties that make human society possible; they do more, they make it noble. To them we owe it that a man will sacrifice ease, profit, life itself, for something which wholly transcends his merely personal interests. Therefore, whether mistaken or not, there is always in them a touch of greatness ... But it has to be observed that the kind of loyalty we call patriotism, though it expresses a simple feeling, need have no exclusive application. It may embrace a great deal more than a man's country or a man's race. It may embrace a great deal less. And these various patriotisms need not be, and should not be, mutually exclusive. As civilisation advances it becomes more and more necessary for men to learn how loyalties are to be combined without being weakened ...

As a matter of fact some combination of different patriotisms is almost universal among thinking persons. If I consider the case I know best (namely my own), I find that, within a general regard for mankind, which I hope is not absent or weak, I am moved by a feeling, especially patriotic in its character, for the group of nations who are the authors and the guardians of western civilization, for the sub-group which speaks the English language, and whose laws and institutions are rooted in British history, for the communities which compose the British Empire, for the United Kingdom of which I am a citizen, and for Scotland where I was born, and is my home, as it was the home of my father before me.

A. J. BALFOUR
Nationality and Home Rule, 1913

THE ENGLISH GRAVES

Were I that wandering citizen whose city is the world,
I would not weep for all that fell before the flags were furled;
I would not let one murmur mar the trumpets volleying forth
How God grew weary of the kings, and the cold hell in the north.
But we whose hearts are homing birds have heavier thoughts of home,
Though the great eagles burn with gold on Paris or on Rome,
Who stand beside our dead and stare, like seers at an eclipse,
At the riddle of the island tale and the twilight of the ships.

For these were simple men that loved with hands and feet and eyes,
Whose souls were humbled to the hills and narrowed to the skies.
The hundred little lands within one little land that lie,
Where Severn seeks the sunset isles or Sussex scales the sky.

And what is theirs, though banners blow on Warsaw risen again,
Or ancient laughter walks in gold through the vineyards of Lorraine,
Their dead are marked on English stones, their loves on English trees,
How little is the prize they win, how mean a coin for these –
How small a shrivelled laurel-leaf lies crumpled here and curled:
They died to save their country and they only saved the world.

G. K. CHESTERTON

'Without victory, there is no survival'

I have nothing to offer but blood, toil, tears and sweat. We have before us an ordeal of the most grievous kind. We have before us many many long months of struggle and of suffering. You ask, what is our policy? I will say it is to wage war, by sea, land and air, with all our might and with all the strength that God can give us; to wage war against a monstrous tyranny, never surpassed in the dark, lamentable catalogue of human crime. That is our policy. You ask, what is our aim? I can answer in one word: it is victory, victory at all costs, victory in spite of all terror, victory however long and hard the road may be; for, without victory, there is no survival.

WINSTON CHURCHILL, 1940

'What it is that binds us together'

Backward travels our gaze ... and there at last we find them, or seem to find them, in many a village church, beneath the tall tracery of a perpendicular East window and the coffered ceiling of the chantry chapel. From brass and stone, from line and effigy, their eyes look out at us, and we gaze into them, as if we would win some answer from their inscrutable silence. 'Tell us what it is that binds us together; show us the clue that leads us through a thousand years; whisper to us the secret of this charmed life of England, that we in our time may know how to hold it fast.'

ENOCH POWELL
Speech to the Royal Society of St George, 1964

'The noble hymn'

We declare ourselves the unsleeping opponents of all class, all official or all Party privilege, which denies the genius of our island race, whose sparks fly upwards unceasingly from the whole people, its rightful career, reward and pre-eminence alike in peace and war. How, then, do we draw the lines of political battle? The British race is not actuated mainly by the hope of material gain. Otherwise we should long ago have sunk in the ocean of the past. It is stirred on almost all occasions by sentiment and instinct, rather than by programmes or worldly calculation. When this new Parliament first met all the Socialist

Members stood up and sang 'The Red Flag' in their triumph.

Peering ahead through the mists and mysteries of the future, so far as I can I see the division at the next Election will be between those who wholeheartedly sing 'The Red Flag' and those who rejoice to sing 'Land of Hope and Glory'. There is the noble hymn which will rally the wise, the sober-minded and the good to the salvation of our native land.

WINSTON CHURCHILL
Conservative Party Conference, 1946

'I went to war because it was my duty'

TZARA: Wars are fought for oil wells and coaling stations; for control of the Dardanelles or the Suez Canal; for colonial pickings to buy cheap in and conquered markets to sell dear in. War is capitalism with the gloves off and many who go to war know it but they go to war because they don't want to be a hero. It takes courage to sit down and be counted. But how much better to live bravely in Switzerland than to die cravenly in France, quite apart from what it does to one's trousers.

CARR: My God, you little Rumanian wog – you bloody dago – you jumped-up phrase-making smart-alecy arty-intellectual Balkan turd!!! Think you know it all! – while we poor dupes think we're fighting for ideals, you've got a profound understanding of what is *really* going on, underneath! – you've got a phrase for it! You pedant! Do you think your phrases are the true sum of each man's living of each day? – *capitalism with the gloves off?* – do you think that's the true experience of a wire-cutting party caught in a crossfire in no-man's-land? – Why not infantile sexuality in khaki trews? Or the collective unconscious in a tin hat? (*Viciously*) It's all the rage in Zurich! – You slug! I'll tell you what's *really* going on: I went to war because it was my *duty*, because my country needed me, and that's *patriotism*. I went to war because I believed that those boring little Belgians and incompetent Frogs had the right to be defended from German militarism, and that's *love of freedom. That's* how things are underneath, and I won't be told by some yellow-bellied Bolshevik that I ended up in the trenches because there's a profit in ball-bearings!

TOM STOPPARD
Travesties, 1975

'No merely utilitarian definition of civic loyalty'

Another, and related, consequence of the disestablishment of religion as a publicly sanctioned mythos has been the inability of liberal society ever to come up with a convincing and generally accepted theory of political obligation. Liberal philosophers have proposed many versions of utilitarianism to this end, but these have remained academic exercises and have not had much popular impact. Nor is this surprising: No merely utilitarian definition of civic loyalty is going to convince anyone that it makes sense for him to die for his country. In actual fact, it has been the secular myth of nationalism which, for the past century and a half, has provided this rationale. But this secular myth, though it has evolved hand in hand with bourgeois society, is not intrinsically or necessarily bourgeois. Nationalism ends by establishing 'equal sacrifice' as the criterion of justice; and this is no kind of bourgeois criterion. We have seen, in our own day, how the spirit of nationalism can be utterly contemptuous of bourgeois properties, and utterly subversive of the bourgeois order itself.

IRVING KRISTOL

'Patriotism in a pure form'

Now a conservative is likely to value the institution of monarchy, and the kind of patriotism that it engenders. For the legitimacy of monarchical rule arises 'transcendentally', in the manner of the duties and obligations of family life. The monarch is not chosen for his personal attributes, nor does he have obligations and expectations which are the subject-matter of any 'social contract'. He is simply the representation of sovereignty, and its ceremonial presence. His will as monarch is not his individual will, but the will of state. The monarch forms part of that surface of concepts and symbols whereby the citizen can perceive his social identity, and perceive society not as a means to an end, but as an end in itself. Attachment to the monarch is therefore patriotism in a pure form, a form that could not be translated into attachment to a policy, or to a choice of means.

ROGER SCRUTON

The Meaning of Conservatism, 1981

'The spirit of Britain at her best'

This is not going to be a speech about the Falklands campaign, though I would be proud to make one. But I want to say just this, because it is true for all our people: the spirit of the South Atlantic was the spirit of Britain at her best. It has been said that we surprised the world, that British patriotism was rediscovered in those spring days. It was never really lost. But it would be no bad thing if the feeling that swept the country then were to continue to inspire us. For if there was any doubt about the determination of the British people it was removed by the men and women who, a few months ago, brought a renewed sense of pride and self-respect to our country.

They were for the most part young. Let all of us here, and in the wider audience outside, pause and reflect on what we who stayed at home owe to those who sailed and fought, and lived and died – and won. If this is tomorrow's generation, Britain has little to fear in the years to come.

In what by any standards was a remarkable chapter in our island's history, it is they who this year wrote its brightest page. In remembering their heroism, let us not forget the courage shown by those same armed forces nearer home. We see them and the other forces of law and order display these qualities day after day in Northern Ireland. Yes, and even closer at hand. I have seen no more moving sight in the last year than the Blues and Royals bearing their tattered standard proudly past the spot in Hyde Park where their comrades had been murdered in a cruel and cowardly bomb attack only two days before.

MARGARET THATCHER
Conservative Party Conference, 1982

15

'England has Saved Herself by her Exertions, and will, as I Trust, Save Europe by her Example'

This chapter deals with the Conservative attitude over the years towards the rest of the world. Most Conservatives have tended to favour the adventurous outward-going policies that led Britain to become for a time the most powerful country in the world. Conservatives were proud of our nation's achievements – the expansion of British trade and influence in the eighteenth century, and the consolidation of a great empire in the nineteenth century. The Liberal Party, and later the Labour Party, were more hesitant and critical. In the late nineteenth and early twentieth centuries they became advocates first of a loose federation and then of independence for the constituent parts of the Empire.

The large expansion of empire generally occurred under the administrations of Tory Prime Ministers, although it was a Tory Prime Minister who was responsible for the fiasco of the American War of Independence when the wiser counsels of Burke were overlooked. There were clearly trading and economic advantages in British domination of Canada, India, parts of the Far East and Africa. However, the cost of maintaining this policy with soldiers, sailors and administrators involved heavy financial burdens. If an imperial profit and loss account were ever to be drawn up, it is by no means clear that the balance would be in the black.

In the nineteenth century, a new philosophy emerged that went beyond the 'fruits of conquest' approach. An imperial mission evolved which was proclaimed and reached its eloquent apogee in Kipling's verses. It was the 'white man's burden' to spread European civilization – Christian values, education, justice, impartial administration and democracy – together with roads, telegraphs and railways. Disraeli

made Queen Victoria Empress of India, and her army and navy
maintained a Pax Britannica across the world. When Edward VII
ascended the throne that passionate advocate of imperialism, Joe
Chamberlain, decided that his title should be 'King of All the British
Dominons Beyond the Seas'. Those infused with these noble senti-
ments were contemptuous of the traders and box-wallahs. They con-
sidered Britain's role in the nineteenth and early twentieth century was
to give the world a legacy of civilization comparable to the legacy of
Greece and Rome.

Many Conservative politicians – Pitt, Canning, Disraeli, Salisbury
and Baldwin – made eloquent and stirring speeches on this theme,
though a small minority of Tories were deeply suspicious of such
grandiose policies. Enoch Powell in the 1960s urged the Tory Party to
abandon the twin myths of believing that there had been an age of
imperial splendour and that consequently we were living through a
period of decline. The first led to a morbid nostalgia, the second to a
lack of national self-confidence.

In the twentieth century the move from Empire to Commonwealth
and from sovereignty to independence became irresistible. The grant-
ing of independence to India in 1947 was followed by the secession of
virtually every colonial territory over the following fifteen years. It fell
to Harold Macmillan's administration in particular to handle this
transfer of power. This raised the whole question of Britain's role in
the world following the loss of an empire. Macmillan recognized that
change had to be accepted. In a celebrated and much quoted speech in
South Africa, he referred to the 'winds of change sweeping over that
continent'. But these winds were also blowing across the world.

In the 1950s the European Community was formed. Conservatives
instinctively regarded this with caution. Many preferred a wider
grouping involving the Scandinavian countries and retaining some
transatlantic link as well. Macmillan persuaded the party that Britain
should join the European Community. He cited the twin arguments
that membership would bring to an end the intra-European rivalries
that had led to two World Wars, and that a single economic market of
300 million people would replace Britain's preferential arrangements
with the old empire and provide an economic force as great as
America. But de Gaulle turned down the British application to join the
Community in 1962. Ted Heath, in the act for which he will be best
remembered, took Britain into the Community ten years later.

The Tories became the party of Europe, and Labour became vehemently opposed to membership of the European Community, although after three successive general election defeats Labour did an about-turn when they saw the possibility of promoting socialist objectives through the Community. Some Tories, notably Enoch Powell, were always deeply suspicious of and actively hostile towards the centralizing powers of Brussels. Sovereignty over many matters had been transferred from the Westminster Parliament, and the petty interference by Brussels into trivial but everyday concerns irritated many British people. Margaret Thatcher in her Bruges speech advocated a 'Europe des Patries' which recognized the individual characteristics of each country. Ironically, the spirit of de Gaulle lived on in the sentiments expressed by a British Conservative Prime Minister.

There is no doubt that Britain's future destiny lies in Europe. But the increasingly centralist thrust of the Community's organization today is unlikely to be the pattern for the future as the Community welcomes more and more new members. The role of the Conservative Party is to argue for a European Community in which individual nations cooperate on the basis of shared interests rather than submerge their identities under the weight of some imposed federalist goal.

'The dignity of the British name'

Many are the motives which have induced us to enter into the war. I have heard of wars of honour, and such, too, have been deemed wars of prudence and policy. On the present occasion, whatever can raise the feelings, or animate the exertions of a people, concurs to prompt us to the contest. The contempt which the French have shown for a neutrality, on our part most strictly observed; the violations of their solemn and plighted faith; their presumptuous attempts to interfere in the government of this country, and to arm our subjects against ourselves; to vilify a monarch, the object of our gratitude, reverence and affection; and to separate the Court from the people, by representing them as influenced by different motives, and acting from different interests. After provocation so wanton, so often repeated, and so highly aggravated, does not this become, on our part, a war of honour; a war necessary to assert the spirit of the nation, and the dignity of the British name? . . .

We are at war with those who would destroy the whole fabric of our Constitution. When I look at these things they afford me encouragement and consolation; and support me in discharging the painful task to which I am now called by my duty. The retrospect to that flourishing state in which we were placed previous to this war, ought to teach us to know the value of the present order of things; and to resist the malignant and envious attempts of those who would deprive us of that happiness which they despair themselves to attain.

WILLIAM PITT, March 1793

I return you many thanks for the honour you have done me: but Europe is not to be saved by any single man. England has saved herself by her exertions, and will, as I trust, save Europe by her example.

WILLIAM PITT

Reply to a toast from the Lord Mayor of London after Trafalgar, November 1805

'War never leaves, where it found a nation'

I am sure you cannot forget with how much uneasiness we heard in conversation the language of more than one gentleman at the opening of this contest, 'that he was willing to try the war for a year or two, and, if it did not succeed, then to vote for peace.' As if war was a matter of experiment! As if you could take it up or lay it down as an idle frolick! As if the dire goddess that presides over it, with her murderous spear in her hand, and her gorgon at her breast, was a coquette to be flirted with! We ought with reverence to approach that tremendous divinity, that loves courage, but commands counsel. War never leaves, where it found a nation. It is never to be entered into without a mature deliberation; not a deliberation lengthened out into a perplexing indecision, but a deliberation leading to a sure and fixed judgment. When so taken up, it is not to be abandoned without reason as valid, as fully and as extensively considered.

EDMUND BURKE
Letters on a Regicide Peace, 1795–7

'On grounds clearly British'

But wherefore this dread of a neutrality? If gentlemen look to the page of history, they will find that for centuries past, whenever there has been a war in Europe, we have almost always been belligerent. The fact is undoubtedly so; but I am not prepared to lay it down as a principle, that if, at the beginning of a war, we should happen to maintain a species of neutrality, it was an unnatural thing that we should do so. Gentlemen say, that we must be drawn into a war, sooner or later. Why, then, I answer, let it be later. I say, if we are to be drawn into a war, let us be drawn into it on grounds clearly British. I do not say – God forbid I should – that it is no part of the duty of Great Britain to protect what is termed the balance of power, and to aid the weak against the insults of the strong. I say, on the contrary, that to do so is her bounden duty; but I affirm also, that we must take care to do our duty to ourselves. The first condition of engaging in any war – the *sine qua non* of every such undertaking – is, that the war must be just; the second, that being just in itself, we can also with justice engage in it; and the third, that being just in its nature, and it being possible for us justly to embark in it, we can so interfere without detriment or prejudice to ourselves. I contend that he is a visionary politician who leaves this last condition out of the question; and I say further, that though the glorious abandonment of it may sound well in the generous speech of an irresponsible orator – with the safety of a nation upon his lips, and none of the responsibility upon his shoulders – it is matter deeply to be considered; and that the Minister who should lay it out of his view, in calling on the country to undertake a war, would well deserve that universal censure and reprobation with which the noble lord opposite has this night menaced me.

GEORGE CANNING

'England has outgrown the continent of Europe'

England has outgrown the continent of Europe. The abstention of England from any unnecessary interference in the affairs of Europe is the consequence, not of her decline of power, but of her increased strength. England is no longer a mere European power; she is the metropolis of a great maritime empire ... she is really more an Asiatic Power than a European ... Therefore, it is not because England does not recognise her duty to interfere in the affairs of the Continent of Europe that persons are justified in declaring that she has relinquished her imperial position, and has taken refuge in the *otium cum dignitate*, which agrees with the decline of life, of power, and of prosperity. On the contrary, she has a greater sphere of action than any European Power, and she has duties devolving upon her on a much larger scale ...

BENJAMIN DISRAELI, July 1866

Disraeli said this ten days after the Prussian victory over the Austrians at Sadowa. He was recognizing that Britain had a role and interests right around the world and what was needed was a blue-seas policy and not one just concerned with the internal waterways of Europe. This was always the tug at the heart of British foreign policy, and it was echoed in Churchill's 'Three Circles' speech in 1948.

'The working classes of England'

That Act [the 1867 Reform Act] was founded on a confidence that the great body of the people of this country were 'Conservative'. When I say 'Conservative', I use the word in its purest and loftiest sense. I mean that the people of England, and especially the working classes of England, are proud of belonging to a great country, and wish to maintain its greatness – that they are proud of belonging to an Imperial country, and are resolved to maintain, if they can, their empire – that they believe, on the whole, that the greatness and the empire of England are to be attributed to the ancient institutions of the land.

I say with confidence that the great body of the working class of England are English to the core. They repudiate cosmopolitan principles. They adhere to national principles. They are for maintaining the greatness of the kingdom and the empire, and they are proud of being subjects of our Sovereign and members of such an Empire.

BENJAMIN DISRAELI, 1872

'British interests'

As to the future, he had nothing to add to the statement which was made by a colleague of his very early last session – namely, that her Majesty's Government would pursue British interests, and British interests alone.

'We have been reproached with selfishness in this view; in fact the reproach of selfishness has been addressed to us from both sides. Now, there is nothing easier than to be brave with other people's blood, or generous with other people's money. If her Majesty's Government had in the course of the war to sacrifice all their own fortunes, and then to go into the field to be shot, you would fairly say that it was a brave and generous action for them to undertake such a war. But as long as these two duties fall, one of them exclusively, and the other mainly, upon other people, I dispute entirely the application of these two adjectives of "brave" and "generous" to the acts of a Government which plunges a nation into war.'

ROBERT CECIL, MARQUESS OF SALISBURY

England has neither lasting enemies, nor even a providential destiny, only interests.

ROBERT CECIL, MARQUESS OF SALISBURY

THE WHITE MAN'S BURDEN

Take up the White Man's burden –
    Send forth the best ye breed –
Go bind your sons to exile
    To serve your captives' need;
To wait in heavy harness,
    On fluttered folk and wild –
Your new-caught, sullen peoples,
    Half-devil and half-child.

Take up the White Man's Burden –
    In patience to abide,

To veil the threat of terror
  And check the show of pride;
By open speech and simple,
  An hundred times made plain,
To seek another's profit,
  And work another's gain . . .

Take up the White Man's burden –
  No tawdry rule of kings,
But toil of serf and sweeper –
  The tale of common things.
The ports ye shall not enter,
  The roads ye shall not tread,
Go make them with your living,
  And mark them with your dead . . .

Take up the White Man's burden –
  Have done with childish days –
The lightly proffered laurel,
  The easy, ungrudged praise.
Comes now, to search your manhood
  Through all the thankless years,
Cold, edged with dear-bought wisdom,
  The judgment of your peers!
    RUDYARD KIPLING, 1899

'I believe in a British Empire'

My proposition is that a true Zollverein for the Empire, that a free trade established throughout the Empire, although it would involve the imposition of duties against foreign countries, and would in that respect be a derogation from the high principles of free trade, and from the practice of the United Kingdom up to the present time, would still be a proper subject for discussion and might possibly lead to a satisfactory arrangement if the colonies on their part were willing to consider it . . .

    I say it is the business of British statesmen to do everything they can, even at some present sacrifice, to keep the trade of the colonies with Great Britain, to increase that trade, to promote it, even if in doing so we lessen somewhat our trade with our foreign competitors . . . the

germs of a federal union that will make the British Empire powerful ...
the germs of that union are in the soil; but it is a tender and delicate
plant and requires careful handling.

You want an Empire. Do you think it is better to cultivate the trade
with your own people or to let that go in order that you may keep the
trade of those who ... are your competitors.

I believe in a British Empire ... and I do not believe in a Little
England which shall be separated from all those to whom it would in
the natural course look for support and affection.

JOSEPH CHAMBERLAIN
Speech in Birmingham, 1903

Joseph Chamberlain (1836–1914) divided and broke the Liberal Party in 1886
over home rule for Ireland. He then headed the Liberal–Unionists, joined
Salisbury's government as Colonial Secretary in the 1890s, and in 1903 divided
and broke the Tory Party over Imperial Preference. He was determined to
strengthen the British Empire by turning it into a closed trading block. He was
careful to use the language of free trade but his proposals were highly protectionist
and had the unpopular consequence of increasing the cost of food. He was seeking
to protect not the landed interests but the commercial and manufacturing interests
from which he himself sprang. The Conservative Party was divided; it paid the
heavy price of a Liberal landslide victory in 1906 and had a very troubled time up
to 1914. However, Chamberlain's policies remained Tory policy up to the Second
World War. Later the Common Market was created as another highly protected
trading area and for a time the Tories supported, as an alternative, the European
Free Trade Area, but this never became a significant trading block. The principal
advantage for Britain in joining the Community in 1973 was that its economic and
commercial interests were best served by being a member of a large trading block.
The development of a single market where goods and services could be traded
freely was also very much in line with the Conservatives' traditional preference for
free trade.

'Let India be my judge'

A hundred times in India have I said to myself, 'Oh, to every Englishman in this country, as he ends his work, might be truthfully applied
the phrase, "thou hast loved righteousness and hated iniquity" ...'
Perhaps there are a few of us who make anything but a poor approximation to that ideal. But let it be our ideal all the same. To fight for the
right, to abhor the imperfect, the unjust, or the mean, to swerve neither
to the right-hand or to the left, to care nothing for flattery or applause
or odium or abuse – it is so easy to have any of them in India – never to
let your enthusiasm be soured or your courage grow dim, but to

remember that the Almighty has placed your hand on the greatest of his ploughs, in whose furrow the nations of the future are germinating and taking shape, to drive the blade a little forward in your time and to feel that somewhere among those millions you have left a little justice, or happiness or prosperity, a sense of manliness or moral dignity, a spring of patriotism, a dawn of intellectual enlightenment, or a stirring of duty where it did not exist before – that is enough, that is the Englishman's justification in India. It is good enough for his watchword while he is here, for his epitaph when he is gone. I have worked for no other aim. Let India by my judge.

LORD CURZON

Bombay, 1906

Curzon was one of the great Viceroys of India, serving from 1898 to 1906. Taken from his farewell speech in Bombay, this extract sets out the noble mission that he fulfilled. He loved India and, in particular, helped to preserve the great ancient buildings and monuments, including the Taj Mahal.

'The ripple of a restless tide'

The British Empire has spread with the ripple of a restless tide over tracts and islands and continents. Pioneers, adventurers, preachers, traders: all in their day, and with their several motives, have been its architects. We see in its history the human hand that hath built it, the human lives that have been laid down for it; but, as we study its destiny, we are bound to think of it less as a human achievement than as an instrument of Divine Providence for the promotion of the progress of mankind. Through all changes of political relations and vicissitudes of trade, it has dug channels, innumerable channels, wide and deep, for the spread of what is noblest in human achievement to the remotest corners of the earth, and one of those greatest gifts of civilisation is freedom, which we seek not only to enjoy ourselves but to share increasingly with others.

STANLEY BALDWIN, 1929

THE WORLD STATE

Oh, how I love Humanity,
    With love so pure and pringlish,
And how I hate the horrid French,
    Who never will be English!

The International Idea,
  The largest and the clearest,
Is welding all the nations now,
  Except the one that's nearest.

This compromise has long been known,
  This scheme of partial pardons,
In ethical societies
  And small suburban gardens –

The villas and the chapels where
  I learned with little labour
The way to love my fellow-man
  and hate my next-door neighbour.
  G. K. CHESTERTON

'Three great circles'

As I look out upon the future of our country in the changing scene of human destiny I feel the existence of three great circles among the free nations and democracies. I almost wish I had a blackboard. I would make a picture for you. I don't suppose it would get hung in the Royal Academy, but it would illustrate the point I am anxious for you to hold in your minds. The first circle for us is naturally the British Commonwealth and Empire, with all that that comprises. Then there is also the English-speaking world in which we, Canada, and the other British Dominions play so important a part. And finally there is United Europe. These three majestic circles are co-existent and if they are linked together there is no force or combination which could overthrow them or ever challenge them. Now if you think of the three inter-linked circles you will see that we are the only country which has a great part in every one of them. We stand, in fact, at the very point of junction, and here in this Island at the centre of the seaways and perhaps of the airways also we have the opportunity of joining them all together.

If we rise to the occasion in the years that are to come it may be found that once again we hold the key to opening a safe and happy future to humanity, and will gain for ourselves gratitude and fame.
  WINSTON CHURCHILL
  Conservative Party Conference, 1948

'We, at least, have work to do'

I cannot promise you a popular colonial policy. There will be toil and sweat and tears; but I hope not blood and I hope not bitterness – although in the turmoil that is Africa today, of even that one cannot be certain. But this is the road we must walk and we can walk no other.

The Socialists can scheme their schemes and the Liberals can dream their dreams, but we, at least, have work to do. I make you one pledge only; nothing more than this and nothing less – that we will at all times, to all peoples, in all these territories, carry out our duty faithfully, steadfastly and without fear.

IAIN MACLEOD
Conservative Party Conference, 1960

'The wind of change is blowing through the continent'

The most striking of all the impressions I have formed since I left London a month ago is of the strength of this African national consciousness. In different places it may take different forms, but it is happening everywhere. The wind of change is blowing through the continent. Whether we like it or not, this growth of national consciousness is a political fact. We must all accept it as a fact. Our national policies must take account of it. Of course, you understand this as well as anyone. You are sprung from Europe, the home of nationalism. And here in Africa you have yourselves created a full nation – a new nation. Indeed, in the history of our times yours will be recorded as the first of the African nationalisms . . .

As a fellow member of the Commonwealth, it is our earnest desire to give South Africa our support and encouragement, but I hope you won't mind my saying frankly that there are some aspects of your policies which make it impossible for us to do this without being false to our own deep convictions about the political destinies of free men, to which in our own territories we are trying to give effect.

I think we ought as friends to face together – without seeking to apportion credit or blame – the fact that in the world of today this difference of outlook lies between us . . .

HAROLD MACMILLAN
South Africa, 1960
This speech was made to the two Houses of the South African Parliament in Cape

Town. This one phrase rang round the world; it had a greater effect in reinforcing nationalist and independence movements in the rest of Africa than in South Africa itself.

AN ODE FOR TRAFALGAR DAY

As I was crossing Trafalgar Square
whose but the Admiral's shadow hand
should tap my shoulder. At my ear:
'You Sir, stay-at-home citizen
poet, here's more use for your pen
than picking scabs. Tell them in England
this: when first I stuck my head in the air,

'winched from a cockpit's tar and blood
to my crow's nest over London, I
looked down on a singular crowd
moving with the confident swell
of the sea. As it rose and fell
every pulse in the estuary
carried them quayward, carried them seaward.

'Box-wallah, missionary, clerk,
lancer, planter, I saw them all
linked like the waves on the waves embark.
Their eyes looked out – as yours look in –
to harbour names on the cabin-
trunks carrying topees to Bengal,
maxims or gospels to lighten a dark

'continent. Blatant as the flag
they went out under were the bright
abstractions nailed to every mast.
Sharpshooters since have riddled most
and buried an empire in their rags –
scrivener, do you dare to write
a little 'e' in the epilogue

'to an empire that spread its wings
wider than Rome? They are folded,
you say, with the maps and flags; awnings

and verandahs overrun
by impis of the ant; sun-
downers sunk, and the planter's blood
turned tea or siphoned into rubber saplings.

'My one eye reports that their roads
remain, their laws, their language
seeding all winds. They were no gods
from harnessed clouds, as the islanders
thought them, nor were they monsters
but men, as you stooped over your page
and you and you and these wind-driven crowds

'are and are not. For you have lost
their rhythm, the pulse of the sea
in their salt blood. Your heart has missed
the beat of centuries, its channels
silted to their source. the muscles
of the will stricken by distrophy
dishonour those that bareback rode the crest

'of untamed seas. Acknowledge
their energy. If you condemn
their violence in a violent age
speak of their courage. Mock their pride
when, having built as well, in as wide
a compass, you have none. Tell them
in England this.'
               And a pigeon sealed the page.
   JON STALLWORTHY

'It was our own private hell"

Of course nothing halted, because nothing could halt, the continued
decline in the relative size of Britain in the industrial and commercial
world; but the longer it continued, the more firmly the British
embraced the myth of the world's workshop as a lost Golden Age, and
the more they flagellated themselves for the supposed latter-day sins
which had earned them expulsion from that economic Garden of Eden.
The Americans did not do this; the Dutch and Belgians did not do this;

the Germans did not do this; but the British did. It was our own private
hell, as the myth of empire was our own private heaven, and under
both hallucinations together two generations have laboured.

ENOCH POWELL

Dublin, 1964

Enoch Powell had a personal fascination for India, having served there. He wanted
to show up two myths, namely that the Victorians' great power rested on the Pax
Britannica and that much of the twentieth century was a story of decline from
imperial power and industrial dominance. Powell's clear message was to disregard
the myths and get on with the business of creating a confident and successful
economy and nation. As shadow defence spokesman in 1967 he received a
standing ovation for arguing that Britain should abandon its military role east of
Suez, on the grounds that the powers in Asia would have to find their own
equilibrium, and that Britain should look to its own defences in Europe.

'Our rightful place in a truly United Europe'

When we came to the end of the negotiations in 1963, after the Veto
had been imposed, the negotiator on behalf of India said: 'When you
left India some people wept. And when you leave Europe tonight some
will weep. And there is no other people in the world of whom these
things can be said.' That was a tribute from an Indian to the British.
But tonight when this House endorses this Motion many millions of
people right across the world will rejoice that we have our rightful
place in a truly United Europe.

EDWARD HEATH

House of Commons, 28 October 1971

'The centre of a European conglomerate'

My first guiding principle is this: willing and active cooperation
between independent sovereign states is the best way to build a successful European Community.

To try to suppress nationhood and concentrate power at the centre
of a European conglomerate would be highly damaging and would
jeopardize the objectives we seek to achieve.

Europe will be stronger precisely because it has France as France,
Spain as Spain, Britain as Britain, each with its own customs, traditions
and identity. It would be folly to try to fit them into some sort of
identikit European personality.

Some of the Founding Fathers of the Community thought that the United States of America might be its model, but the whole history of America is quite different from Europe. People went there to get away from the intolerance and constraints of life in Europe. They sought liberty and opportunity and their strong sense of purpose has, over two centuries, helped to create a new unity and pride in being American, just as our pride lies in being British or Belgian or Dutch or German.

I am the first to say that on many great issues the countries of Europe should try to speak with a single voice. I want to see us work more closely on the things we can do better together than alone. Europe is stronger when we do so, whether it be in trade, in defence or in our relations with the rest of the world, but working more closely together does not require power to be centralised in Brussels or decisions to be taken by an appointed bureaucracy. Indeed, it is ironic that just when those countries such as the Soviet Union which have tried to run everything from the centre are learning that success depends on dispersing power and decisions away from the centre, there are some in the Community who seem to want to move in the opposite direction.

We have not successfully rolled back the frontiers of the state in Britain only to see them reimposed at a European level with a European super-state exercising a new dominance from Brussels.

Certainly, we want to see Europe more united and with a greater sense of common purpose, but it must be in a way which preserves the different traditions, parliamentary powers and sense of national pride in one's own country, for these have been the source of Europe's vitality through the centuries.

MARGARET THATCHER
Speech to College of Europe, Bruges, September 1988

'Serious risks for the future of our nation'

The second thing that happened was, I fear, even more disturbing. Reporting to this House, my right hon. Friend almost casually remarked that she did not think that many people would want to use the hard ecu anyway – even as a common currency, let alone as a single one. It was remarkable – indeed, it was tragic – to hear my right hon. Friend dismissing, with such personalised incredulity, the very idea that the hard ecu proposal might find growing favour among the peoples of Europe, just as it was extraordinary to hear her assert that the whole

idea of EMU might be open for consideration only by future generations. Those future generations are with us today.

How on earth are the Chancellor and the Governor of the Bank of
England, commending the hard ecu as they strive to, to be taken as
serious participants in the debate against that kind of background
noise? I believe that both the Chancellor and the Governor are
cricketing enthusiasts, so I hope that there is no monopoly of cricketing
metaphors. It is rather like sending your opening batsmen to the crease
only for them to find, the moment the first balls are bowled, that their
bats have been broken before the game by the team captain . . .

The tragedy is – and it is for me personally, for my party, for our
whole people and for my right hon. Friend herself, a very real tragedy –
that the Prime Minister's perceived attitude towards Europe is running
increasingly serious risks for the future of our nation. It risks mini-
mising our influence and maximising our chances of being once again
shut out. We have paid heavily in the past for late starts and squan-
dered opportunities in Europe. We dare not let that happens again. If
we detach ourselves completely, as a party or a nation, from the middle
ground of Europe, the effects will be incalculable and very hard ever to
correct . . .

The conflict of loyalty, of loyalty to my right hon. Friend the Prime
Minister – and, after all, in two decades together that instinct of loyalty
is still very real – and of loyalty to what I perceive to be the true
interests of the nation, has become all too great. I no longer believe it
possible to resolve that conflict from within this Government. That is
why I have resigned. In doing so, I have done what I believe to be right
for my party and my country. The time has come for others to consider
their own response to the tragic conflict of loyalties with which I have
myself wrestled for perhaps too long.

GEOFFREY HOWE

House of Commons, November 1990

In this resignation speech Geoffrey Howe made clear that he and the Prime
Minister had fundamentally different views about the future of the European
Community. Many wondered why he had not resigned earlier, but he chose to
strike at a moment of particular vulnerability for the PM. The excuse was
Margaret Thatcher's attitude towards the British proposal for a hard ecu but the
real reason was his continuing and long-held opposition to her views and her style
of expressing them. A few scores had to be settled.

The central issue was, and it remains, what sort of Europe the party wants – a
growingly centralized community, federal in all but name, or a community of

nation states, cooperating but not compelled. The Maastricht negotiations in December 1991 did not resolve this, but the mood in the country and party has shifted to a broader and looser Europe.

'A problem of far greater magnitude'

One of the better examples of alternative comedy with which politics has lately provided us came last Saturday, in Sir Geoffrey Howe's response to advice on the national question given to voters by his former colleague Mr Nicholas Ridley. Mr Ridley, like Mr Enoch Powell, articulates the basic instincts of ordinary, unpolitical people, and in our democracy is, therefore, regarded as a nutter. Sir Geoffrey articulates the refined prejudices of a very small group of Tory grandees, and in our democracy is, therefore, regarded as a key figure in political debate. Mr Ridley advised those faced with a federalist Tory candidate at the general election to vote if possible, for someone against European union. Sir Geoffrey, in that impeccable *de haut en bas* tone that former foreign secretaries can get away with using to a chap who only ever roughed it as trade secretary, said Mr Ridley was mistaken: popular feeling was very much in favour of involvement in Europe.

To be charitable to Sir Geoffrey, the Surrey seat for which he sits is hardly typical. It is just possible that in the saloon bar of the Jolly Stockbrokers at Oxted the talk is of little other than the excitement the regulars feel at the 'deal' about to be done at Maastricht. Mr Ridley would claim this does not reflect the view of the nation. There is no way of telling who is right, because the signals from the public are not as clear as they are, say, on the health service, or as they were on the poll tax . . .

Politicians, civil servants, columnists, lobbyists and a few other psychiatric cases are obsessively fired up about Europe. Despite being bombarded with arguments about it in the media, and being told their liberties are under threat, the voters so far seem not to give a damn, and are not writing in their millions to MPs and newspapers about it. The parallels with the 1930s are obvious. Perhaps when Mr Major returns from Maastricht waving his piece of paper, like his hero Neville Chamberlain, the public will be motivated to press for political re-armanent. But by then it will be too late . . .

The blame for the current confusion of direction can be laid at two doors. First, as in all administrations top-heavy with inexperienced ministers, the civil service has too much influence. Second, the poll tax has been a great, but misleading, lesson to the Government about how to treat public opinion. The theory goes that if you listen to the people in the first place (as a substitute for offering them any vision) you don't have to spend years undoing the damage. That depends, though, on reading opinion properly in the first place, and not everything is as clear an issue as the poll tax.

Europe, though, seems to be the one issue on which the Government is reluctant to pursue this theory, no doubt because it would mean being different from the rest of the EEC. More to the point, though, a government that follows opinion cannot have a policy on Europe because the people have yet to express their opinion. This creates a further problem. Poll taxes and their like can, if things go wrong, be undone relatively simply, as the Government has found. Undoing a commitment to European Union is likely to prove a problem of far greater magnitude. Spouting 'trust the people' is all very well, but it should be clear to politicians of all parties that the public are so uninterested in most political questions that they are liable to regard this trust as something of an imposition. It would be far better to look to the principles that delivered the last three election victories, and trust them instead.

SIMON HEFFER

Spectator, November 1991

In this perceptive article, written before the summit of the European Community at Maastricht in December 1991, Simon Heffer, a leading Euro-sceptic, posed the dilemma for the Conservative Party. It became a major issue after the Danes rejected the treaty in a referendum. This reawakened the debate in the party about Britain's place in Europe. The debate continues.

16

'Gentleman, I am a Party Man'

This chapter is about the Tory Party as an organization. It does not attempt to be a history of the party, for there are several already, but it contains some reflections upon the organized force of the party. It starts with Burke's famous definition of the role of an MP – 'A representative and not a delegate'. This is a crucial statement that distinguishes the Tory MP from the Labour MP, giving him an independence and strength which is almost unique in the constitutional arrangements of the country. The Tory MP is essentially a territorial representative who draws his strength, and indeed his continuing service as an MP, from his local party and local electorate. He is not an apparatchik imposed by the central party machine.

The first practical advice on electioneering was given by Peel, who urged the Conservative Party to get down to the practical business of registering the voters. Later, Randolph Churchill, who had tried to take over the newly created central organization of the party, urged Conservatives to embrace Tory democracy under the slogan, 'Trust the people'. Throughout its history the Tory Party has been better organized than its opponents and Meredith reflected upon the fact that other parties have always stood in awe of the Tory Party's organization – perhaps too much in awe.

But the enduring success of the Tory Party is that it has succeeded in remaining one party. Disraeli's advice of 'damn your principles – stick to your party' has seen the Conservative Party through some of its darkest days. It has allowed the party to survive when other parties under great pressure have sundered. What is undeniable is that the politics of the last 200 years can really only be understood through the existence of strong parties. That is the way that power is gained, that *policies are determined and programmes implemented. In the 1980s the Social Democrats tried to break the mould of British politics by splitting away from the Labour Party. They failed for many reasons, some to do with policies and some to do with personalities. But the essential weakness was revealed by Roy Jenkins in his memoirs, when he admitted that he was more interested in creating a movement than a party. This patrician concept, which paradoxically also has a strong appeal to some demagogues, fails to recognize the reality of Britain's political make-up. It is rightly rejected by serious politicians who are interested in acquiring and holding power over a long period.*

'Not *his industry only, but his judgment*'

Certainly, gentlemen, it ought to be the happiness and glory of a representative to live in the strictest union, the closest correspondence, and the most unreserved communication with his constituents. Their wishes ought to have great weight with him; their opinions high respect; their business unremitted attention. It is his duty to sacrifice his repose, his pleasure, his satisfactions, to theirs – and above all, ever, and in all cases, to prefer their interest to his own.

But his unbiased opinion, his mature judgment, his enlightened conscience, he ought not to sacrifice to you, to any man, or to any set of men living. These he does not derive from your pleasure – no, nor from the law and the Constitution. They are a trust from Providence, for the abuse of which he is deeply answerable. Your representative owes you, not his industry only, but his judgment; and he betrays, instead of serving you, if he sacrifices it to your opinion.

My worthy colleague says, his will ought to be subservient to yours, If that be all, the thing is innocent. If government were a matter of will upon any side, yours, without question, ought to be superior. But government and legislation are matters of reason and judgment, and not of inclination; and what sort of reason is that in which the determination precedes the discussion, in which one set of men deliberate and another decide, and where those who form the conclusion are perhaps three hundred miles distant from those who hear the arguments?

To deliver an opinion is the right of all men; that of constituents is a weighty and respectable opinion, which a representative ... ought always most seriously to consider. But *authoritative* instructions, *mandates* issued, which the member is bound blindly and implicitly to obey, to vote, and to argue for, though contrary to the clearest convictions of his judgment and conscience – these are things utterly unknown to the laws of this land, and which arise from a fundamental mistake of the whole order and tenor of our constitution.

Parliament is not a *congress* of ambassadors from different and hostile interests, which interests each must maintain, as an agent and advocate, against other agents and advocates; but Parliament is a *deliberative* assembly of *one* nation, with *one* interest, that of the whole – where not local purposes, not local prejudices, ought to guide, but the general good, resulting from the general reason of the whole.

You choose a member, indeed; but when you have chosen him, he is not a member of Bristol, but he is a member of *Parliament*.

EDMUND BURKE

'Letter to John Farr and John Harris Esquires,' 1774

In 1774 some of the merchants of Bristol, which had become the second port in the country, wanted Edmund Burke to become their MP in order to defend their interests at Westminster. In his famous letter to two citizens of Bristol, Burke set out the classic definition of the relationship between an MP and his constituents. This is a much-quoted passage, especially by MPs who intend to disregard their constituents' views.

Burke represented Bristol for six years, parting company when his constituents disagreed with his liberal views on the penal laws against Catholics and his refusal to maintain trade restrictions against Ireland. Burke found the pocket borough of Malton much easier.

'The advice which I give you'

It may be disagreeable, and, indeed, inconvenient, to attend to the registration of voters which annually takes place throughout the country. All this may be revolting; but you may depend upon it that it is better you should take that trouble than you should allow the Constitution to become the victim of false friends, or that you should be trampled under the hoofs of a ruthless democracy. The advice which has been given by some persons was, 'Agitate, agitate, agitate!' The advice which I give you is this – 'Register, register, register!'

ROBERT PEEL

Speech to Conservative Party agents, 1837

In 1830 Wellington and Peel had decided to oppose the reform of the rotten boroughs on the grounds that it would open the way to a whole army of radicals. The Great Reform Bill was passed in 1832 and Peel set about persuading the Conservative Party to accept the reality of reform and to turn it to its own advantage. In 1834 in the Tamworth Manifesto he asserted that 'the Reform Bill is a final and irrevocable settlement of a great Constitutional question.' In this speech he advised the party agents of the many Conservative associations which had been set up to get down to the practical work of registering the voters. This had to be done each year at the cost of one shilling per voter. So the job of the local party workers was then as it is today, to register and to canvass.

'Let 'em go'

The Party! What is the meaning of a Party if they don't follow their leaders? Damn 'em; let 'em go.

ARTHUR WELLESLEY, DUKE OF WELLINGTON

'He is just fit now, after being twice discarded by the people, to become a Conservative'

He is a living lie; and the British Empire is degraded by tolerating a miscreant of his abominable description. The language is harsh, I must confess; but it is no more than deserved, and if I should apologize for using it, it is because I can find no harsher epithets in the English language by which to convey the utter abhorrence which I entertain for such a reptile. He is just fit now, after being twice discarded by the people, to become a Conservative. He possesses all the necessary requisites of perfidy, selfishness, depravity, want of principle, etc., which would qualify him for the change. His name shows that he is of Jewish origin. I do not use it as a term of reproach; there are many most respectable Jews. But there are, as in every other people, some of the lowest and most disgusting grade of moral turpitude; and of those I look upon Mr Disraeli as the worst. He has just the qualities of the impenitent thief on the Cross, and I verily believe, if Mr Disraeli's family herald were to be examined and his genealogy traced, the same personage would be discovered to be the heir at law of the exalted individual to whom I allude. I forgive Mr Disraeli now, and as the lineal descendant of the blasphemous robber, who ended his career besides the Founder of the Christian Faith, I leave the gentleman to the enjoyment of his infamous distinction and family honours.

DANIEL O'CONNELL, 1835

In the general election in 1835 Disraeli, standing in Taunton, accused O'Connell of being 'an incendiary and a traitor'. He responded with this vitriolic racist abuse which today would certainly have landed him in the courts.

I deduce from your communication that you do not consider yourself responsible for any insults offered by your father, but only bound to resent the insults that he may receive. Now, Sir, it is my hope that I *have* insulted him; assuredly it was my intention to do so. I wished to express the utter scorn in which I hold his character, and the disgust

with which his conduct inspires me. If I failed in conveying this
expression of my feelings to him, let me more successfully express them
now to you. I shall take every opportunity of holding your father's
name up to public contempt. And I fervently pray that you, or some of
his blood, may attempt to avenge the unextinguishable hatred with
which I shall pursue his existence.

BENJAMIN DISRAELI, 1835

Disraeli responded to O'Connell by challenging his son to a duel, and on his refusal
sent off this letter.

'A sound Conservative government'

'Ah! Tadpole,' said Mr Taper, getting a little maudlin; 'I often think, if
the time should ever come, when you and I should be joint Secretaries
of the Treasury.'

'We shall see, we shall see. All we have to do is to get into Parliament, work well together, and keep other men down.'

'We will do our best,' said Taper. 'A dissolution you hold
inevitable?'

'How are you and I to get into Parliament if there be not one? We
must make it inevitable. I tell you what, Taper, the lists must prove a
dissolution inevitable. You understand me? If the present Parliament
goes on, where shall we be? We shall have new men cropping up every
session.'

'True, terribly true,' said Mr Taper. 'That we should ever live to see a
Tory government again! We have reason to be very thankful.'

'Hush!' said Mr Tadpole. 'The time has gone by for Tory governments; what the country requires is a sound Conservative government.'

'A sound Conservative government,' said Mr Taper, musingly. 'I
understand: Tory men and Whig measures.'

BENJAMIN DISRAELI

Coningsby, 1844

In this, his finest political novel Disraeli holds up to ridicule these two characters,
whose only interest in politics is getting any job in any government.

'Shipwrecked, lost and gone to pieces'

Then there is my Lord Boodle, of considerable reputation with his
party, who has known what office is and who tells Sir Leicester

Dedlock with much gravity, after dinner, that he really does not see to what the present age is tending. A debate is not what a debate used to be; the House is not what the House used to be; even a Cabinet is not what it formerly was. He perceives with astonishment, that supposing the present Government to be overthrown, the limited choice of the Crown, in the formation of a new Ministry, would lie between Lord Coodle and Sir Thomas Doodle – supposing it to be impossible for the Duke of Foodle to act with Goodle, which may be assumed to be the case in consequence of the breach arising out of that affair with Hoodle. Then, giving the Home Department and the leadership of the House of Commons to Joodle, the Exchequer to Koodle, the colonies to Loodle, and the Foreign Office to Moodle, what are you to do with Noodle? You can't offer him the Presidency of the Council; that is reserved for Poodle. You can't put him in the Woods and Forests; that is hardly good enough for Quoodle. What follows? That the country is shipwrecked, lost, and gone to pieces (as is made manifest to the patriotism of Sir Leicester Dedlock), because you can't provide, for Noodle!

On the other hand, the Right Honourable William Buffy, MP, contends across the table with some one else, that the shipwreck of the country about which there is no doubt; it is only the manner of it that is in question – is attributable to Cuffy. If you had done with Cuffy what you ought to have done when he first came into Parliament, and had prevented him from going over to Duffy, you would have got him into alliance with Fuffy, you would have had with you the weight attaching as a smart debater to Guffy, you would have brought to bear upon the elections the wealth of Huffy, you would have got in for three counties Juffy, Kuffy, and Luffy; and you would have strengthened your administration by the official knowledge and the business habits of Muffy. All this, instead of being, as you now are, dependent on the mere caprice of Puffy!

As to this point, and as to some minor topics, there are differences of opinion; but it is perfectly clear to the brilliant and distinguished circle, all round, that nobody is in question but Boodle and his retinue, and Buffy and *his* retinue. These are the great actors for whom the stage is reserved. A People there are, no doubt – a certain large number of supernumeraries, who are to be occasionally addressed, and relied upon for shouts and choruses, as on the theatrical stage; but Boodle and Buffy, their followers and families, their heirs, executors, administrators, and assigns, are the born first-actors, managers, and leaders, and no others can appear upon the scene for ever and ever.

CHARLES DICKENS

Bleak House, 1852

Over dinner at Sir Leicester Dedlock's great house, Chesney Wold in Lincolnshire, the eternal verities of politics are discussed.

'Gentleman, I am a party man'

There is another powerful and most beneficial influence which is also exercised by the Crown. Gentlemen, I am a party man. I believe that, without party, Parliamentary government is impossible. I look upon Parliamentary government as the noblest government in the world, and certainly the one most suited to England. But without the discipline of political connection, animated by the principle of private honour, I feel certain that a popular Assembly would sink before the power or the corruption of a minister. Yet, gentlemen, I am not blind to the faults of party government. It has one great defect. Party has a tendency to warp the intelligence, and there is no minister, however resolved he may be in treating a great public question, who does not find some difficulty in emancipating himself from the traditionary prejudice on which he had long acted. It is, therefore, a great merit in our Constitution that before a minister introduces a measure to Parliament, he must submit it to an intelligence superior to all party, and entirely free from influences of that character.

BENJAMIN DISRAELI

'The Stupid Party'

The Stupid Party.

J. S. MILL

I said a lot of stupid things when I was in the Conservative Party and I left them because I did not want to go on saying stupid things.

WINSTON CHURCHILL

Churchill left the Tory Party in 1903; he gave this answer to a heckler in the 1906 election when challenged over his apostasy.

'There is more danger in conferring political power on the middle classes'

Among the events of last week one of the most interesting was the Queen's visit to Birmingham, where she was received by the whole of that enormous population with an enthusiasm which is said to have exceeded all that was ever displayed in her former receptions at Manchester or elsewhere. It is impossible not to regard such manifestations as both significant and important. They evince a disposition in those masses of the population in which, if anywhere, the seeds of Radicalism are supposed to lurk, most favourable to the Conservative cause, by which I mean not to this or that party, but to the Monarchy and the Constitution . . . This great fact lends some force to the notion entertained by many political thinkers, that there is more danger in conferring political power on the middle classes than in extending it far beneath them, and in point of fact that there is so little to be apprehended from the extension of the suffrage, that universal suffrage itself would be innocuous.

CHARLES GREVILLE

Memoirs, describing 1858

Charles Greville was Clerk to the Council for nearly forty years, from 1821 to 1859. This position gave him a ringside seat for nearly all the major political events of his time. Here he recognizes that the working people of England were instinctively conservative, respectful of authority and fiercely loyal to the Crown. In the twentieth century the royal family has always received its warmest welcome in the East End of London.

'All classes, from the highest to the most homely'

Now, my lords and gentlemen, I have always considered that the Tory party was the national party of England. It is not formed of a combination of oligarchs and philosophers who practise on the sectarian prejudices of a portion of the people. It is formed of all classes, from the highest to the most homely, and it upholds a series of institutions that are in theory, and ought to be in practice, an embodiment of the national requirements and the security of the national rights. Whenever the Tory party degenerates into an oligarchy, it becomes unpopular; whenever the national institutions do not fulfil their original intention, the Tory party becomes odious; but when the people are led by their natural leaders, and when, by their united influence, the national institutions fulfil their original intention, the Tory party is triumphant, and then, under Providence, will secure the prosperity and the power of the country.

BENJAMIN DISRAELI, Edinburgh, 1867

Gentlemen, the Tory party, unless it is a national party, is nothing. It is not a confederacy of nobles, it is not a democratic multitude; it is a party formed from all the numerous classes in the realm – classes alike and equal before the law, but whose different conditions and different aims give vigour and variety to our national life.

BENJAMIN DISRAELI
Speech at the Crystal Palace, 1872
In 1867 Disraeli had carried through the Reform Act, which many had considered was a betrayal of basic Conservative interests. Ever resourceful, Disraeli claimed that only this truly national party could benefit from the opportunities he had thus created.

'The Tory's cry'

Liberalism gave the heading cry, devoid of which parties are dogs without a scent, orators mere pump-handles. The Tory's cry was but a whistle to his pack, the Radical howled to the moon like any chained hound. And no wonder, for these parties had no established current, they were as hard-bound waters; the Radical being diked and damned most soundly, the Tory resembling a placid lake of the plains, fed by springs and no confluents.

Tories dread the restlessness of Radicals, and Radicals are in awe of the organization of Tories.

GEORGE MEREDITH
Beauchamp's Career, 1876

'An essentially popular flavour'

You tell me that you find the designation 'Tory' a great difficulty to you. I cannot see any good reason for this. After all, since the Revolution the designation 'Tory' has always possessed an essentially popular flavour, in contradistinction to the designation 'Whig'. It has not only a popular but a grand historical origin; it denotes great historical struggles, in many of which the Tory party have been found on the popular side. Lord Beaconsfield – who, if he was anything, was a man of the people and understood the popular significance of names and words – invariably made use of the word 'Tory' to characterise his party; and whatever the Tory party may be deemed to be at particular moments, I have always held, from the commencement of my political life, that, rightly understood and explained, it ought to be, and was intended to be, the party of broad ideas and a truly liberal policy.

LORD RANDOLPH CHURCHILL, 1892

'Trust the people'

'Trust the people' – I have long tried to make that my motto; but I know, and will not conceal, that there are still a few in our party who have that lesson yet to learn and have yet to understand that the Tory party of to-day is no longer identified with that small and narrow class which is connected with the ownership of land; but that its great strength can be found, and must be developed, in our large towns as well as in our country districts. Yes, trust the people. You, who are ambitious, and rightly ambitious, of being the guardians of the British Constitution, trust the people, and they will trust you – and they will follow you and join you in the defence of that Constitution against any and every foe. I have no fear of democracy ... Modern checks and securities are not worth a brass farthing. Give me a fair arrangement of the constituencies, and one part of England will correct and balance the other.

LORD RANDOLPH CHURCHILL

Letter to Member of Parliament Unseated at General Election

Dear Mr Posby-Burford,

Though I am myself an ardent Tory, I cannot but rejoice in the crushing defeat you have just suffered in West Odgetown. There are moments when political conviction is overborne by personal sentiment; and this is one of them. Your loss of the seat that you held is the more striking by reason of the splendid manner in which the northern and eastern divisions of Odgetown have been wrested from the Liberal Party. The great bulk of the newspaper-reading public will be puzzled by your extinction in the midst of our party's triumph. But then, the great mass of the newspaper-reading public has not met you. I have. You will probably not remember me. You are the sort of man who would not remember anybody who might not be of some definite use to him. Such, at least, was one of the impressions you made on me when I met you last summer at a dinner given by our friends the Pelhams. Among the other things in you that struck me were the blatant pomposity of your manner, your appalling flow of cheap platitudes, and your hoggish lack of ideas. It is such men as you that lower the tone of public life. And I am sure that in writing to you thus I am but expressing what is felt, without distinction of party, by all who sat with you in the late Parliament.

The one person in whose behalf I regret your withdrawal into private life is your wife, whom I had the pleasure of taking in to the aforesaid dinner. It was evident to me that she was a woman whose spirit was well-nigh broken by her conjunction with you. Such remnants of cheerfulness as were in her I attributed to the Parliamentary duties which kept you out of her sight for so very many hours daily. I do not like to think of the fate to which the free and independent electors of West Odgetown have just condemned her. Only, remember this: chattel of yours though she is, and timid and humble, she despises you in her heart.

I am, dear Mr Pobsby-Burford,
Yours very truly,

Harold Thistlake

MAX BEERBOHM, 1910
This was written in the wake of the general election which saw a lot of Tory gains, but this was one Max Beerbohm was glad to see go the other way.

'The rank and file'

I have had forty years experience of politics, most of it in the rank and file. There is nothing I ask you to do that I have not done myself. I have marked off polling cards. I have addressed envelopes (*laughter*), and I have shepherded the last batch of voters from the public house (*cheers, and laughter*). I gained my experience in an old borough and there is nothing you can teach me . . .

I am proud to lead such a party with such a tradition. I sprang from the rank and file and they have supported me in good times and bad. They stood by me after the general election of 1923, when many stout hearts wavered. They have stood by me since . . . They have trusted me. (*Prolonged cheers.*)

STANLEY BALDWIN

Conservative Party Conference, 1928

Baldwin was the first leader really to identify himself with the party workers in the constituencies: none of his predecessors could ever have made a speech like this. They loved it and him, and for much of the 1920s and the 1930s Baldwin was the Conservative Party and the Conservative Party was Baldwin. He was an experienced campaigner and knew both defeat and success. In the 1923 general election the Tories lost eighty-eight seats and after a few weeks Baldwin resigned to allow Ramsay MacDonald to form the first Labour government. This lasted for six months, then in the general election of 1924 Baldwin won 154 seats. He had campaigned vigorously across the country, which he was able to do as he was lucky enough not to be opposed in his own seat at Bewdley.

'Lawlor for Redbridge'

It had not been my intention originally to take any part in the by-election in the Redbridge division beyond writing three verses of a hymn in praise of Boko Lawlor and sending him a congratulatory wire if he won. But two things combined to make me change my mind. The first was the fact that it occurred to me – always the keen young journalist – that there might be a couple of guineas of *Interesting Bits* money in it ('How a Modern Election is Fought: Humours of the Poll'); the second, that, ever since his departure Ukridge had been sending me a constant stream of telegrams so stimulating that eventually they lit the spark.

I append specimens:

Going strong. Made three speeches yesterday. Election song a sensation. Come on down. – UKRIDGE.

Boko locally regarded as walk-over. Made four speeches yesterday. Election song a breeze. Come on down. – UKRIDGE.

Victory in sight. Spoke practically all yesterday. Election song a riot. Children croon it in cots. Come on down. – UKRIDGE.

I leave it to any young author to say whether a man with one solitary political lyric to his credit could have resisted this. With the exception of a single music-hall song ('Mother, She's Pinching My Leg', tried out by Tim Sims, the Koy Komic, at the Peebles Hippodrome, and discarded, in response to a popular appeal, after one performance), no written words of mine had ever passed human lips. Naturally, it gave me a certain thrill to imagine the enlightened electorate of Redbridge – at any rate, the right-thinking portion of it – bellowing in its thousands those noble lines:

No foreign foe's insidious hate
  Our country shall o'erwhelm
So long as England's ship of state
  Has LAWLOR at the helm.

Whether I was technically correct in describing as guiding the ship of state a man who would probably spend his entire Parliamentary career in total silence, voting meekly as the Whip directed, I had not stopped to inquire. All I knew was that it sounded well, and I wanted to hear it. In addition to which, there was the opportunity, never likely to occur again, of seeing Ukridge make an ass of himself before a large audience.

I went to Redbridge.

The first thing I saw on leaving the station was a very large poster exhibiting Boko Lawlor's expressive features, bearing the legend:

LAWLOR

FOR

REDBRIDGE

This was all right, but immediately beside it, evidently placed there by the hand of an enemy, was a still larger caricature of this poster which stressed my old friend's prominent nose in a manner that seemed to me to go beyond the limits of a fair debate. To this was appended the word:

DO YOU

WANT

THIS

FOR A MEMBER?

To which, if I had been a hesitating voter of the constituency, I would certainly have replied 'No!' for there was something about that grossly elongated nose that convicted the man beyond hope of appeal of every undesirable quality a Member of Parliament can possess. You could see at a glance that here was one who, if elected, would do his underhand best to cut down the Navy, tax the poor man's food, and strike a series of blows at the very root of the home. And, as if this were not enough, a few yards farther on was a placard covering almost the entire side of a house, which said in simple, straightforward black letters a foot high:

DOWN WITH
BOKO
THE HUMAN GARGOYLE

P. G. WODEHOUSE
Ukridge, 1924

'Character and ability'

A big effort to improve the intellectual standard of Conservative MPs is behind the Party chief's move to make character and ability rather than wealth, the qualifications for adopting Parliamentary candidates.

Evening Standard, 1944

Harold Macmillan told a story about his attempt to be adopted for a seat in the late 1920s. After the applicants had made their speeches the chairman asked each of them to write down on a piece of paper how much they would give each year to the association if they were elected. This was specifically forbidden after the war, following the Maxwell Fyfe report which recommended that the maximum contribution should not exceed £50 from an MP and £25 from a candidate.

'Loyalty'

Loyalty was the Tories' secret weapon.

DAVID MAXWELL FYFE, 1961

David Maxwell Fyfe held the offices of Attorney General, Home Secretary and Lord Chancellor, but this was the most memorable thing he said. It occurred in an interview given to a young historian, John Mackintosh, who later became a Scottish Labour MP, when he was preparing his book on the British Cabinet.

In the night of the long knives in 1962, Maxwell Fyfe was abruptly sacked by Macmillan, along with six other Cabinet ministers. Macmillan panicked and hoped that by bringing in new blood he would make his government popular. It didn't. Maxwell Fyfe's comment on his speedy despatch was that he doubted whether loyalty 'has ever had to endure so severe a strain'. He went back to his house in Sussex and heard on the radio that he had been made an earl, which Macmillan had forgotten to mention. On the same day Macmillan had also forgotten to offer Selwyn Lloyd a CH when he sacked him as Chancellor of the Exchequer. Later the Prime Minister's secretary rang up the Chancellor's secretary to apologize for the Prime Minister's oversight, and it was said that Selwyn Lloyd's initial comment was 'Tell him to stuff it.' None the less, he did accept it.

If you go, I go.

IAIN MACLEOD

Letter to Nigel Fisher, 1968

Nigel Fisher was the Conservative MP for Surbiton and was under threat of deselection for his left-wing views. Iain stood by his friends and I am quite sure that he meant what he said. Nigel was a delightful man who canvassed for me in the Acton by-election, followed up every path by his two King Charles spaniels, and I spoke for him in Surbiton. His son Mark entered the House as a Labour MP.

'The magic circle'

The key day was Thursday, October 17, a day which for me began as an ordinary working day and ended with my firm decision that I could not serve in the Administration that I knew Lord Home was to be invited to form . . .

Curiouser and curiouser it seemed, and Maudling and I decided to stay in touch. I joined him and Mrs Maudling for lunch. Butler we discussed a good deal. Hailsham we mentioned once, but we both knew that his bandwagon had long ago stopped rolling: indeed, the opposition to Hailsham (not, of course, on personal grounds) was and was known to be so formidable that it remains astonishing that he was not given clear warning of it in advance of his declaration that he would disclaim his peerage. Home we never mentioned in any connection. Neither of us thought he was a contender, although for a brief moment his star seemed to have flared at Blackpool. It is some measure of the tightness of the magic circle on this occasion that neither the Chancellor of the Exchequer nor the Leader of the House of Commons had any inkling of what was happening . . .

I have argued that when the office of the leader of a great political party has to be filled it is wholly proper that all those who feel strongly should do their utmost to ensure that their view prevails. Such actions must sometimes cut across personal friendships. They need not destroy them. In this case I think they did not.

The decisive roles in the selection of Lord Home as Prime Minister were played by Macmillan and Redmayne. I am certain that they acted at each stage in the interest as they saw it of the sort of Tory Party in which they believe. So did I.

IAIN MACLEOD

Spectator, 17 January 1964

Iain Macleod wrote this celebrated article as a response to an account by Randolph Churchill of the change in the leadership of the Tory Party in October 1963, in which he was very favourable to Macmillan. Macleod said that Macmillan was the villain of the piece. From his hospital bed, with the connivance of Martin Redmayne, the Chief Whip and the Lord Chancellor, Macmillan dished the chances of R. A. Butler to succeed him, preferring Alec Douglas Home. Macleod used the phrase 'the magic circle' to describe the inner workings of the Tory establishment. But this was the last occasion when a leader of the party emerged in this way. When Douglas Home stood down in 1965 there was an election which Edward Heath won; in 1975 he lost to Margaret Thatcher and in 1990 John Major won. Democracy came late to the leadership of the Tory Party. The 1990 election showed that the party could change its leader within four weeks. Labour takes months and the primaries in the USA drag out the process for nearly a year.

After his departure, a roseate glow settled over the ageing Macmillan. But Bernard Levin was in no doubt that he was an old fraud: 'Advancing through life with a paralysed shuffle, an assortment of facial ticks, a voice that was the distilled essence of all the confidence tricksters . . . The eyes were hooded, they seemed to hover always on the verge of a wink, at his fantastic good fortune in being set down in the country of the blind where none could see through him. Where de Gaulle proudly proclaimed the destiny of the French nation Macmillan, by nods and winks, proclaimed the end of the British . . . Few things in his career became Macmillan like the leaving of it – the stag at bay with the mentality of a fox at large.'

'I am extremely careful never to be extreme'

I am *extremely* careful never to be extreme. I am *extremely* aware of the dangerous duplicity of Socialism, and *extremely* determined to turn back the tide before it destroys everything we hold dear. I am *extremely* disinclined to be deceived by the mask of moderation that Labour adopts whenever an Election is in the offing, a mask now being worn, as we saw last week, by all who would 'keep the red flag flying here'. Not if I can help it! The Conservative Party, now and always, flies the flag of one nation – and that flag is the Union Jack. So much for my so-called 'extremism'.

MARGARET THATCHER
Conservative Party Conference, 1977

'A city that is worth belonging to'

Elite is not a word to conjure with among Conservatives. But it is a conception that has to be faced. England today is a suburban country and run by middle-class professionals. So is the Conservative party; it is run by middle-class professionals and will go on being run by them for a long time in the future. If the failing of aristocratic politicians was a tendency to pick up a second-rate intellectual language in the hope of reconciling the thinking classes to them, the failing of middle-class professionals is to think solemnly and speak earnestly as if it were enough merely to say what they mean in order to be understood. In order to be understood and followed in a democratic system (as indeed under any other form of government) it is necessary to do something more. In particular it is necessary to persuade citizens that they belong to a city that is worth belonging to.

MAURICE COWLING

Conservative Essays, 1978

17

'Hostility to Radicalism, Incessant, Implacable Hostility'

In this chapter I have included some attacks on the Tories' main opponents – the Whigs in the eighteenth century, the Liberals in the nineteenth century and Socialists in the twentieth century. Some of the strongest attacks I have included are on Liberalism, despite the fact that some Conservatives like to consider themselves to be on the liberal wing of their party. Because it is a broad church the Tory Party is happy to accommodate many shades of opinion, but conservatism and liberalism are quite distinct. They both seek to enhance the opportunities for individuals to develop their talents in a free and open society. But Conservatives have a tougher core; they recognize that it's not only the law but also conventions, customs and practices which hold society together. And an unfettered liberalism can destabilize society by its refusal to recognize that there are some boundaries that should not be crossed and some traditions that have to be defended.

No one chastises and condemns the essential weakness of liberalism better than Malcolm Muggeridge. Liberals frequently have the right sentiments but they are too sentimental, pursuing the trivial by allowing the free play of any passing idea. There is also a streak of piety in liberalism. However, this does not prevent some Liberal candidates, particularly in local elections, from indulging in sleazy politics. This is an accusation which Conservative and Labour candidates, who have no particular love for each other, would readily confirm.

MY OPINION

After thinking this Fortnight of Whig and of Tory,
This to me is the long and the short of the Story:
They are all Fools and Knaves; and they keep up this pother,
On both sides, designing to cheat one another.

Poor *Rowley* (whose Maxims of State are a riddle)
Has plac'd himself much like the Pin in the middle:
Let which corner so ever be tumbled down first,
'Tis ten Thousand to one, but he comes by the worst.

'Twixt Brother and Bastard (those Dukes of Renown)
He'l make a wise shift to get rid of his Crown.
Had he half common Sense (were it ne'r so uncivil)
He'd have had 'em long since tipt down to the Devil.

The first is a Prince well fashion'd, well featur'd,
No Bigot to speak of, not false, nor ill natur'd:
The other for Government can't be unfit,
He's so little a Fop, and so plaguy a Wit.

Had I this soft Son, and this dangerous Brother,
I'd hang up the one, then I'd piss upon t'other.
I'd make this the long and the Short of the Story;
The Fools might be Whigs, none but Knaves should be Torye.
    CHARLES SACKVILLE, EARL OF DORSET

ON JACOBINISM

Such is the lib'ral Justice which presides
In these our days, and modern Patriots guides –
Justice, whose blood-stain'd book one sole decree,
One statute fills – 'the People shall be Free.'
Free by what means? – by folly, madness, guilt,
By boundless rapines, blood in oceans spilt;
By confiscation, in whose sweeping toils
The poor man's pittance with the rich man's spoils,
Mix'd in one common mass, are swept away –
To glut the short-liv'd tyrant of the day.

By laws, religion, morals all o'erthrown,
– Rouse then, ye Sov'reign People, claim your own –
The license that enthrals, the truth that blinds,
The wealth that starves you, and the pow'r that grinds.
– So Justice bids – 'twas her enlighten'd doom,
LOUIS, thy head devoted to the tomb –
'Twas Justice claim'd, in the accursed hour,
The fatal forfeit of too lenient pow'r.
Mourn for the Man we may – but for the King –
Freedom, oh! Freedom's such a charming thing . . .

　　GEORGE CANNING, 1797/8

This is an extract from a poem in the weekly magazine the *Anti-Jacobin*. This was written by a group of politicians who detested Jacobinism and all its works. The poems were often written by two or three people, but this passage is by George Canning, who later became Prime Minister. He has been the only occupant of No. 10 who wrote verse successfully.

WHIG ROBBERY AND DESTRUCTION OF PROPERTY UNDER THE NAME OF LAW

The perfidious, perjured, peculating, persecuting, paltry, purse-proud, pernicious, pandering, pharasaitical, partial, puffing, patch-working patibulary, paunch-puffed, peccant, pedling, place and pension loving, pertinacious, pestiferous, pettifogging, phlebotomizing, piratical, picaroon, pig-headed, pimping, pledge-breaking, plotting, potwolloping, pot-valiant, pragmatical, prating, predatory, presumptious, priest-ridden, puling, profligate, prowling, pseudo, pudding-headed, puddling, pugnacious, purloining, purblind, pusillanimous, peasant-starving, poor-people-hating, pilfering, plundering WHIGS, SMASHING THE UNSTAMPED.

　　C. J. GRANT

This passage was provoked by an increase in stamp duties on certain items including pamphlets. It appeared as the caption to a political cartoon, a woodcut by C. J. Grant.

A RADICAL WAR SONG

Awake, arise, the hour is come,
   For rows and revolutions;
There's no receipt like pike and drum
   For crazy constitutions.
Close, close the shop! Break, break the loom!
   Desert your hearths and furrows,
And throng in arms to seal the doom
   Of England's rotten boroughs . . .

In chains we'll hang in fair Guildhall
   The City's famed Recorder,
And next on proud St. Stephen's fall,
   Though Wynne should squeak to order.
In vain our tyrants then shall try
   To 'scape our martial law, sir;
In vain the trembling Speaker cry
   That 'Strangers must withdraw,' sir . . .

The peer shall dangle from his gate,
   The bishop from his steeple,
Till all recanting, own, the State
   Means nothing but the People.
We'll fix the church's revenues
   On Apostolic basis,
One coat, one scrip, one pair of shoes
   Shall pay their strange grimaces.

We'll strap the bar's deluding train
   In their own darling halter,
And with his big church bible brain
   The parson at the altar.
Hail glorious hour, when fair Reform
   Shall bless our longing nation,
And Hunt receives command to form
   A new administration . . .

Down with your sheriffs, and your mayors,
   Your registrars, and proctors,
We'll live without the lawyer's cares,
   And die without the doctor's.

No discontented fair shall pout
  To see her spouse so stupid;
We'll tread the torch of Hymen out,
  And live content with Cupid.

Then, when the high-born and the great
  Are humbled to our level,
On all the wealth of Church and State,
  Like aldermen, we'll revel.
We'll live when hushed the battle's din,
In smoking and in cards, sir,
In drinking unexcised gin,
  And wooing fair Poissardes, sir.
    LORD MACAULAY, 1820

This poem was written just after the Peterloo Massacre, at a time of revolutionary ferment.

MAXIMS

'Lord Auckland is understood to be appointed permanently on Constitutional grounds.' *Globe*, Jan. 14, 1834.

If a Tory is ever found out
  In pocketing twenty pence,
The thing is a job, no doubt,
  It admits of no defence:
If a Whig has the luck to secure
  Some twenty thousand pounds,
It is all arranged, be sure,
  On 'Constitutional grounds.'

If a Tory dares distrust
  The faith of our fiercest foe,
Suspicion is quite unjust,
  And jealousy vastly low:
If a Whig with a bold blockade
  Our ancient friend confounds,
It is done, for the good of trade,
  On 'Constitutional grounds.'

If a Tory punishes crimes
   In Kerry or in Clare,
The wisdom of the *Times*
   Proclaims it quite unfair;
If a Whig with a troop of horse
   The Murphys and Macs astounds,
He cuts and thrusts of course
   On 'Constitutional grounds.'

If a Tory gives a place
   To a nephew or a son,
Good lack! a thing so base
   Was never, never done!
If a Whig, with his countless kin,
   The nation's purse surrounds,
They slip their fingers in
   On 'Constitutional grounds.'

Then take, my Lord, oh, take
   The gift the Greys provide,
For the Constitution's sake,
   And for no ends beside.
And think, on quarter-day,
   Of the friend who thus expounds
The rights of place and pay
   On 'Constitutional grounds.'
   WINTHROP MACKWORTH PRAED

'Very convenient opinions'

Liberal opinions are the opinions of those who would be free from certain constraints and regulations, from a certain dependence and duty which are deemed necessary for the general and popular welfare. Liberal opinions are very convenient opinions for the rich and the powerful. They ensure enjoyment and are opposed to self-sacrifice. The holder of Liberal opinions, for example, maintains that the possession of land is to be considered in a commercial light and no other. He looks to the income which it will afford him. It is not a Liberal principle that the holder of land should incur the duty of executing justice and maintaining truth among the multitude for nothing. That, gentlemen, is a popular principle, a principle of government for the benefit of the people, not a Liberal opinion.

BENJAMIN DISRAELI
Address to the electors of the County of Buckinghamshire, 1847

'Hostility to Radicalism'

Hostility to Radicalism, incessant, implacable hostility, is the essential definition of Conservatism. The fear that the Radicals may triumph is the only final cause that the Conservative Party can plead for their own existence.

ROBERT CECIL, MARQUESS OF SALISBURY
English Politics and Parties, 1859

Until he succeeded to the title of the Marquess of Salisbury and to the Cecil estates in 1868, Robert Cecil was so short of money that he resorted to journalism and taking directorships. In particular he wrote for the *Political Quarterly* and in a series of articles over several years he set out his own philosophy. Like Peel, he regarded the radicals as dangerous and subversive groups who threatened society; he thought that democracy through the extension of the suffrage would lead to envy and expropriation, and this led him to resign from Derby's Cabinet in 1867 over Disraeli's Reform Act. For him, any changes had to be as limited as possible and as late as possible. His cast of mind was bleak, sceptical and defensive, but he was a shrewd politician who enjoyed power and as Prime Minister he kept his own die-hards in control, keeping Chamberlain's Liberal Unionists alongside as well.

'Strong Arms'

The socialist, seeing a strong man oppress a weak one cries out – 'Break the strong man's arms' but I say 'Teach him to use them to better purpose.'

JOHN RUSKIN
Unto This Last, 1860

'The Boneless Wonder'

I remember, when I was a child, being taken to the celebrated Barnum's Circus, which contained an exhibition of freaks and monstrosities; but the exhibit on the programme which I most desired to see was the one described as 'The Boneless Wonder.' My parents judged that the spectacle would be too revolting and demoralizing for my youthful eyes, and I have waited fifty years to see The Boneless Wonder sitting on the Treasury Bench.

WINSTON CHURCHILL
(describing Ramsay MacDonald)

'Left-wing parties'

The weakness of all left-wing parties is their inability to tell the truth about the immediate future.

GEORGE ORWELL, 1945

'An illusionist without ideals'

No one knows what role the Prime Minister is playing at any given moment. The Prime Minister in his first one hundred days until Leyton was a combination of J. F. Kennedy and Napoleon . . . Then there was the Dunkirk spirit, the reincarnation of Sir Winston Churchill, and then for a time – and, Heaven help us, over Rhodesia – the Prime Minister was Abraham Lincoln, with malice towards none. He has emerged recently as the Duke of Wellington. J. F. Kennedy described himself in a brilliant phrase as an idealist without illusions. I would describe the Prime Minister as an illusionist without ideals. Abraham Lincoln said that you cannot fool all of the people all of the time . . . he wants to know if he can fool fifty per cent of the people for three weeks . . . He was seen through at Westminster long ago; and it becomes the task of the Tory Party in this month to make sure he is seen through in the country.

IAIN MACLEOD, March 1966

This is one of the best pieces of invective since the war, but in the ensuing election Harold Wilson increased his majority.

'Between freedom and tyranny'

We can choose a system in which the amount and kind of goods produced is determined by the *impersonal* mechanism of the market, issuing its decrees in the form of fluctuating prices. Or we can choose a system in which this is determined by commands issuing from a *personal* authority backed by armed force. You cannot dodge this issue by talking about a 'mixed economy.' The economy is inevitably mixed;

nobody in his right mind proposes a total abandonment of government enterprise. You can not dodge it by insisting the state must *regulate* the market or *intervene* in its operations. If carefully defined, that statement is obvious. The question is whether the economy is mixed to the point of destroying the essential directing function of the market, whether the regulations are a substitute for the market or a framework within which it shall operate, whether intervention is compatible or incompatible with the general control of the economy by the whole people as consumers of goods. That is the difference between collectivism and the market economy. That is the alternative with which mankind is confronted. You can not dodge it, or pray it away, or hide it from yourself with smokescreens of ideas. It is a fact, not an idea. We have to choose. And the choice is between freedom and tyranny.

MAX EASTMAN

Reflections on the Failure of Socialism, 1955

Max Eastman (1883–1969) was an American poet, critic and social thinker. A pacifist in the First World War, he preached socialist revolution in the 1920s. He became increasingly disenchanted with Marxism and turned instead to market forces and he helped to rescue American political thought from socialist interventionist orthodoxy.

'An unfocused dissatisfaction with the way things are'

Let me just read you, if I can find it, my analysis of the Lefty consciousness. The Lefty starts from an unfocused dissatisfaction with the way things are. One need not drag Freud into the argument in order to suggest that 'the way things are', the social system, will strike the young or the youngish as a product of authority, of parents, schoolmasters, vicars and employers, the people who seem to limit freedom for the sake of doing so. Stage two prolongs this: the frustrations of trying to get on in a competitive society where most people by definition cannot get on very far. Then, like the fire from heaven, the hint of an explanation and an ideology. The reason we are failing to get on, or are simply not having a good enough time, is not because we are lazy and stupid but because of the system. So we now oppose the system.

The reason why prominent Leftists or Lefties go on opposing the system long after having got on pretty well by most standards is perhaps threefold. First of all, political habit dies hard – and it has in my case, though it *has* died. Secondly, success is always relative: the controversial poet gets bad reviews from the pundits, the popular actress (especially her) finds an extra and even more appreciative audience at political rallies. Thirdly, an increasing bitterness develops as the system, having been repeatedly shouted at to pull itself together, chugs on much as before.

KINGSLEY AMIS
'Lucky Jim's Politics', 1968

'Socialism as a concept is unjust'

If I were asked a simple reason why Socialism as a concept is unjust, I would say that one at least was because it operates against the natural instincts of man to own a little property, and to share in the good material things of life and to pass them on to his children, instead of trying to use those natural instincts for the common good. Society is for the *homme moyen sensual* as well as for the saint, and the *homme moyen sensual* is a man of mixed instincts and various and different inclinations.

QUINTIN HOGG, VISCOUNT HAILSHAM, 1974

'The Mild and the Bitter'

I sometimes think the Labour Party is like a pub where the mild is running out. If someone does not do something soon, all that is left will be bitter, and all that is bitter will be Left.

MARGARET THATCHER, 1975

'Throw out Marxism bodily'

Why has the Party become a repository of destructive envy and militant failure, a Party of green-eyed monsters! The answer is that Labour has starved itself of intellectual nourishment and the stimulus of debate . . . It was inevitable that the Marxists should fill Labour's intellectual vacuum. Alas, Labour has never been able or willing to throw out Marxism bodily; it has always held that there must be *something* in it. Such feeble resistance as it once offered has been overwhelmed, and the crudest kind of Marxists now roam through the Party at all levels.

PAUL JOHNSON
'Farewell to the Labour Party', *New Statesman*, 1976

'The Great Liberal Death Wish'

Searching in my mind for an appropriate name for the seventies, I settle for The Decade of The Great Liberal Death Wish. It seems to me that this process of death-wishing, in the guise of liberalism, has been eroding the civilization of the West for a century and more, and is now about to reach its apogee. The liberal mind, effective everywhere, whether in power or in opposition, particularly so during the present period of American world domination, has provided the perfect instrument. Systematically, stage by stage, dismantling our Western way of life, depreciating and deprecating all its values so that the whole social structure is now tumbling down, dethroning its God, undermining all its certainties, and finally mobilizing a Praetorian Guard of ribald students, maintained at the public expense, and ready at the drop of a hat to go into action, not only against their own weak-kneed, bemused academic authorities, but also against any institution or organ for the maintenance of law and order still capable of functioning, especially the police. And all this, wonderfully enough, in the name of the health, wealth and happiness of all mankind.

Previous civilizations have been overthrown from without by the incursion of barbarian hordes; ours has dreamed up its own dissolution in the minds of its own intellectual élite. It has carefully nurtured its own barbarians – all reared on the best Dr. Spock lines, sent to progressive schools and colleges, fitted with contraceptives or fed birth pills at puberty; mixing D. H. Lawrence with their Coca-Cola, and imbibing the headier stuff (Marcuse, Chairman Mao, Malcolm X) in evening libations of hot chocolate. Not Bolshevism, which Stalin liquidated along with all the old Bolsheviks; not Nazism, which perished with Hitler in his Berlin bunker; not Fascism, which was left hanging upside down, along with Mussolini and his mistress, from a lamp-post – none of these, history will record, was responsible for bringing down the darkness on our civilization, but liberalism. A solvent rather than a precipitate, a sedative rather than a stimulant, a slough rather than a precipice; blurring the edges of truth, the definition of virtue, the shape of beauty; a cracked bell, a mist, a death wish.

MALCOLM MUGGERIDGE
Things Past, 1979

The Inadequacies of Liberalism

One is bound to wonder at the inadequacies of bourgeois liberalism that have made it so vulnerable, first to the Old Left and now to the New . . .

Certainly, one of the key problematic aspects of bourgeois-liberal society has long been known and announced. This is the fact that liberal society is of necessity a secular society, one in which religion is mainly a private affair. Such a disestablishment of religion, it was predicted by Catholic thinkers and others, would gradually lead to a diminution of religious faith and a growing scepticism about the traditional consolations of religion – especially the consolations offered by a life after death. That has unquestionably happened, and with significant consequences. One such consequence is that the demands placed upon liberal society, in the name of temporal 'happiness,' have become ever more urgent and ever more unreasonable. In every society, the overwhelming majority of the people lead lives of considerable frustration, and if society is to endure, it needs to be able to rely on a great measure of stoical resignation. In theory, this could be philosophical rather than religious; in fact, philosophical stoicism has never been found suitable for mass consumption. Philosophical stoicism has always been an aristocratic prerogative; it has never been able to give an acceptable rationale of 'one's station and one's duties' to those whose stations are low and whose duties are onerous. So liberal civilization finds itself having spiritually expropriated the masses of its citizenry, whose demands for material compensation gradually become as infinite as the infinity they have lost. All of this was clearly foreseen by many of the anti-modern critics who witnessed the birth of modernity.

IRVING KRISTOL

'Government by the Left – Yes'

The Labour Party claimed that they lost the election because they failed to get their message across. Nothing could be further from the truth. They lost because they got their message across beyond their wildest dreams. Britain stared into the eyes of the Left and it rejected what it saw. Once we could all rally to that simple but so fine a message 'Government of the people, by the people for the people'. Now that is all changed.

Government by the Left – yes. They will go along with that.

Government for the Left – yes. That is the name of the game. But Government of the Left – that is not the way they see it at all. For the Left today sees itself as about Government. It sees Parliament increasingly as a constitutional convenience to be used when they control it, to be frustrated, bypassed or ultimately discarded when they do not. And there is no way, by simply changing the Leader, that the Left will surrender its appetite for power or compromise with the workings of the free institutions of Western society. They seek their destruction and the destruction of the liberal economies that support them.

MICHAEL HESELTINE
Conservative Party Conference, 1983

18

'The Essence of Toryism is Enjoyment'

Conservatives and enjoyment go hand in hand. This has been elo-
quently asserted by David Hume, Bagehot and by Quintin Hogg in his
The Case for Conservatism. *It is a very important strand in the make*
up of the Conservative. Politics is not the be-all and end-all in life —
indeed, one can have too much of it. Men and women are not simply or
principally political and economic animals. They have a wide range of
interests, hobbies, amusements and diversions, and the political party
that does not recognize and revel in that is a narrow, crimped and
unrewarding body.

Michael Oakeshott frequently uses the word 'conversation' to des-
cribe the Conservative attitude to social behaviour. It does not have the
earnest compulsion of the radical. Instead people come together for no
particular purpose other than friendship and fellowship. The pub is
unique to our country and is one of the places where this happens. As
Dr Johnson said, 'No, Sir, there is nothing which has yet been con-
trived by man, by which so much happiness is produced as by a good
tavern or inn.'

I cannot in all conscience claim that, in Milton's phrase, 'Laughter
holding both his sides' is a unique conservative quality. But the smile
rather than the sneer, the laugh rather than the snigger, and the desire
to find the more cheerful aspects of life are things that come readily to
conservatives.

'So goes the world'

Lord Radnor and I were walking in the Mall this evening: and Mr Secretary Bolingbroke met us and took a turn or two, and then stole away, and we both believed it was to pick up some wench; and tomorrow he will be at the cabinet with the Queen; so goes the world.

JONATHAN SWIFT

Philandering is not a pastime exclusive to Conservative politicians, for that would overlook the expertise of Palmerston and Lloyd George. Bolingbroke was a rake but also a gifted orator, a writer, and a statesman, and it was for these qualities that Disraeli admired him.

'There are in England, in particular, many honest gentlemen'

There are in England, in particular, many honest gentlemen, who being always employed in their domestic affairs, or amusing themselves in common recreations, have carried their thoughts very little beyond those objects, which are every day exposed to their senses. And indeed, of such as these I pretend not to make philosophers, nor do I expect them to be associates in these researches or auditors of these discoveries. They do well to keep themselves in their present situation; and instead of refining them into philosophers, I wish we could communicate to our founders of systems, a share of this gross earthy mixture, as an ingredient, which they commonly stand much in need of, and which would serve to temper those fiery particles, of which they are composed.

DAVID HUME

A Treatise of Human Nature, 1751

Hume also believed that 'celibacy, fasting, penance, mortification, self-denial, humility, silence, solitude and the whole train of monkish virtues' were to be shunned since all they did was 'stupify the understanding and harden the heart, obscure the fancy and sour the temper'.

'At a tavern there is a general freedom from anxiety'

We dined at an excellent inn at Chapel-house, where he expatiated on the felicity of England in its taverns and inns, and triumphed over the French for not having, in any perfection, the tavern life. 'There is no private house, (said he,) in which people can enjoy themselves so well, as at a capital tavern. Let there be ever so great plenty of good things, ever so much grandeur, ever so much elegance, ever so much desire that every body should be easy; in the nature of things it cannot be: there must always be some degree of care and anxiety. The master of the house is anxious to entertain his guests; the guests are anxious to be agreeable to him: and no man, but a very impudent dog indeed, can as freely command what is in another man's house, as if it were his own. Whereas, at a tavern, there is a general freedom from anxiety. You are sure you are welcome: and the more noise you make, the more trouble you give, the more good things you call for, the welcomer you are. No servants will attend you with the alacrity which waiters do, who are incited by the prospect of an immediate reward in proportion as they please. No, Sir, there is nothing which has yet been contrived by man, by which so much happiness is produced as by a good tavern or inn.'

JAMES BOSWELL
The Life of Samuel Johnson, 1791

'A gathering of the Tory'

But tomorrow, if we live,
Our ponderous squire will give
A grand political dinner
To half the squirelings near;
And Maud will wear her jewels,
And the bird of prey will hover,
And the titmouse hope to win her
With his chirrup at her ear.

*

A grand political dinner
To the men of many acres,
A gathering of the Tory,
A dinner and then a dance
For the maids and marriage-makers,
And every eye but mine will glance
At Maud in all her glory.

*

For I am not invited,
But, with the Sultan's pardon,

I am all as well delighted,
For I know her own rose-garden,
And mean to linger in it
Till the dancing will be over;
And then, oh then, come out to me
For a minute, but for a minute,
Come out to your own true lover,
That your true lover may see
Your glory also, and render
All homage to his own darling,
Queen Maud in all her splendour.

*

Come into the garden, Maud,
    For the black bat, night, has flown,
Come into the garden, Maud,
    I am here at the gate alone;
And the woodbine spices are wafted abroad,
    And the musk of the rose is blown.

ALFRED, LORD TENNYSON
Maud, 1855

It is not often remembered that the most famous quotation from Victorian poetry
was uttered by an ardent lover who was persuading a girl to leave a Tory ball. The
one to which she but not he was invited seems to have had as its main purpose
matchmaking, a function which the Young Conservatives now provide. Tory balls
have now become major fundraising, rather joyless events, and the modern-day
Maud would be well advised to take her lover's advice.

'The essence of Toryism is enjoyment'

The essence of Toryism is enjoyment. Talk of the ways of spreading a
wholesome Conservatism throughout this country: give painful lec-
tures, distribute weary tracts (and perhaps this is as well – you may be
able to give an argumentative answer to a few objections, you may
diffuse a distinct notion of the dignified dullness of politics); but as far as
communicating and establishing your creed are concerned – try a little
pleasure. The way to keep up old customs is, to enjoy old customs; the
way to be satisfied with the present state of things is, to enjoy that state of
things. Over the 'Cavalier' mind this world passes with a thrill of delight;
there is an exultation in a daily event, zest in the 'regular thing,' joy at an

old feast. Sir Walter Scott is an example of this. Every habit and practice of old Scotland was inseparably in his mind associated with genial enjoyment. To propose to touch one of her institutions, to abolish one of those practices, was to touch a personal pleasure – a point on which his mind reposed, a thing of memory and hope. So long as this world is this world, will a buoyant life be the proper source of an animated Conservatism.

WALTER BAGEHOT
'Essay on Macaulay', 1856

'Cheerful and hopeful men'

The men I have seen succeed best in life have always been cheerful and hopeful men who went about their business with a smile on their faces.

C. M. KINGSLEY
A Little Book of Cheerfulness

'It is a grand thing to rise in the world'

'It is a grand thing to rise in the world. The ambition to do so is the very salt of the earth. It is the parent of all enterprise, and the cause of all improvement. They who know no such ambition are savages and remain savage. As far as I can see, among us Englishmen such ambition is, healthily and happily, almost universal, and on that account we stand high among the citizens of the world. But, owing to false teaching, men are afraid to own aloud a truth which is known to their own hearts. I am not afraid to do so, and I would not have you afraid. I am proud that, by one step after another, I have been able so to place you and so to form you, that you should have been found worthy of rank much higher than my own. And I would have you proud also and equally ambitious for your child. Let him be the Duke of Brotherton. Let him be brought up to be one of England's statesmen, if God shall give him the intellect for the work. Let him be seen with the George and Garter, and be known throughout Europe as one of England's worthiest worthies. Though not born as yet, his career should already be a care to you. And that he may be great, you should rejoice that you yourself are great already.'

ANTHONY TROLLOPE
Is He Popenjoy?, 1878
The Dean of Brotherton cannot conceal his joy that his daughter is to become the Marchioness of Brotherton, but as to her child nothing is beyond his grasp – a dukedom, the Garter and a European statesman.

Disraeli's Primroses

The primrose is now generally supposed to have been Lord Beaconsfield's favourite flower, but I cannot say for certain that I ever heard him express any particular partiality for it, though I daresay he may have done so.

As a matter of fact, I believe that Queen Victoria at the proper season invariably sent Lord Beaconsfield primroses from the slopes at Windsor, and it is probable that, having expressed to someone his warm appreciation of these flowers, it was in consequence assumed that the great statesman had a strong partiality for the primrose.

I sat next to Mr Gladstone at a dinner some time after Lord Beaconsfield's death [1881], and in the course of conversation he suddenly said: 'Tell me, Lady Dorothy, upon your honour, have you ever heard Lord Beaconsfield express any particular fondness for the primrose?' I was compelled to admit that I had not, upon which he said: 'The gorgeous lily, I think, was more to his taste.'

LADY DOROTHY NEVILL
Reminiscences, 1881

It was said that primroses were Disraeli's favourite flowers and they were exchanged between the Queen and her Prime Minister. This was one of the many romantic myths which swirled around Disraeli and which Gladstone instinctively distrusted. After his death some Tories formed the Primrose League to cherish his memory. This flourished for a time but became the refuge for Tories of the old school who still today lay a wreath of primroses on his tomb at Hughenden. Disraeli can have the last word through one of his characters, Lord St Jerome in *Lothair*: 'They say primroses make a capital salad.'

'Good digestions'

The healthy stomach is nothing if not conservative. Few radicals have good digestions.

SAMUEL BUTLER
Notebooks, 1912

'Glittering Prizes'

For as long a time as the records of history have been preserved human societies passed through a ceaseless process of evolution and adjustment. This process has been sometimes pacific; but more often it has resulted from warlike disturbance. The strength of different nations, measured in terms of arms, varies from century to century. The world continues to offer glittering prizes to those who have stout hearts and sharp swords; it is therefore extremely improbable that the experience of future ages will differ in any material respect from that which has happened since the twilight of the human race. It is for us, therefore, who in our history have proved ourselves a martial, rather than a military, people to abstain, as has been our habit, from provocation; but to maintain in our own hand the adequate means for our own protection; and, so equipped, to march with heads erect and bright eyes along the road of our Imperial destiny.

F. E. SMITH, LORD BIRKENHEAD
Rectorial address, Glasgow University, 1923

This speech to the young of Scotland just five years after the Great War shocked many people. Its subject was 'Idealism in International Politics' and Smith, who had recently relinquished the office of Lord Chancellor, asserted that war would never be abolished and that martial superiority was a key policy for any country. The famous phrase about the glittering prizes referred to countries but it came to characterize the rumbustious, combative attitude of the political adventurer, and there were three such politicians at that time: Smith, Churchill and Lloyd George. The Bishop of St Albans described it as the doctrine of the jungle, Asquith condemned its 'cynical barbarities', and in the *Daily News* A. A. Milne drew the public's attention to the absence of any military service in Smith's career:

GALLOPER SMITH

(Lines in honour of the great gentleman who said to the youth of Glasgow University: 'The idealists had the temerity to exploit the Great War for their own controversial purposes – a war to end war.')

He says: 'Man's fighting instinct never dies,
'War hath, no less than, Peace, her glittering prize,'
No need for him to tell us, who can see
What happened in the case of Smith, F. E.
For him no barren bloodstained victories!
For 'human nature being what it is,'
He stuck to England – and became a Knight,
Leaving the less articulate to fight.
The which they did. And after three long years
Of blood and bitter agony and tears,
'Sir Frederick' became a Baronet –
Showing the Lord of Hosts was with him yet.

And now (an Earl) the first Lord Birkenhead,
Feeling that, after all, the dead are dead
(And dead, whatever they were fighting for),
Holds up to Youth the 'glittering prize' of War
And pours his scorn on the 'idealist'
(The 'sloppy fool' the 'sentimentalist')
Through whom some of these prizes might be missed.

'A curious sense of humour'

Then, above all, the English people have a curious sense of humour,
rather than wit. Humour comes from the heart; wit comes from the
brain. We can laugh at ourselves. Do you remember what Ruskin said?
'The English laugh is the purest and truest in the metals that can be
minted,' and indeed, only heaven can know what the country owes to
it. Well, laughter is one of the best things that God has given us, and
with hearty laughter neither malice nor indecency can exist. And of all
men who have shown us what that laughter can mean, none was like
Dickens, every one of whose characters is English to the marrow; and if
I might mention a living writer, I think the truest Englishmen are found
in Mr Priestley's novels.'

STANLEY BALDWIN
'Our National Character', radio broadcast, 1933

'A very great gentleman'

Mr Zitelli says that no one who can select a fine cigar with the unerring
instinct of Winston Churchill 'can possibly be anything but a very great
gentleman'.

News Chronicle, 1942

Alcohol

All I will say is that I have taken more out of alcohol than alcohol has
taken out of me.

WINSTON CHURCHILL

'The wisest religion'

For Conservatives do not believe that political struggle is the most important thing in life. In this they differ from Communists, Socialists, Nazis, Fascists, Social Creditors and most members of the British Labour Party. The simplest among them prefer fox-hunting – the wisest religion. To the great majority of Conservatives, religion, art, study, family, country, friends, music, fun, duty, all the joy and riches of existence of which the poor no less than the rich are the indefeasible freeholders, all these are higher in the scale than their handmaiden, the political struggle. This makes them easy to defeat – at first. But, once defeated, they will hold to this belief with the fanaticism of a Crusader and the doggedness of an Englishman. One of the earliest English Conservatives, the author of Hudibras, expressed in a single savage couplet his contempt for those

'Who think religion was intended
For nothing else than to be mended'.

This sentiment still animates the Conservative when he faces the political bigots of our time. It will win in the end. Whatever the fanatics may think, in this at least Conservatives have the vast majority on their side. The man who puts politics first is not fit to be called a civilised being, let alone a Christian.

QUINTIN HOGG
The Case for Conservatism, 1947
Quintin's famous comment about fox hunting occasioned some controversy since as written it implies that fox hunting is the wisest religion. The meaning would have been clearer if he had put a comma after 'wisest'.

'The disposition to be conservative'

The disposition to be conservative is, then, warm and positive in respect of enjoyment, and correspondingly cool and critical in respect of change and innovation: these two inclinations support and elucidate one another. The man of conservative temperament believes that a known good is not lightly to be surrendered for an unknown better. He is not in love with what is dangerous and difficult; he is unadventurous; he has no impulse to sail uncharted seas; for him there is no magic in being lost, bewildered or shipwrecked. If he is forced to navigate the unknown, he sees virtue in heaving the lead every inch of the way. What others plausibly identify as timidity, he recognizes in himself as rational prudence; what others interpret as inactivity, he recognizes as a disposition to enjoy rather than to exploit. He is cautious, and he is disposed to indicate his assent or dissent, not in absolute, but in graduated terms. He eyes the situation in terms of its propensity to disrupt the familiarity of the features of this world.

MICHAEL OAKESHOTT
Rationalism in Politics, 1962

'Cricket is not entirely irrelevant to political philosophy'

My argument is deeply hostile to the premises of much liberal thought. Liberals ought to be shocked by it. For instance, cricket is a profound and absorbing activity, closely attuned to man's spiritual needs. Albert Camus said that most of what he had learnt that was of moral significance was learnt on the football field. But Camus had no knowledge of cricket, a game in which technique and teamwork and planning strategically to win, often by adapting more quickly to the land and the weather, are taken to their highest levels. Of course, cricket can be boring and silly, but it can also be profound and deeply satisfying and it has fewer disadvantages than war. Should cricket, then, be compulsory? In principle and up to a point, yes. Where it would work and not cause a reaction against the activity itself, children should be obliged to make some acquaintance with cricket, as with music. But this would not work where cricket is alien to a culture, nor with individuals who have begun to react against it. Thus it should only be compulsory in a very limited sense for some children in some cultures. In any case, there are other activities with spiritual qualities and it may be more efficient that individuals find their own. These are questions of judgement; there is no question of a philosophic ban on interference with matters of taste.

It is not, of course, a plausible objective of political philosophy to specify precisely how people should spend their leisure time, to prescribe (for instance) universal compulsory cricket. Societies can thrive without cricket; in the interests of cultural diversity it is desirable that they do. Within a cricket-playing society decent individuals can live rich lives while abhorring the game. But cricket is not entirely irrelevant to political philosophy. It is the *kind* of activity which gives people's lives meaning and makes them satisfying. Whether or not people's tastes are directed to such activities and whether or not suitable opportunities are available to them is in part, but necessarily, a consequence of the decisions of governments.

LINCOLN ALLISON, 1986

This is the noblest case for cricket I have yet found. Cricket has a compulsive and absorbing appeal to players, watchers and listeners. Cricket's positive virtues are fairness, patience, teamwork and letting the other side in, and these can be reflected in political attitudes. Including those who play in the Indian subcontinent, cricketers are numbered in the millions, though the game's effect on politics has yet to be seen. I could claim that cricket stands for England and Conservatism, but then that wouldn't be cricket.

But what about bowls, darts and shove ha'penny? One of my teachers called cricket 'an organized waste of time'.

The Tory Party does not like brains'

'The Tory Party does not like brains,' Willie Whitelaw once remarked to an aide as he walked down the committee room corridor of the House of Commons. Then he paused, shaking his head sadly, 'Thank God I don't have any!'

JOHN RANELAGH
Thatcher's People

Acknowledgements

For permission to reprint copyright material the pulishers gratefully acknowledge the following:

LINCOLN ALLISON: Blackwell Publishers for an extract from *Right Principles: A Conservative Philosophy* (1986)

LEO AMERY: the Rt Hon Lord Amery for extracts from *Ashridge Journal* (1943) and *Thoughts on the Constitution* (1947)

W. H. AUDEN: Faber and Faber Ltd for 'Doggerel by a Senior Citizen' from *W. H. Auden: Collected Poems*, ed. Edward Mendelson, copyright © 1969 by W. H. Auden

MARY BAKER: the author for an extract from *Opening Doors for Women* (Macmillan, 1987)

STANLEY BALDWIN: Earl Baldwin of Bewdley for extracts entitled 'With no help from governments' (1933), 'The prerogative of the harlot' (1930), 'To me, England is the country, and the country is England' (1924), 'The ripple of a restless tide' (1929), and 'A curious sense of humour' (1933)

SIR ISAIAH BERLIN: the author for extracts from *Four Essays on Liberty* (1969) and *The Crooked Timber of Humanity* (1990)

JOHN BETJEMAN: John Murray (Publishers) Ltd for an extract from 'Mildenhall, Wilts', 'Church of England Thoughts', 'Anglo-Catholic Congresses' and 'County' from *Selected Poems*

SIR ARTHUR BRYANT: HarperCollins Publishers for an extract from *The Lion and the Unicorn* (1970)

R. A. BUTLER: the Master and Fellows of Trinity College Cambridge for extracts from the Butler Papers

LORD HUGH CECIL: the Marquess of Salisbury for extracts from *Conservatism, Religion and Politics* and 'Liberty: A Definition'

GEOFFREY CHAUCER: Penguin Books Ltd for an extract from *The Canterbury Tales*, translated by Nevill Coghill (Penguin Classics, fourth revised edition, 1977), copyright © Nevill Coghill, 1951, 1958, 1960, 1975, 1977

CHURCHILL, SIR WINSTON: extracts reproduced with permission of Curtis Brown

the World Order (1979), copyright © E. R. Norman, 1979

GEORGE ORWELL: A. M. Heath Ltd, the Estate of the late Sonia Brownell Orwell and Martin Secker & Warburg for extracts from *Coming Up for Air* (1939), *The Lion and the Unicorn* (1941) and *Rudyard Kipling* (1942)

SIR KARL POPPER: the author for an extract from *The Open Society and Its Enemies*, Volume II (Routledge & Kegan Paul, 1945)

RT HON J. ENOCH POWELL: the author for extracts from *Freedom and Reality* (1969)

J. B. PRIESTLEY: Peters Fraser & Dunlop Group Ltd for 'An Unrepentant Bourgeois' (*Sunday Telegraph*, 1975)

SIR ANTHONY QUINTON: the author for an extract from *The Politics of Imperfection*

JOHN RANELAGH: HarperCollins Publishers Ltd for an extract from *Thatcher's People*

LORD REES-MOGG: the author for an extract from *An Humbler Heaven* (1977)

LORD RIDLEY OF LIDDESDALE: the author for an extract from 'From the role of manager to the role of enabler'

VITA SACKVILLE-WEST: Nigel Nicolson for 'The Coronation of George V' (1910)

ROGER SCRUTON: the author for extracts from *The Meaning of Conservatism* (1981)

GEORGE BERNARD SHAW: the Society of Authors on behalf of the Bernard Shaw Estate for extracts from *The Apple Cart* and *Pygmalion*

C. H. SISSON: the author and Carcanet Press Ltd for 'The Commonplace' and 'For Canon Brown, Who Likes Contemporary Speech' from *Collected Poems*

STEVIE SMITH: James MacGibbon for 'The Past' from *The Collected Poems of Stevie Smith* (Penguin)

TOM STOPPARD: Faber and Faber Ltd for an extract from *Travesties* (1975)

RT HON LORD TEBBIT: the author for an extract from a 1978 Conservative Party conference speech

MARGARET THATCHER: Lady Thatcher for extracts from her speeches

T. E. UTLEY: Conservative Political Centre for extracts from *Capitalism: The Moral Case* (1980), *Essays in Conservatism* (1949), and a Summer School lecture (1953)

PETER VIERECK: the author for an extract from *Conservatism Revisited* (1949), reprinted in 1978 in an expanded edition by Greenwood Press, 88 Post Rd West, Westport, Conn. 06881, USA, under the title *Conservatism Revisited and the New Conservatism: What Went Wrong*, copyright Professor Peter Viereck.

EVELYN WAUGH: Peters Fraser & Dunlop Group Ltd for extracts from *The Seven Deadly Sins*, *The Private Man* and *Robbery under Law*

DAVID WILLETS: Penguin Books Ltd for extracts from *Modern Conservatism* (Penguin Books, 1992) copyright © David Willets, 1992

P. G. WODEHOUSE: A. P. Watt Ltd and Random House UK Ltd on behalf of the Trustees of the Wodehouse Estate for extracts from *Ukridge* (Hutchinson)

SIR PEREGRINE WORSTHORNE: the author for extracts from *The Politics of Manners* and 'The Essence of Toryism'

Faber and Faber Limited apologize for any errors or omissions in the above list and would be grateful to be notified of any corrections that should be incorporated in the next edition or reprint of this volume.

General Index

Index of Authors